Everything You

Always Wanted to Know

About the Catholic Church

---

but Were Afraid to Ask

---

for Fear of Excommunication

Everything You

Always Wanted to Know

About the Catholic Church

---

but Were Afraid to Ask

---

for Fear of Excommunication

PAUL L. WILLIAMS

DOUBLEDAY

NEW YORK · LONDON · TORONTO · SYDNEY · AUCKLAND

Published by Doubleday, a division of
Bantam Doubleday Dell Publishing Group, Inc.
666 Fifth Avenue, New York, New York 10103

DOUBLEDAY and the portrayal of an anchor with a dolphin
are trademarks of Doubleday, a division of
Bantam Doubleday Dell Publishing Group, Inc.

Scriptural references are taken from the *Revised Standard* and *The New Jerusalem Bibles*. Citations from Vatican II and the post-conciliar doctrines are taken from *Vatican Council II: The Conciliar and Post Conciliar Documents,* copyright © 1975 by Costello Publishing Company, Inc., and Reverend Austin Flannery, O. P.

Library of Congress Cataloging-in-Publication Data

Williams, Paul L., 1944–
Everything you always wanted to know about the
Catholic Church but were afraid to ask for fear of
excommunication.

Includes index.
1. Catholic Church—Doctrines.
I. Title.
BX1751.2.W55   1989   282   88-33556

ISBN 0-385-24882-2
Copyright © 1989 by Paul L. Williams
All Rights Reserved
Printed in the United States of America
September 1989
First Edition
BG

Contents

Everything You

———————

Always Wanted to Know

———————

About the Catholic Church

———————

but Were Afraid to Ask

———————

for Fear of Excommunication

ONE

A Primer to Church History

---

and the Papacy

And I will tell you, you are Peter and upon this rock [*petrus*] I will build my Church, and the gates of hell shall not prevail against it. I will give to you the keys of the kingdom of heaven, and whatsoever you bind on earth shall be bound in heaven, and whatsoever you loose on earth shall be loosed in heaven.

Matthew 16:18–19

If anyone says that Christ the Lord did not constitute the Blessed Peter prince of all the Apostles and head of the whole Church militant; or if he says that this primacy is one of mere honor and not of real jurisdiction received directly and immediately from our Lord Jesus, let him be anathema.

"On the Church," *Proclamations of Vatican I, 2*

1. *What does the Catholic Church say about itself yesterday and today?*

In the Confession of the Council of Nicea (325), the phrase "We believe in one holy, Catholic, and apostolic Church" referred unambiguously to that Christian community which was united in faith and obedience to the Bishop of Rome. Prior to Vatican II, the expression "the one true Church founded by Jesus Christ" was used in Catholic catechetical texts (including the Baltimore Catechism) to refer to the Roman Catholic Church.

The Second Vatican Council (1965) formally admitted that Christian communities separated from the Catholic Church are used by the Holy Spirit as "means of salvation" for those who belong to them (*Unitatis Redintegratio,* 4). This affirmation opened up friendly outreach to other churches, but did not retract the Church's claim in another Vatican document on Oriental churches which identified the Mystical Body of Christ with "the holy and Catholic Church" (*Lumen Gentium,* 7).

2. *What function does the Catholic Church claim to perform?*

The major function of the Church is to proclaim the "good news" of eternal salvation through Jesus Christ. According to Vatican II, the Church accomplishes this task through its liturgy, its sacraments, and its preaching and ministry.

3. *Does the Catholic Church call itself divine?*

Yes, the Catholic Church maintains that it is divine because it was established by Jesus (Matt. 16: 18–19) and because it brings the presence of Christ to people in its preaching and sacraments. Nevertheless the Church throughout the ages has acknowledged its own humanity.

It has affirmed that its divine mission has been conducted by human beings with their fair share of foibles and shortcomings.

4. Who were the earliest Christians?

The earliest Christians were a group of Jews, initially not more than a handful, who began to gather in Jerusalem in the weeks between Easter and Pentecost. This nuclear group consisted mostly of Galileans, including the apostles (who had become Twelve again with the election of Matthias) and women such as Mary Magdalene, who had followed Jesus and attended to his and the group's needs. In addition, the group included "Mary, the mother of Jesus, and his brethren" (Acts 1:14). These "Nazarenes," as they were called, made their presence known in the Holy City and soon were joined by other "adherents of the Way" so that by Pentecost "the company of persons was in all one hundred and twenty" (Acts 1:15).[1] Each night they gathered in the upper room of a private home that belonged to a wealthy widow, since she is mentioned in Acts not by her husband's name but as "Mary, the son of John whose name was Mark" (Acts 12:12). This room, which was probably the site of the Last Supper, served the primitive community as a makeshift dormitory, a meeting room, and a place of worship.

By day, the Nazarenes gathered at the eastern wall of the Great Temple, an area known as Solomon's Portico (Acts 2:46; 3:11). They gathered at this location to pray, to share the warmth of faith and fellowship, and to spread the Good News of Jesus to those who passed by. But, above all, they came to this site simply to be there when the heavens parted and the Crucified One descended from the clouds in triumphant glory to judge the living and dead and to bring forth the Kingdom of God.[2] They believed that this glorious return of Jesus— an event known as the Parousia—would occur unexpectedly, "in the twinkling of an eye," as the Apostle Paul later put it, and it would occur *soon*. "The end of the world is near," Peter wrote in what some believe to be one of the earliest of Christian documents, "be serious, therefore, and pray" (1 Peter 4:7). The temple was the proper place for the Nazarenes to gather and wait, for the prophet Malachi had written: "Behold, I will send my messenger to prepare the way before

me, and the Lord whom you seek will suddenly come to his Temple"
(Mal. 3:1).

5. Did the early Christians seek to establish a new religion?

No. Although the Nazarenes endeavored to form an assembly or
ecclesia of believers in Jesus as Lord *(Kyrios)* within the confines of
traditional Judaism, they did not seek to establish a new religion.
Quite to the contrary, they saw themselves as devout Jews. They
strictly obeyed the dietetic and ceremonial regulations of their faith,
and, at first, proclaimed the Gospel solely to fellow Jews.[3]

6. How did Christianity become a religious movement?

Christianity became a movement at Pentecost, the day when the
apostles received the gift of tongues, known in the Greek as *glossolalia.*
This gift inspired them to proclaim the message of the Parousia to
other nations (i.e., primarily to the Jews of the Diaspora—those dis-
persed in faraway lands). They carried the message first northward to
Syria and Cilicia. Soon there were believers in Damascus and Antioch.
Within two years of Pentecost, the number of Nazarenes had multiplied from 120 to 8,000 (Acts 2:42; 4:4). By A.D. 40, these "adherents
of the Way" were no longer known as Nazarenes but as *Christianoi,*
"men of Christ."[4] At this time the movement began to be looked
upon as a threat to official Judaism. Stephen, a Hellenist sympathizer,
became the first martyr. The first persecutions, ordered by the Jewish
King Herod Agrippa I, occurred between 41 and 44. At the same time,
a number of early disciples lost their lives, including James, the son of
Zebedee, and Peter was cast into prison (Acts 12:2).

7. Was Peter the leader of the primitive Christian community?

Yes. Peter's role as leader of the early Christians is reported in
several early Christian documents.[5] In Matthew 16:18–20, Peter receives from Jesus "the Great Commission" of Church leadership. In its
exegesis of this passage the Catholic Church maintains that "the keys
of the kingdom" were given to Peter in a special way. Non-Catholics
assume that Jesus was speaking through Peter to the apostles as a
group. This latter position is rather difficult to justify scripturally since

the crucial passage begins by Christ singling out Peter by the words, "You are Peter and upon this rock [*petrus*] I will build my Church." Many modern biblical scholars, however, maintain that these words do not represent an authentic "Jesus-saying," but rather a pious interpolation by the primitive community. If this be the case, such an interpolation further serves to affirm Peter's position of primacy.

Peter's position of leadership is reasserted in other passages of Scripture, including most clearly the following closing passage from John's Gospel: "When they had finished breakfast, Jesus said to Simon Peter, 'Simon, son of John, do you love me more than these?' He said to him, 'Yes, Lord; you know that I love you.' He said to him, 'Feed my lambs.' A second time, he said to him, 'Simon, son of John, do you love me?' He said to him, 'Yes, Lord; you know that I love you.' He said to him, 'Tend my sheep.' He said to him the third time, 'Simon, son of John, do you love me?' And then he said to him, 'Lord, you know everything; you know that I love you.' Jesus said to him, 'Feed my sheep' " (John 21:15–17). This passage, which parallels Peter's threefold denial (John 26:69–75) presents an ecclesiastical prefiguring of Peter as Shepherd of the Christian flock.

Of equal importance for doctrinal development is Luke 22:31–32 in which Jesus says to Peter: "I have prayed for you that your faith will never fail. You, in turn, must strengthen your brothers." This became the pivotal test for Vatican I's affirmation of papal infallibility.

Throughout the first eight chapters of Acts, the primary source of information about the early Church, Peter is represented as the unquestioned leader and chief spokesman for the apostles.

8. *But wasn't the early Church governed by a council?*

Yes. While Peter was in prison and otherwise engaged in carrying the Gospel to Samaria, the Christian mission was supervised by a Church Council in Jerusalem under the supervision of James "the Just," the "brethren of Jesus."[6] This Council was responsible for deciding not to impose on pagan converts the Jewish requirement of circumcision. By this momentous decision, the Christian community clearly severed itself, in the eyes of its contemporaries, from its Jewish roots and began to appear publicly as a new and distinctive religious body (Acts 15:19–20).

9. *What was the structure of the first Christian assemblies?*

The first Christian congregations were structured as simple associations of believers. Each association or *ecclesia* chose one or more elders or priests—*presbyteroi*—to lead them, and at least one deacon *(diakonos)* to assist the priests. As the worshippers grew in number and their affairs became more complex, the congregations chose a priest or layman in each city to be an *episcopos*—overseer or bishop to coordinate their functioning.

The members of these communities lived in trustful simplicity, contributing all their possessions to a common pool. This communal living is described as follows in Acts 4:32–37: "There was but one heart and one soul in the multitude who had become believers, and not one of them claimed anything that belonged to him as his own, but they shared everything they had with one another. . . . No one among them was in any want, for any who had lands or houses would sell them and bring the proceeds and put them at the disposal of the apostles; then, they were shared with everyone in proportion to his need."

This Christian "communism," as it is sometimes called, persisted throughout the first three hundred years. Tertullian, circa 190, wrote in his "Apology" that Christians are "true brothers" who share "all things in common," adding with his characteristic sarcasm, "but their wives."[7]

10. *How quickly did Christianity spread through the Roman Empire?*

The first major church outside of the confines of Palestine was Antioch (in modern Syria), then the third city of the Empire and the main source of missionary activity (beginning with St. Paul) throughout Asia Minor. Later churches appeared in Greece, Armenia, Romania, and southern Russia. Christianity existed in Rome thirty years after the Crucifixion. There also is evidence of several Christian communities in France during the second century and in Spain during the third century. Alexandria in northern Africa was an important catechetical center by the third century, led by St. Clement of Alexandria (d. 215) and Origen (d. 251). After the conversion of Constantine (312), Egypt fell under Christian influence.

11. *Did Peter establish a Church* (ecclesia) *at Rome?*

Yes. Several early Church Fathers, including St. Irenaeus in "Against the Heretics," speak of the labors of Peter in establishing a Christian congregation in Rome.[8] Moreover, there is internal evidence of a Roman origin in the Petrine Epistles. For example, in 1 Peter 5:13, the apostle speaks and sends greetings from "the church that is in Babylon." Rome was likened to Babylon by the early Fathers since the ancient Babylonian and Roman armies both had conquered Jerusalem and destroyed the temple.

12. *Did Peter hand over his authority to his episcopal successors in the Church of Rome?*

Tradition says that he did. For example, St. Irenaeus in 187 wrote that Peter ". . . committed to the hands of Linus the office of the episcopate. Of this Linus, Paul makes mention in his Epistle to Timothy. To him succeeded Anacletus; and after him in the third place from the apostles, Clement was allotted the bishopric . . . To this Clement there succeeded Evaristus. Alexander followed Evaristus; then, sixth from the apostles, Sixtus was appointed; after him, Telesphorus, who was gloriously martyred; then Hyginus; after him, Pius; then, after him, Anicetus. Soter succeeded Anicetus; Eleutherius does now, in the twelfth place from the apostles, hold the inheritance of the episcopate. . . ."[9]

The early Bishops Linus and Anacletus left practically no mark on Church history save for their presumed martyrdoms. However, the third successor to the Roman See—Clement, who was said to have been ordained by Peter—made the history books. Only a generation after the death of Peter, Pope Clement (92–101) wrote a rather sharp letter to the congregation of Corinth in Greece demanding their obedience to their presbyters.[10]

13. *Was the primacy of Peter's successors universally recognized?*

By the end of the second Christian century, the primal importance of the See of Rome was recognized by bishops and theologians from St. Ignatius of Antioch in the Middle East to Tertullian of Carthage in Africa. St. Irenaeus, Bishop of Lyons in Gaul (France), urged all Christians to avoid heresy by looking to the Church of Rome, which had preserved the glorious tradition of the holy apostles Peter and Paul through the process of apostolic succession.[11] Similarly, St. Cyprian, Bishop of Carthage (249–258), in his treatise *De Catholicas Ecclesiae Unitate* (On the Unity of the Catholic Church) proclaimed the Chair of Peter *(cathedra Petri)* as "the source and landmark of the Church's oneness."[12]

Pope Victor (circa 190) made a dramatic display of his authority by excommunicating recalcitrant Eastern churches who refused to accept the Western date for the celebration of Easter. The Eastern churches celebrated Easter on the fourteenth day of the Jewish month of Nisan, whatever day of the week that might be; the Western churches postponed the feast until the following Sunday.[13]

14. *When did the Christian Church become the "Catholic Church"?*

The Greek word *Catholic* means universal. St. Ignatius, Bishop of Antioch in Syria for forty years, was the first to speak of "the Catholic Church."[14] He died between A.D. 110 and 120.

15. *When did the phrase* Roman Catholic *come into existence?*

It was first used during the Protestant Reformation in the sixteenth century as a term of derision. However, it became a useful designation to identify Christians who remained in communion with the Bishop of Rome.

16. *Whence comes the title "Pope"?*

The word *papa*, which in English became "pope," means "father." It was applied in the first four centuries to every Christian bishop.

17. *How did Roman Catholicism become the official religion of the Roman Empire?*

The Roman Catholic Church was firmly established in power and majesty not by a saint but a pagan. In 312, Constantine, before going into battle with his imperial rival Maxentius, beheld a vision of the cross with the words *In hoc signo vinces* (By this sign, you will conquer). He inscribed the sign of the cross on the shields of his soldiers and thoroughly routed the forces of Maxentius at the Milvian Bridge. Upon becoming sole Emperor, Constantine issued the Edict of Milan which made Christianity an approved religion of Rome.

18. *What effect did the Edict of Milan (313) have on the life and order of the Church?*

It had an enormous effect. Every aspect of Christian life and worship achieved public status. Christianity spread and imperial legislation approved of its growth. Eventually, the Pope was crowned like a temporal prince as "the representative of Jesus Christ" and came to rule over his fellow Christians from the Lateran Palace in Rome, a gift from Constantine for "every successor of the Blessed Apostle Peter." Rome's central place of worship henceforth was not a simple chapel but a great basilica, which was erected on Vatican Hill with the stone and marble from the pagan temples that had formerly stood there.[15] Prior to this time, a basilica was a pagan building whose central area—the apse—was filled with the statues of emperors who were worshipped as divinities.

Numerous other effects occurred. As the official religion of the Empire, Christianity began to synthesize many aspects of Roman life and organization into the faith. The Church, e.g., began to utilize the stole and other vestments of the pagan priesthood into its ritual, along with the use of holy water and incense for purification, the burning of candles before the images of the saints, and an everlasting flame before the altar. And Latin became the official language for Christian worship.

19. *How did Constantine become involved in the first Ecumenical Council at Nicaea (325)?*

Once he reunited the Roman Empire, Constantine was intent upon safeguarding it from division. Then, he discovered that an African priest named Arius was creating a schism within the Church by his assertion that Christ had been created in time by the Father and was therefore not eternal. To restore unity and order, Constantine summoned all the bishops of the Roman world to Nicaea, a town not far from the capital, Constantinople. Three hundred bishops took part in this council under the presidency of the Emperor and his principal religious adviser Hosius, Bishop of Cordova. Pope Sylvester I was represented by two priests, whose signatures validated the decrees, the most important of which proclaimed "the Nicene Creed," said every Sunday at Mass to this day, which proclaimed Jesus as "consubstantial with the Father." Arius was condemned and for the first time a civil punishment—heresy—was inflicted on a heretic.[16] The Bishop of Rome henceforth became known as the Supreme Pontiff. Local bishops, too, acquired civil jurisdiction over all localities in the western half of the Roman Empire, with the Supreme Pontiff asserting supreme civil jurisdiction.

20. *Whence comes the title "Pontifex Maximus"?*

In the ancient Roman religion, public worship was conducted by several associations of priests *(collegia)* under the lead of a chief priest or *pontifex maximus.*[17] In 63 B.C., the emperor Julius Caesar reserved for himself the title *pontifex maximus.* Successive emperors retained the title until the establishment of Christianity as the official religion of the Empire. The title, at this time, was transferred to the Bishop of Rome. The College of Priests became the College of Cardinals.

21. *What is the origin of the ecclesiastical office of cardinal?*

Cardinal comes from the Latin *cardo* meaning "hinge" or "support." In the fourth century, cardinals were clerics who were *incardinated* to support the Pope in his jurisdiction of the Church of Rome. By the time of Pope Stephen III (768–72), the number of such supportive clerics (cardinal-bishops, cardinal-priests, cardinal-deacons) was fixed at twenty-eight, seven for each of the four patriarchal churches in Rome.[18] Stationed at the Vatican, they formed a *collegium* or college of ecclesiastical administrators.

22. Is there a fixed number of Cardinals?

No. However, since the time of Pope Sixtus V (1586), the number of cardinals was around 70. This particular number was upheld to commemorate the seventy ancient scholars at Alexandria who were said to have been the translators of the Hebrew Bible. In 1965, Pope Paul VI raised the number to 101; and, by 1976, in spite of the cardinals who died in the intervening time, he raised the number to 136.

23. How did the Church acquire such early influence?

After the collapse of the Roman Empire, caused by internal corruption and the waves of barbarian invasions, the Roman Church became the one stable force in Western Europe. It was the font of learning throughout the medieval epoch, the body that transformed the ravaging hordes of Huns, Goths, Visigoths, Lombards, and Vandals into civilized men. To safeguard this force against the powers of darkness (which the barbarians really represented), the Church assumed a worldly role that the early Christians would have found inconceivable. Bishops replaced the Roman prefects, becoming the central source of order in the cities. Archbishops supplanted the provincial governors. The Synod of Bishops succeeded the provincial assembly. Moreover, the Bishop of Rome assumed the authority that was hitherto the property of kings and emperors.

While the barbarian invasions persisted until the time of the millennium, this new civilization had to be continuously fortified. Numerous bulls and decrees in support of the papacy helped to accomplish this. Without this support, the edifice now known as Christendom was likely to collapse, leaving the Western world in chaos.

24. What was the role of missionaries in the early Church?

By and large, the task of converting and civilizing the barbarian hordes fell to Christian missionaries and the monks who followed them. The most famous of the former was St. Patrick (389–461), whose conversion of Ireland was only one segment of an enduring historical saga. For two hundred years after his death, Irish monks carried the faith to Scotland and throughout continential Europe. It is not unusual to find ancient churches in modern Europe named for "St. Bridget of Ireland."

St. Benedict (480–547) so reorganized monastic life that his monks became models for later founders of those religious orders which had influence on the structure of Europe's Middle Ages. Benedictine monks were missionaries to England and France as early as the sixth century.

25. Why was Pope Leo I called "the Great"?

Pope Leo I (440–461), more clearly than any of his predecessors, set out the concept that the papacy was Peter's own office, not only as founder but also as present ruler of the Church through his servant, the Bishop of Rome. Leo claimed that it did not matter how immoral or inept an individual pope might be as long as he was the rightful successor of Peter and acted according to the rule of faith.

Leo strengthened the union of church and state by urging Emperor Valentinian III to enforce papal dictates by imperial law. Valentinian complied and, in 445, ordered Aëtius, the Roman commander in Gaul, to compel the attendance at the papal court of any bishop who refused to come voluntarily.

At the same time, Leo played an important role in doctrinal development. Faced with the Nestorian controversy regarding the nature of Christ (is Christ by nature God or man?), Leo issued his skillful Tome to the Council of Chalcedon in 451. In the Tome, Leo affirmed that Christ was true God and true man: two natures combined in one divine being *(hypostasis)*. When the Tome was read, it was greeted with the cry: "St. Peter has spoken through Leo."

In 451, Atilla, with a horde of barbarians, invaded Italy. After sacking Milan, the Huns set out in 452 for Rome. Helpless to prevent the conquest of the city, the Emperor abdicated his responsibility to the Pope. Pope Leo met Atilla at the gates of the city, and, by means of masterful negotiations, turned the horde from the city, thereby forever altering the course of Western civilization.[19]

26. *Of the early popes, who was the greatest?*

Arguably, Pope Gregory I (590–604) was the greatest. When he became Pope, Rome's situation was truly desperate. The Romans faced the invading Lombards with no help from the imperial governor at Ravenna. Moreover, famine and plague ravaged the city. Pope Gregory assumed command without hesitation. He collected taxes, provisioned the city, and provided for its defense. He sent orders to the generals in the field, and, after a series of skirmishes, managed to negotiate a lasting peace with the Lombards without the Emperor's authorization.[20]

In the midst of this, Pope Gregory, who like Pope Leo would later be canonized and called "the Great," administered the papal estates, strengthened papal ties to the churches in Gaul and Spain, defended the rights of the Bishop of Rome against the claims of the Patriarch of Constantinople for the title of "Ecumenical Patriarch," and sent missionaries to England.

Gregory's prolific writings include a basic textbook for the training of the medieval clergy *(Liber pastoralis curae)* and *Magna moralia*, a six-volume commentary on the Book of Job, which increased the popularity of allegorical interpretations of the Bible. In his *Dialogues,* he gave medieval Catholicism many of its distinctive characteristics by stressing the cult of the saints and relics, demonology, and ascetic virtues. In these works, he set forth his vision of *societas Christiana.* Christian society, he argued, must be structured in imitation of the heavenly kingdom, where every spirit has its proper place and function. This society was to be ordered by a chain of command leading from local prelates to bishops to the Supreme Pontiff. Gregory's vision animated much of medieval Christianity and received its fullest crystallization during the triumphant papacy of Pope Innocent III (1198–1216).

27. *How did succeeding popes deal with the problems that followed upon the spread of Catholic influence throughout Europe?*

Fortunately great popes continued to appear at the opportune moment.

By the year 1000 the Church in Europe had become subject in many places to the secular power of kings. It was almost a universal practice by then that a temporal prince would invest the local bishop with the symbols of his episcopal office, his ring and crozier, and in many cases would confer the office on relatives or cronies. Lay investiture, as it was called, frequently was linked with simony. A new Pope Gregory VII (1073–85), the monk Hildebrand as he was known, looked upon the practice with displeasure. He had not sought the papacy, but he was a born ruler who imprinted on the Church a form of asceticism that had gone out of style. The keynote of his administration was reform. He expected a pope to be a saint like St. Peter and a sovereign, entitled to depose all princes, temporal as well as spiritual. He vigorously fought against secular interference in Church appointments and began to nominate his own choices not only for the sees of Italy but in Germany. When Henry IV resisted the incursion of papal power into his realm, Hildebrand excommunicated him, forcing the king to promise penance and obedience in exchange for absolution. It was this pope who began to send his legates to various countries, who insisted that archbishops come to Rome to receive the pallium (the symbol of their metropolitan jurisdiction), who established the Roman liturgy, defended the Church's teaching on the Eucharist (against Berengarius), and worked to restore unity with the Eastern Church. Gregory had his share of failures, but he was an impressive figure in the early medieval period.

Innocent III (1198–1216) was also given the name "Great." Also born to rule, he ascended the papacy in his thirty-seventh year, the man who gave currency to the papal title "Vicar of Christ." For him the fullness of the Pope's power was spiritual, inclining him to resist involvement in temporal affairs. But he quickly established his authority in Rome by reasserting personal control over the Papal States. He crowned Otto IV King of Germany but excommunicated him when the latter invaded southern Italy. His overriding concerns during his eighteen-year reign were reform of the Church, a crusade against Islam, and combatting heresy. He simplified the living standards of the clergy, took steps to improve their quality and moral behavior, and insisted that bishops visit Rome every four years. He encouraged the preaching of the Franciscans with their stress on poverty. His fourth Lateran Council (1215) defined the Eucharist in terms of transubstantiation and decreed that Catholics should make yearly confession. He is considered one of the great Catholic popes.

28. What is a papal bull?

A bull is an official communication from the Pope. It comes from the Latin word *bulla,* which refers to a round, leaden seal attached to formal papal correspondence. The seal attests to the genuineness of the document.

29. What is a papal encyclical?

In addition to bulls, popes in more recent years have issued briefs (usually for grants, privileges, and concessions) and rescripts (usually for dispensations), and encyclical letters or "encyclicals." The latter are the most important since they often deal with matters of faith and morals. Notable encyclicals include Pope Leo XIII's "On the Condition of Labor" *(Rerum Novarum)* in 1891, Pope Pius XII's "On Biblical Studies" *(Divino afflante Spiritu)* in 1943, Pope John XXIII's "Peace on Earth" *(Pacem in Terris)* in 1961, and Pope Paul VI's "On the Development of People" *(Populorum Progressio)* in 1967.

30. What is a decretal?

A decretal, an early form of letter writing, was used by popes for direct pronouncements on urgent matters of morals and doctrine. Initiated by Pope Damasus in 384, the first decretals concerned such matters as the requirements of candidacy for Holy Orders, the degrees of kindred and affinity that constitute a bar to Christian marriage, and the need for requiring celibacy in bishops, priests, and deacons.

31. *What were the False Decretals?*

To establish the supreme authority of the Pope, an ingenious compilation of documents was put together by a French cleric named Isidorus Mercator in 842. Along with a mass of authentic decrees by councils and popes, the compilation included fabricated decrees and letters which were attributed to popes from Clement I (91–100) to Melchiades (311–314). These forged documents purported to show that in the oldest traditions and practice of the Church no bishop might be deposed, no Church Council might be convened, and no major issue might be decided without the consent of the Pope. The earliest pontiffs, these documents alleged, claimed absolute and universal authority as Vicars of Christ on earth. In one document, Pope Sylvester I (314–335) was represented as having received the famous "Donation of Constantine," by which the papacy was said to have received full secular and religious authority over Western Europe.[21] For eight hundred years the popes assumed the authenticity of these false decretals and used them to support their policies and to expand their worldly possessions. In 1440, Lorenzo Valla conclusively exposed the fraudulent nature of these decretals by demonstrating that they quoted Scripture from the translation by St. Jerome who was born twenty-six years after the death of Pope Melchiades.

32. *Why is the Vatican called the Holy See?*

The word *See* is a corruption of the Latin *sedes* meaning "seat." It refers to the official headquarters or "seat" of a bishop. Since the Bishop of Rome represents the highest authority in the Church, his place of residence is known as the Holy Seat or Holy See.

33. *What is the difference between a cathedral and a basilica?*

A cathedral is the local bishop's main church. The name comes from the Latin *cathedra,* meaning "chair." This is a reference to what used to be called "the bishop's throne," which occupied a prominent place within the altar of the bishop's church.

A basilica is usually an ancient church that either received special recognition by a reigning Pope or possessed a papal altar. In Rome, for example, the churches of St. Peter, St. John Lateran, and St. Paul Outside the Walls are called basilicas. The word derives from a Greek word meaning "kingly" or "royal."

34. Can a pope sin?

Yes. Despite their exalted position as Vicars of Christ, the popes can and do commit moral sins and are in need of the sacrament of penance. For this reason, all popes have a private confessor.

35. Were any popes married?

Peter, according to Mark 1:30, was married. Regarding the popes of the first three Christian centuries, records of their personal lives are sparse, to say the least. St. Hormisdas (514–523), however, appeared to have enjoyed the pleasures of connubial bliss and was the father of another Pope who became a saint, St. Silverius (536–538).[22] The last married Pope was Adrian II (867–872).

36. Was there ever a female pope?

No. The fable of Pope Joan or Johanna was first mentioned in the thirteenth century by two Dominicans, John de Mailly and Stephen de Bourbon, who placed her pontificate in 1100, and by the papal chamberlain, Martin of Troppau, who maintained that a woman was Pope in 855. The legend of Pope Joan appears to have originated either in a rumor concerning a woman patriarch of Constantinople, which was mentioned by Pope Leo IX in a letter to Cerularius in 1053, or in a medieval satire that ridiculed the domination of the papacy by the notorious Theodora and her seductive daughter, Marozia.

37. Who were Theodora and Marozia?

Theodora, the wife of Theophylact, a chief official of the papal court, and her daughter Marozia made and unmade popes practically at will throughout much of the tenth century, a period aptly known as "the nadir of the papacy." In 906, Marozia, at the age of fifteen, became the mistress of Pope Sergius III. They had one child, John, who subsequently became Pope John XI.[23] In 914, Theodora's lover, Bishop John of Ravenna, became Pope John X. Marozia, after having enjoyed a succession of lovers, married Guido, Duke of Tuscany. The newlyweds conspired to unseat the Pope, who was her mother's lover. Joining with John's enemies, Marozia and Guido cast Pope John X in prison and, in 928, had him suffocated. In 931, Marozia raised to the Holy See Pope John XI, her illegitimate son by Pope Sergius III. One year later, Alberic, one of Marozia's legitimate sons, imprisoned the new pontiff (his half brother) in the Castle of Sant' Angelo, but graciously permitted him to exercise his papal duties from his cell. In 955, Marozia's grandson became Pope John XII and distinguished his pontificate with debauched orgies in the Lateran Palace. By this time, the degradation of the papacy had become so outrageous that Otto of Germany with the aid of the transalpine clergy felt compelled to intervene for the simple sake of Christian decency. Otto summoned the depraved Pope John XII to a trial before an ecclesiastical council. At the trial, the cardinals gave evidence that the Pope had taken bribes for consecrating bishops, had made a boy of ten a bishop, had committed adultery with his father's concubine and niece, and had transformed the Lateran Palace into a veritable brothel.[24] With characteristic arrogance, Pope John refused to attend the council and went out on a hunting party. In 963, the council dutifully deposed the profligate pontiff and unanimously elected Otto's candidate, a layman, as Pope Leo VIII.

38. Who was the worst pope?

The worst appears to have been Pope Alexander VI (1492–1503). After purchasing the votes of thirteen cardinals, including that of the ninety-six-year-old cardinal of Venice for a measly five thousand ducats, Cardinal Rodrigo Borgia became Pope Alexander VI. By this time, he had already fathered four children, including the infamous duo Caesar and Lucrezia Borgia, by his mistress, Vannozza dei Catanei, a member of one of the lesser noble families in Rome. In addition, he boasted a considerable number of illegitimate children from his legion of lovers. Upon ascending to the throne of Peter, Pope Alexander abandoned his faithful mistress Vannozza for a young beauty named Guila Farnese. He lived openly with his new mistress in the Lateran Palace, and Guila was soon dubbed *Sponsa di Cristo* (the Bride of Christ) by a witty contemporary recorder of events.[25]

Pope Alexander proved himself to be a ruthless erotomaniac who cared for little else than the immediate interests of his personal friends and immediate family. Upon becoming Pope, he elevated nineteen of his Catalan compatriots to the cardinalate, along with his fourteen-year-old son Caesar.

To raise money for his pleasure-loving government, Pope Alexander in 1500 created twelve new cardinals who paid a total of 120,000 ducats for their appointments. "These appointments," wrote the historian Guicciardini, "were made not of such as had the most merit, but of those that offered the most money."[26] In 1503, the Pope continued to swell the cardinalate by appointing nine additional cardinals at a commensurate price. In the same year, Pope Alexander created *ex nihilo* eight new offices in the Curia, which were sold at 760 ducats each. To create additional positions, the Pope is said to have poisoned several ecclesiastics, including Cardinal Michiel and Cardinal Orsini in 1503.[27] Alexander's contemporaries further charged that the Pope and his son Caesar made a practice of arresting rich clergymen on trumped up charges, only to release them when they received payment of outlandish ransoms and fines. The Bishop of Cerena, it was alleged, was cast into Sant' Angelo by the avaricious pope and freed only upon the payment of 100,000 ducats.[28]

The most incredible allegation appeared in the usually reliable diary of the papal master of ceremonies, Burchard. On October 30, 1501, Burchard described a dinner in the apartment of Caesar in the Vatican at which fifty naked Roman harlots chased chestnuts that were scattered over the floor, while Pope Alexander and Lucrezia looked on with amusement.[29]

The death of the Borgia Pope in 1503 was the cause of riotous rejoicing in Rome, as the citizens chased the Catalan cardinals from the city and burned their dwelling places to the ground. Guicciardini writes:

> The whole city of Rome ran together with incredible alacrity, and crowded about the corpse in St. Peter's Church, and were not able to

satisfy their eyes with the sight of the dead serpent, who, with his immoderate ambition and detestable treachery, with manifold instances of horrid cruelty and monstrous lust, and exposing all things without distinction, both sacred and profane, had intoxicated the whole world.[30]

Pope Alexander's reputation hasn't improved with age.

39. Can a pope go to hell?

Yes. According to Catholic doctrine, popes, despite their gift of infallibility, can go to hell. The popes are mortal, sinful men and have to earn their way to eternal salvation like any other Catholic. Fr. Bertrand Conway points this out in his book, *The Question Box,* by writing: "While we naturally expect the popes to be of the highest moral character—and most of them have been—the official prerogative of infallibility has nothing to do with the Pope's personal goodness or wickedness."[31] Dante in his *Divine Comedy* did not hesitate to consign pontiffs to hell, including such simoniacs as Pope Nicholas III and Pope Boniface VIII.

40. Were any popes mentally unbalanced?

Yes. Pope Stephen VI (nicknamed "the Trembler" because of a nervous disorder) is commonly assumed to have been clinically insane. He is noted for exhuming the corpse of his predecessor, Pope Formosus (891–896), in 897 and placing the rotting cadaver on trial before an ecclesiastic council on the charge of violating certain Church laws. The body of the dead Pope was dutifully found guilty, condemned to death, stripped, mutilated, and tossed into the Tiber.[32]

Pope Urban VI, the first Italian Pope in seventy-four years, is also thought to have been mentally deranged. In 1378, he was elected by a college of predominantly French cardinals under the sway of an angry crowd demanding a Roman Pope. The cardinals would have been hard pressed to make a worse choice. Upon his election, the new Pope, who had been a creditable bishop, singled out each of the cardinals for a blistering personal attack. For hours, the Pope continued to harangue the befuddled cardinals in scandalous language and with a face purple with rage. He called one cardinal a liar, another a fool, and dismissed Cardinal Orsini as a "half wit" *(sotus).*[33]

Nor did his political compatriots escape his furious tirades. When ambassadors from Queen Johanna of Naples came to congratulate Pope Urban, he proceeded to insult them and their queen, threatening to place Johanna in a nunnery for her failure to pay the dues of Naples as a papal fief.

Throughout his first year of rule, Pope Urban's behavior grew steadily more outrageous, culminating in a violent physical attack on the cardinal of Limoges.

By this time, the cardinals who had elected Urban fancied that the sudden delirium of power had made him *furiosus et melancholicus,* i.e., hopelessly insane.[34]

Realizing that they had made a ghastly mistake in electing Pope Urban, the disgruntled French cardinals met at Anagni and elected a new Pope: Robert of Geneva who became Antipope Clement VII. In an effort to legitimize Clement's claim to the throne of Peter, they maintained that Urban's election was invalid since it had been conducted under duress. From this date in 1378 to the Council of Constance in 1417, there would be at least two popes (antipopes) in Western Christendom, each excommunicating and invalidating the sacraments of the other.

In the midst of this madness, Pope Urban set out on an ill-fated campaign to capture the Kingdom of Naples. As they neared their military destination, the Pope and his troops were besieged at a castle outside of Nocera by the army of Charles of Durazzo. This siege set the scene for one of the most bizarre incidents in Church history. Charles of Durazzo had promised to pay ten thousand florins to the man who captured the Pope dead or alive. The soldiers, therefore, began the siege with a good deal of bloodthirsty enthusiasm. As the siege progressed, Pope Urban appeared at a window of the castle with bell, book, and candle, raving curses at the army below and excommunicating every man in it. The Pope continued this rite, onlookers reported, three times a day throughout the siege, each time miraculously escaping the shower of arrows that greeted his every appearance. The attack finally came to an end several weeks later with the Holy Pontiff still physically, if not mentally, intact.[35]

At this time, he decided to abandon his military plans and return to Rome. Faced with the Pope's increased paranoia on the journey home, a group of seven cardinals conspired to depose him. When the plot haplessly misfired, the furious pontiff committed the unprecedented atrocity of having five of the cardinals subjected to unspeakable torture (while he read from his breviary) and later executed. The two remaining co-conspirators managed to escape and joined the ranks of Antipope Clement VII at Avignon.

Pope Urban VI died, the object of general hatred, in 1389.

41. *How did it come about there were three popes at the same time?*

As stated in the previous answer, Pope Urban VI, albeit quite mad, was elected Bishop of Rome under bizarre circumstances in 1378. In response to his verbal and physical assaults upon them, the French cardinals declared Urban's election "invalid" since it had been conducted under duress, and elected a cardinal from their own ranks as Antipope Clement VII. The result of this schism on the spiritual and financial state of the Catholic Church was catastrophic. Half the Christian world held the other half to be blasphemous and heretical. Each claimed that the sacraments administered by the priests of the opposing obedience were null and void. Thus, children baptized by priests loyal to the opposing pope were not shriven of original sin; the priests ordained by bishops loyal to the opposing pope were invalid; the sins forgiven by prelates loyal to the opposing pope were unforgiven. At the same time, revenues were cut in half. To fill the empty coffers, simony redoubled, chancery taxes on all documents required from the Curia quadrupled, and indulgences were sold for every possible occasion and with the crassest of all possible techniques.[36]

To resolve this crisis, a General Council of all Christians was convoked at Pisa in 1409. The Council consisted of 26 cardinals, 4 patriarchs, 12 archbishops, 80 bishops, 87 abbots, delegates from the major universities, 300 doctors of canon law, and ambassadors from all the European governments save Hungary, Spain, Scandinavia, and Scotland.

Declaring itself to be canonical and ecumenical, the Council of Pisa summoned the two reigning pontiffs—Antipope Benedict XIII in Avignon and Pope Gregory XII in Rome—to appear before it. Both popes stubbornly refused. Faced with these refusals, the Council officially deposed both popes and elected a third Supreme Pontiff: Antipope Alexander V.

When the Council adjourned, the newly elected third pope almost immediately dropped dead. He was replaced by the most notorious of antipopes: John XXIII.

The ill-fated Council of Pisa only succeeded in worsening a terrible condition. This became apparent with John XXIII, in order to claim the papal states for himself, declared war on Pope Gregory XII, the reigning Bishop of Rome.

42. *How was the papal schism (division) finally resolved?*

The schism came to an end at the Council of Constance in 1414. By this time, socioeconomic pressures throughout Christendom forced a solution to the crisis. The Council, which ironically was summoned by the power-hungry Antipope John XXIII, attracted 24,000 knights-at-arms, 800 laymen, 18,000 prelates, 300 doctors of theology, and representatives of the chief nations of Europe. The Council sentenced John XXIII to prison on charges of prostitution, gambling, and usury.[37] Antipope Benedict XIII refused to submit to the Council and was subsequently driven from the papal palace at Avignon and fled to Aragon, Spain. The reigning Bishop of Rome, Gregory XII, gracefully resigned for the sake of Christian unity on July 4, 1415. Upon receiving his resignation, a new papal conclave elected Pope Martin V, who began his reign as the sole Supreme Pontiff in 1417.

43. *Didn't the Council of Constance, an official council of the Church, formally declare that a General Council is superior in authority to the Bishop of Rome?*

Yes. The Council of Constance declared itself superior in power and authority to the Pope by the following decree: "The Holy Synod of Constance . . . ordains, declares, and decrees . . . that this synod represents the Church Militant, and has authority directly from

Christ; and everybody, of whatever rank and dignity, including also the pope, is bound to obey the Council in those things that pertain to the faith."[38]

This decree, which has been used by Conciliarists to undermine the dogma of papal infallibility, directly conflicts with the traditional Catholic teaching that the Pope has the sole right to convoke a General Council and the sole authority to give its decrees binding force. For this reason, the above decree from the Council of Constance was pronounced null and void by Pope Martin V on April 22, 1418, and by Pope Eugenius IV on July 22, 1446. The traditional Catholic position was formally restated in the following manner by the Council of Florence in 1438: "We define that the Holy Apostolic See of the Bishop of Rome possesses a primacy throughout the whole world; that the Roman Pontiff is the successor of Blessed Peter, Prince of the Apostles; that he is the true Vicar of Christ, the Head of the Universal Church and of all Christians; that to him was given in Blessed Peter by our Lord Jesus Christ the fullness of power to feed, to rule, and to govern the Universal Church."[39]

44. How is a pope elected?

When the death of a pope is officially proclaimed, the College of Cardinals meets in solemn conclave (i.e., in locked chambers) within the Vatican Palace. This conclave must be held not earlier than fifteen nor later than eighteen days after the death of the pope. The Cardinals must remain in seclusion until the election takes place. Two ballots are taken each morning and evening until a decision is reached. A candidate must receive a two-thirds plus one vote for election. When no selection is made, the ballots are burned with damp straw to produce a heavy black smoke, which ascends from the chimney of the Sistine Chapel. When a two-thirds plus one majority is attained, the ballots are burned without the damp smoke to produce a light smoke. The Apostolic Constitution allows for the following alternative methods in difficult cases: (1) the cardinals can delegate a limited number (nine to twelve) from their ranks to make the decision; (2) they can vote to change the majority rule from two-thirds plus one to an absolute majority plus one; (3) they can limit the final choice between the two candidates who receive the largest number of votes.

45. What is the origin of conclave?

Since the economic life of medieval Europe revolved around the papacy, it was imperative for a vacant Holy See to be filled without delay in order for day-to-day life to go on without interruption in its rhythm. By the end of the twelfth century, however, the political loyalties of the College of Cardinals were sharply divided. As a consequence of rabid nationalism, cardinals often tarried for months—even years—before reaching a consensus about a suitable papal candidate. Such delays often brought on civil unrest, prompting the ordinary laity to take canon law into their own hands. For this reason, the laity began literally to "lock up" the cardinals in a single room and slowly starve them until they made a decision.

The first "lock-up" or "conclave" took place after the death of Pope Gregory IX on August 21, 1241. Knowing the immediate need of a new pontiff to ward off the threat of foreign intrusion in Rome, Senator Matteo Orsini physically forced the cardinals to choose a new pope. By his orders, the cardinals were tied hand and foot, flung to the ground, and beaten by sticks. Then they were thrown into the main hall of a building known as the Septizodium. The windows were nailed shut and the doors were locked so that no one could leave. Armed guards were commanded to kill any cardinal who attempted to escape. The living conditions were abominable. Nevertheless, it took the cardinals over fifty-five days to reach a decision, finally settling on Godfrey, Bishop of Santa Sabina, who took the name of Pope Celestine IV.

Unfortunately, as a result of the rigors of the conclave, the new Pope died two weeks after his election. Fearing another lock-up, the cardinals fled from Rome to their individual palaces and fortresses. Nearly two years passed before a new successor to the throne of Peter was named.

When Pope Clement IV died on November 29, 1268, his successor was not chosen until September 1, 1271. This decision was made only after the cardinals were locked in a room in Viterbo and placed on a diet of bread and water. Still reluctant to make a decision, the roof was removed from their room so that the cardinals were exposed to the heat of the day, the cold of the night, and occasional downpours of heavy rain. Only after St. Bonaventure made a fiery plea to them for Christian unity did they reach a decision. The new Pope—Gregory X—convoked a General Council at Lyons, where the rules for the election of all future popes were outlined once and for all.[40]

46. What is the dogma of papal infallibility?

Vatican I defined papal infallibility as follows:

Faithfully adhering to the tradition received from the beginning of the Christian faith, we teach and define that it is a dogma divinely revealed that the Roman Pontiff when he speaks *ex cathedra,* that is, when in discharge of the office of pastor and teacher of all Christians by virtue of his supreme Apostolic authority, he defines a doctrine regarding faith and morals to be held by the Universal Church by the divine assistance promised him in Blessed Peter, is possessed of that infallibility with which the Blessed Redeemer willed that His Church should be endowed for defining doctrine regarding faith and morals; and that, therefore, such definitions of the Roman Pontiffs are irreformable of themselves, and not from the consent of the Church.

This dogma, which was elaborated upon and promulgated by Vatican II's Dogmatic Constitution of the Church *(Lumen Gentium),* states that the pope is infallible in the following circumstances:

1. When he speaks *ex cathedra,* i.e., when he speaks officially as the supreme pastor of the Church. He is not infallible when he speaks in less solemn ways.

2. When he defines a doctrine regarding faith and morals. To define, in this context, means to settle a doctrinal matter in a definite and irrevocable manner.

3. When he speaks of faith and morals, which includes the whole content of divine revelation, or, as St. Paul puts it, "the deposit of faith."

4. When he intends to bind the whole Church to a common belief. In this instance, the Pope's intention of permanently binding the faith-

ful must be clear from the context, e.g., Pope Pius IX's definition of the Immaculate Conception.

47. How can Catholics claim that Peter was infallible when he denied Christ three times (Matt. 16:70; Mark 14:69–72)?

The infallible primacy was not given to Peter until after the Resurrection.[41] What's more, the dogma of infallibility does not grant a pope immunity from errors of judgment.

48. Were any popes heretics?

Pope Liberius (352–366) was accused of being a semi-Arian. His lapse into alleged heresy occurred when, at the age of 101, he departed from the strict homousia confession of St. Athanasius which upheld that the Father, Son, and Holy Spirit were identical in being or essence, by signing the infamous Second Creed of Sirmium.[42] Moreover, Pope Honorius I (625–638) was condemned as a Monophysite heretic by a General Council, albeit he was probably more culpable of a lack of theological acumen than heresy. When asked about the Chalcedonian formula, he maintained that Christ indeed did possess two natures but only one "energy."[43]

49. How can a pope be a heretic and still be upheld as infallible?

As stated above, the dogma of papal infallibility does not cover the personal errors of popes, even in matters of their private teachings. The charisma of infallibility comes into play only when a pope speaks *ex cathedra* on matters of faith and morals.

50. How can a worldly pope like Alexander VI (see Question 38) be deemed infallible?

Infallibility means freedom from error in official teaching, not freedom from sin—i.e., impeccability.

51. Was Pope Paul V (1605–1621) infallible when he declared the Copernican theory to be "false, heretical and contrary to the Word of God"?

Despite the fact that Pope Paul V's Holy Office did condemn the teachings of Copernicus, the Pope was not speaking *ex cathedra* on a matter to be upheld by the universal Church. In the eyes of the Church, the condemnation was a disciplinary action, prompted in part by the precipitate fashion in which Galileo questioned biblical exegesis.

52. Was Pope Urban VIII (1623–1644) infallible when he condemned Galileo?

The decree of the condemnation of Galileo was an act of a Roman congregation, not a doctrinal declaration by a pope.

53. When have the popes spoken infallibly?

Only two modern statements of the Catholic faith are considered to be *ex cathedra* papal declarations: the Immaculate Conception of Mary (as pronounced by Pope Pius IX in 1854), and the Assumption of Mary (as pronounced by Pope Pius XII in 1950). However, major articles of the Creeds—Christ's divinity, Mary's virginity, and so forth—also would be considered infallible.

54. Is this dogma presently under attack?

Yes. This has been verified by a number of public opinion polls, including one conducted by Yankelovich Clancy Shulman for *Time* magazine (September 7, 1987). This poll showed that while 53 percent of American Catholics believe that the Pope is infallible in matters of faith, only 37 percent accept his infallibility on matters of morality.

Several theologians who call themselves Catholic have openly rejected the dogma of infallibility on historical and religious grounds. Hans Küng in *Infallible?*[44] and Brian Tierney in *Origins of Papal Infallibility, 1150–1350*,[45] have sought to prove that infallibility, despite the claims of Vatican I and II, was not latent in the New Testament, and, indeed, required many centuries to develop into a doctrine. Tierney argues that the notion of infallibility suddenly appeared at the end of the thirteenth century, when it was devised by several disgruntled Franciscans to settle the question of evangelical poverty. These Franciscans, Tierney writes, already had succeeded in obtaining a papal decree in 1299 which espoused their rigorist views of Christ's teaching on poverty, and by having this decree accepted as "infallible," they hoped to ensure that it could not be rescinded by any future pope.

The negative attacks by Küng and Tierney, however, have had little impact on theological academics. For example, George Lindbeck, a Lutheran theologian, argues that a doctrine such as papal infallibility can be neither disproved nor negated simply by historical arguments.[46]

55. What is qualified infallibilism?

Certain modern Catholic theologians, not willing to deny infallibility to the Church or the Pope, espouse a qualified papal infallibility. In his book, *A Church to Believe In,* Fr. Avery Dulles argues that a fundamentalist understanding of infallibility is no longer necessary in the light of the principles set forth by *Mysterium Ecclesiae* (1973). He points to two factors mentioned in this Vatican document which must be considered in dealing with dogmatic pronouncements: the transcendence of divine revelation and the historicity of human formulations to describe such revelations. Dulles argues that dogmatic formulations of divine revelation are merely human attempts to express realities that are ineffable. Concerning the historicity of such formulations, Dulles argues that dogmatic statements are conditioned by "the changeable conceptions of a given epoch" and by the available vocabulary. Therefore, they are completely relative to the pervading temper of the time and are subject to constant change and reinterpretation.[47]

This so-called dynamic and historically conscious approach to dogma permits theologians constantly to question the wording of earlier papal pronouncements in an attempt "to convey more clearly to a new generation what the older expressions really intended."[48] However, such historicism is also a ploy to deny indirectly what the theologian would not dare deny directly. Mary's virginity, for example, was proclaimed in the first century A.D. Since the word "virginity" means today what it meant then, no amount of "changeable conceptions" can make the Church's declaration on that subject any less infallible.

56. Why is the Pope's ring destroyed at the time of his death?

The ring of the Pope is used to authenticate official documents and pronouncements. Because of the belief in papal infallibility, any decree coming from the papal throne must be accepted with intense solemnity. In order to ensure the authenticity of papal correspondence, the Pope's ring is immediately removed from his right hand at the time of his death and destroyed by the papal chamberlain.

57. Describe the institutional structure of the Catholic Church.

The Catholic Church is organized along principal lines leading to and from the papacy. Its adherent bodies of believers are divided into dioceses, and each diocese is divided into parishes. Each diocese is headed by a bishop who is called the "Ordinary" of the diocese. Each parish is headed by a priest. Each parish administers its own spiritual and temporal affairs in conjunction and in alignment with the diocese. Each diocese, through its chancery (the term for the clerical bureaucracy under the supervision of the bishop), manages its own spiritual and temporal affairs in conjunction and in alignment with the diocese of Rome.[49]

The Pope is the Bishop of Rome and his diocese has its own bureaucratic chancery, which is called the "Curia." The Curia, which is run by cardinals, is organized into administrative sections called congregations, tribunals, secretariats, and commissions.

But the Pope is also the absolute ruler of a fully sovereign state—the State of Vatican City, which has its own diplomatic corps, ambassadors, civil service, security systems, police, jails, stamps, coinage, judiciary, and banking system.

Within this enormous infrastructure, each diocese is independent of Rome in its fiscal and monetary administration. As the official representative of the Pope, the bishop exercises supreme authority in his territory. He holds in trust and controls the property of the Church—its liquid assets, its real estate, etcetera. He possesses the power to curb any aberrations in official doctrine through censure and condemnation. The bishop, however, must report to the Curia every five years to give a detailed report of the affairs of his diocese. In addition, he must maintain close contact with the Pope's representative in his province or country, who is called the "pronuncio."[50]

Within Roman Catholicism, the power that is wielded by cardinals, bishops, and prelates in their spiritual and temporal duties comes from the power of the Pope as the representative of Christ on earth. This is why they are appointed to their ecclesiastical offices. Only the position of the Pope is attained by election. Catholicism, in short, represents an absolute monarchy.

NOTES

1. Henry Chadwick, *The Early Church* (Baltimore: Penguin Books, 1969), p. 16; Robert Coughlin, "Who Was This Man Jesus," in *Life*, Vol. 52 (December 25, 1964), p. 93.

2. Coughlin, *loc. cit.*

3. W.H.C. Frend, *The Early Church* (Philadelphia: J. B. Lippincott Company, 1966), pp. 36–37.

4. W.H.C. Frend, *The Rise of Christianity* (Philadelphia: Fortress Press, 1984), p. 499.

5. Raymond Brown, Karl Donfried, and John Reumann, eds., *Peter in the New Testament* (Minneapolis: Augsburg Publishing Company, 1973), p. 159.

6. Frend, *The Early Church*, p. 38; Chadwick, *op. cit.*, p. 18.

7. Tertullian, "Apology," 39, translated by S. Thelwall, in *Latin Christianity: Its Founder, Tertullian*, Vol. III, The Ante Nicene Fathers, edited by Alexander Roberts and James Donaldson (Grand Rapids: William B. Eerdmans Publishing Company, 1980), pp. 46–47.

8. St. Irenaeus, "Against the Heresies," III, in *The Apostolic Fathers: Justin Martyr and Irenaeus,* translated by A. Cleveland Coxe, Vol. I, The Ante Nicene Fathers, edited by Alexander Roberts and James Donaldson (Grand Rapids: William B. Eerdmans Publishing Company, 1981), pp. 415–16.

9. *Ibid.*

10. St. Clement of Rome, "Letter to the Corinthians," 57, in *The Apostolic Fathers, op. cit.* pp. 52–53.

11. St. Irenaeus, *loc. cit.*

12. St. Cyprian, "On the Unity of the Catholic Church," V, in *Ancient Christian Writers,* Vol. 25, edited by Johannes Quasten and Joseph C. Plumpe (London: Longmans, Green and Company, 1957), p. 46.

13. Frend, *The Early Church*, p. 88.

14. St. Ignatius, "Epistle to the Smyrnaeans," 8, in *The Apostolic Fathers, op. cit.,* p. 90.

15. Malachi Martin, *The Decline and Fall of the Roman Church* (New York: G. P. Putnam and Sons, 1981), pp. 33–34.

16. Frend, *The Rise of Christianity*, pp. 539–40.

17. Will Durant, *Caesar and Christ* (New York: Simon and Schuster, 1951), p. 63.

18. *New Catholic Encyclopedia*, Volume III, Can to Col, (New York: McGraw-Hill Book Company, 1967), p. 104.

19. Jeffrey Burton Russell, *A History of Medieval Christianity* (New York: Thomas Y. Crowell Company, 1968), p. 38.

20. Jeffrey Burton Russell, *Counsel of God: The Life and Times of Gregory the Great* (London: Routledge and Kegan Paul, 1980), pp. 51–69.

21. "The Forged *Donation of Constantine*," translated by Sidney Ehler and John B. Morrall, in *Readings in Church History*, Vol. I, edited by Colman J. Barry, O.S.B. (New York: The Newman Press, 1959), pp. 235–40.

22. Hans Kuhner, *Encyclopedia of the Papacy* (New York: Philosophical Library, 1958), pp. 26–27.

23. E. R. Chamberlin, *The Bad Popes* (New York: Dorset Books, 1969), p. 35.

24. *Ibid.*, pp. 56–57.

25. *Ibid.*, p. 175.

26. Guicciardini, quoted in Will Durant's *The Renaissance* (New York: Simon and Schuster, 1953), p. 414.

27. *Ibid.*, pp. 424–26.

28. *Ibid.*

29. Chamberlin, *op. cit.*, pp. 197–98.

30. Guicciardini, quoted in *The Renaissance*, p. 434.

31. Bertrand L. Conway, S.J., *The Question Box* (New York: Paulist Press, 1929), p. 176.

32. Chamberlin, *op. cit.*, p. 154.

33. Barbara Tuchman, *A Distant Mirror* (New York: Alfred A. Knopf, 1978), p. 330.

34. *Ibid.*

35. Chamberlin, *op. cit.*, p. 154.

36. Tuchman, *op. cit.*, p. 335.

37. Martin, *op. cit.*, p. 194.

38. Thomas Bokenkotter, *A Concise History of the Catholic Church* (Garden City, New York: Image Books, 1979), p. 200.

39. Louise Ropes Loomis, trans., and John Hine Mundy and Kennerly M. Woody, eds., *The Council of Constance* (New York: Columbia University Press, 1961), p. 163.

40. Martin, *op. cit.*, pp. 153–66.

41. Conway, *op. cit.*, p. 171.

42. Frend, *The Rise of Christianity*, pp. 539–40.

43. Nicholas Cheetham, *The Keeper of the Keys* (New York: Charles Scribner's Sons, 1982), p. 49.

44. Hans Küng, *Infallible? An Inquiry* (Garden City, New York: Doubleday and Company, 1971), pp. 65–124.

45. Brian Tierney, *Origins of Papal Infallibility, 1150–1350* (Garden City, New York: Doubleday and Company, 1972), p. 281; see also Bokenkotter, *op. cit.*, p. 120.

46. George Lindbeck, "The Reformation and the Infallibility Debate," in *Teaching Authority and Infallibility in the Church* (Minneapolis: Augsburg Publishing Company, 1978), pp. 115–16.

47. Avery Dulles, *A Church to Believe In* (New York: Crossroad Publishing, 1982), p. 145.

48. *Ibid.*

49. Malachi Martin, *Rich Church, Poor Church* (New York: G. P. Putnam's Sons, 1984), p. 124.

50. *Ibid.*

TWO

The Church

and the Scriptures

. . . Tradition transmits in its entirety the Word of God which has been entrusted to the apostles so that, enlightened by the Spirit of truth, they may faithfully preserve, expound and spread it abroad by their preaching. Thus it comes about that the Church does not draw her certainty about all revealed truth from the holy Scriptures alone. . . .

Vatican II, Dei Verbum, 9

1. *Do Catholics accept the primacy of Scripture in determining doctrine?*

No. Catholics place the pronouncements of the Church before the statements of Scripture in determining doctrine. After all, the Magisterium teaches that the Church not only existed before the New Testament but was mother to it.[1] The first written accounts of the New Testament were some of the Epistles of St. Paul which were written almost twenty-five years after the death of Christ. Moreover, Vatican II teaches, it was the Church which determined the canon of Scripture and which alone can give a correct interpretation of its sacred contents. The "Dogmatic Constitution on Divine Revelation" *(Dei Verbum)*, 10, states: ". . . the task of giving an authentic interpretation of the Word of God . . . has been entrusted to the living teaching office of the Church alone."

2. *Do Catholics accept the Old and New Testaments as the Word of God?*

Yes. *Dei Verbum,* 16, says: "God, the inspirer and author of the books of both Testaments, in his wisdom has brought it about that the New should be hidden in the Old and that the Old should be made manifest in the New."

Indeed, one of the most heinous heresies of the early Church was Marcionism. A Gnostic Christian, Marcion (circa 85–160) provided in a treatise called "Antitheses" a list of contradictions between the Old and New Testaments to show that the God of the Jews, the Creator of this miserable world, was far different from the God and Father of Jesus, of whose existence the world had little inkling until the fifteenth year of the reign of Tiberius when Jesus suddenly appeared preaching his Gospel by the Jordon River.[2]

To uphold this distinction between the Old and New Testaments,

Marcion produced a canon of scripture which consisted of the Gospel of Luke and the ten Pauline Epistles. It was largely in response to this threat that the Church finally provided circa 160 its own canon or body of scripture—a canon which consisted of the Old Testament, the four Gospels, and the Pauline and Petrine letters. Believing Christians were required to adhere to these tests for the sake of orthodoxy.

The process of the final selection of texts for the New Testament, however, continued for the next two hundred years. Not until 366 did the Church come to a final agreement regarding the twenty-seven books that became deemed as sacred Scripture.[3]

3. Do Catholics uphold the inerrancy of the Bible?

Throughout the ages, the Church has insisted that there is no error in the Holy Scriptures. Pope Pius XII, for example, in his encyclical, *Divino afflante Spiritu* (1943), maintained: "In our own time, the Vatican Council [I], with the object of condemning false doctrines regarding inspiration, declared that these books were to be regarded by the Church as 'sacred and canonical' . . . not merely because they contain revelations without error, but because 'having been written under the inspiration of the Holy Spirit, they have God as their author, and, as such, were handed down to the Church herself.' "[4] Recent biblical theorists within the Church believe that this rigorist view of biblical inerrancy was somewhat mitigated by Vatican II's *Dei Verbum,* 11, which said: "Since all that the inspired authors, or sacred writers, affirm should be regarded as affirmed by the Holy Spirit, we must acknowledge that the books of Scripture, firmly, faithfully and without error, teach that truth which God for the sake of our salvation, wishes to see confided to the sacred Scriptures."

4. Are Catholics fundamentalists?

No. Catholics believe that certain passages, even entire books like the Book of Revelation, should be understood allegorically and not as literary occurrences. The story of Jonah, for example, may be recognized as true but only anagogically—that is, with reference to a future event in sacred history. Jonah spending three days in the belly of a "big fish" prefigures the death and resurrection of Jesus.

The early Church Fathers were not fundamentalists in the manner of many modern Protestant evangelicals. St. Augustine, for example, in his commentary on Genesis, wrote: "Now to think of God as forming man from the slime of the earth with bodily hands is childish. Indeed, if Scripture had said such a thing, we should be compelled to believe that the writer used a metaphor rather than that God is contained in the structure of members such as we know in our bodies."[5]

5. *Why do Catholics have a larger Bible than Protestants?*

In the wake of the Reformation, the Council of Trent in 1546 decided to readopt the canon of Scripture of seventy-two books—forty-five in the Old and twenty-seven in the New Testament—that had been set forth by the Council of Rome in A.D. 382. Seven books—Tobit, Wisdom, Judith, Sirach, Baruch, and the two Books of the Maccabees—have been called "deutero-canonical" or "a second body of Scripture" because Protestant scholars consider them to be "aprocryphal," or of doubtful authorship. The decision by Fathers of Trent to revert to this expanded canon was meant to provide vivid proof of the Church's authority over the Word of God.

6. *Are Catholics free to provide their own interpretations of the Bible?*

Vatican II's *Dei Verbum,* 10, maintains that the Scriptures are not self-explanatory and require the Church's Magisterium or teaching authority to explain what the more substantive passages mean and how they are to be lived by the faithful. After all, the Council Fathers insist, the writings of the New Testament have their origins in the Church and only the Church can correctly interpret them.[6]

7. *Are Catholics free to engage in the scientific study of Scripture?*

Yes. Pope Pius XII, in his encyclical *Divino afflante Spiritu* (1943), and the Pontifical Biblical Commission under Pope Paul VI (1964) endorsed the "genuine principles of the historical method," which is the commonly used means of modern biblical exegesis.

However, while engaging in such scientific studies, Catholic scholars are obliged to be guided by the Church's *de fide* statements (i.e., statements concerning the faith) on the Scriptures. In other words, while engaging in the quest for the historical Jesus, they must utilize the approach of *fides quarens intellectum* (faith seeking understanding) not *intellectus quarens fidem* (understanding seeking faith). Pope Pius XII in the above-mentioned encyclical said: "The commentators of the Sacred Letters, mindful of the fact that here there is a question of a divinely inspired text the care and interpretation of which have been confined to the Church by God Himself, should no less diligently take into account the explanations and declarations of the teaching authority of the Church, as likewise the interpretation given by the Holy Fathers, and even the 'analogy of faith,' as Leo XIII wisely noted."[7]

8. What is the "analogy of faith"?

The "analogy of faith" refers to the collective teachings of the Church which form a framework. This framework enables Catholic exegetes (or interpreters of the scriptures) to use one truth to explain another. Thus, when a Catholic biblicist attempts to analyze what Matthew and Luke say about Mary, they must keep in mind what the Church infallibly pronounced about her (the Immaculate Conception, the Perpetual Virginity, etcetera).

9. What is the historical-critical method of studying Scripture?

The historical-critical method permits scholars to examine the biblical books as pieces of literature, not as sacred works. The various ancient texts are studied to determine their authenticity, their literary form (narration, poetry, fable of history), their authorship, their source material, and so on.

10. What is the value, according to the Church, in such analysis?

The historical-critical method has been instrumental in establishing various stages of development in the compilation of the Pentateuch (the five Books of Moses) and other Old Testament writings (including the triadic composition of Isaiah). It has also unraveled the complexities of ancient genealogies and uncovered the historic milieu of such apocalyptic works as the Book of Daniel. Similarly, this method has helped to explain the levels of tradition in the New Testament, has provided insight into the actual teachings of the historical Jesus (apart from the *kerygma* or proclamations of the Church), and has established a credible theory for dating the various Gospels and Epistles.

11. *Are there problems, according to the Church, with an historical-critical approach to the Scriptures?*

Yes. By setting aside the sacred nature of the Bible, scholars often become debunkers of biblical history and biblical claims. This is particularly true, according to Vatican spokesman Joseph Cardinal Ratzinger, when the exegetes or biblical interpreters are religious skeptics. Since the historical-critical method holds up natural science as its model, Ratzinger argues, it thereby falls prey to the so-called Heisenberg's principle, i.e., the principle that the outcome of any given experiment is necessarily conditioned by the mind-set of the observer. For this reason, Ratzinger continues, the interpretation of a scriptural event can never be a truly objective reproduction of historical fact but rather a reflection of the point of view of the interpreter.[8]

12. *Do Catholics believe in God because of what they read in the Bible?*

No. Catholicism maintains in its Dogmatic Constitution *(Dei Verbum,* 2) that God can be known with certainty by the natural light of human reason. Indeed, the constitution states that individuals who profess to be seeking God by their intellects but fail to find Him are not excusable for their ignorance.

Catholicism's natural proofs for God's existence, following the arguments set forth by St. Thomas Aquinas in his *Summa Theologiae,* generally take the following forms: (1) the cosmological proof (i.e., proof from the order of the cosmos or universe), which appeals to the principle of causality to explain the existence of motion and change in the world and then posits the necessity of a first cause or an unmoved mover; (2) the teleological proof (i.e., proof from the design and purpose in nature), which explains the existence of order and finality in the world by pointing to the necessity of an infinite intelligent being; (3) the ontological proof (i.e., proof from the metaphysical nature of being), which claims that existence is a necessary attribute of God as the most perfect and necessary being; and (4) the moral proof, which claims that man's intrinsically moral and goal-oriented nature demands a goal that corresponds to his desire for the highest and ultimate good, which is God.[9]

The Church further affirms that reason can establish that God is of one unique spiritual substance, that He is entirely simple and immutable, that He is infinite in intellect, will, and every perfection, and that He is omnipotent, omniscient, and eternal.

13. *Does Catholicism claim that reason alone is sufficient for man to obtain a knowledge of God?*

No. While reason can establish God's existence, it is incapable of comprehending His essence. To know the essential truths about God and thereby to come to a "saving faith," man must rely on revelation.

14. *Where, according to Catholicism, are these revealed truths found?*

In *sacra doctrina,* i.e., the Old and New Testaments and the tradition of the Church, including the writings of the Church Fathers and the pronouncements of the Church Ecumenical Councils in union with the teachings of the popes and the bishops.

15. *Whence comes the dogma of the Trinity?*

The dogma of the Trinity has its origin in the baptismal formula of the early Church as set forth at the close of Matthew's Gospel: "Go, therefore, and make disciples of all nations, baptizing them in the name of the Father, the Son and the Holy Spirit" (Matt. 28:19); and in early Christian doxologies such as St. Paul's blessing to the Church in Corinth: "The grace of our Lord Jesus Christ and the love of God and the fellowship of the Holy Spirit be with you all" (2 Cor. 13:14).

The early Christians were faced with the problem of upholding Judaic monotheism while proclaiming the divinity of Jesus as the son of God. An early solution to this difficult problem came with Monarchianism, the teaching that Jesus was, in fact, the God of the Old Testament incarnate. This solution, however, proved to be unsatisfactory, since Jesus during his ministry made constant references to his Father in heaven.

At the same time, the early Christians were compelled to explain the identity of the Holy Spirit. Was it the Holy Ghost of Jesus still moving through the Christian community or a manifestation of the Presence of God the Father?

Toward the end of the second century, Tertullian, following a line of thought suggested by St. Irenaeus, attempted to define the threeness of Father, Son, and Holy Spirit as a plurality revealed in the working out of the divine plan in history. "All three," he wrote, "are one *unus*." But Tertullian felt obliged to answer the question, "Three what?" And so, he provided the formula that God is "one substance consisting in three persons."[10] By making this distinction in persons, Tertullian was able to refute the claims of the Monarchians, and, at the same time, to attack the heretical position of the Adoptionists, who claimed that Jesus was a mortal man who lived such a saintly life that he was later adopted by God as His divine son.

Tertullian's formula was refined throughout the third century and was cast into its final formation in the so-called Athanasian Creed of the fourth century. The Creed stated the following: "Now the Catholic faith is this: that we worship one God in the Trinity, and the Trinity is a unity. . . . The Father is a distinct Person, the Son is a distinct Person, and the Holy Spirit is a distinct Person; but the Father, the Son, and the Holy Spirit have one divinity, equal glory and majesty."

16. *Do Catholics believe in evolution?*

Catholics are perfectly free to accept the scientific theories of evolution as long as they acknowledge God as their Creator—a Creator not only of the material universe but of each individual soul, regardless of the process of bodily development. Pope Pius XII, in his encyclical *Humani Generis* (1950), said: "The teaching office of the Church does not forbid that the theory of evolution . . . be investigated and discussed by experts in both science and theology . . . [but] the Catholic faith orders us to retain that souls are immediately created by God. They are rash and go too far who act as if the origin of the human body from preexisting and living matter . . . were certain and fully proved. . . ."[11] In 1966, Pope Paul VI re-echoed these words in his letter *Acta Apostolicae Sedis* (58).

17. *Do Catholics accept as history the story of Adam and Eve?*

Yes. The Bible calls the first human being "man," i.e., in Hebrew "Adam." Adam calls his wife Eve because she is the mother of the living. Vatican II in *Gaudium et Spes*, 22, speaks of "Adam, the first man, a type of him who was to come, Christ the Lord, the new Adam." The heart of the Church's teaching is that in the beginning there was "man," i.e., Adam, and he fell from God's grace through pride and disobedience. It teaches that this "original sin" changed the course of human history and necessitated the coming of Jesus Christ.

18. *What is the dogma of original sin?*

One of the major tenets of Catholicism, the dogma of original sin was developed from reflection by the early Church Fathers on two passages of Scripture, Genesis 2 and 3, which relates the story of Adam and Eve and their rebellion against God and subsequent expulsion from the Garden of Eden for eating a forbidden fruit; and Romans 5:12–21, in which St. Paul connects the existence of sin and death with Adam's sin and further juxtaposes the first Adam with Christ inasmuch as men inherited condemnation from Adam and the free gift of justification from Christ.

At first, the Church Fathers, such as Justin Martyr (circa 160), believed that by this "inherited condemnation" men bore the punishment for Adam's sin but not the guilt. Far from believing in an inherent evil nature, they described human corruption in terms of mankind following Adam's bad example.[12]

The idea of a corrupt nature passed on by Adam to his progeny remained to be developed by Tertullian in his work "On the Soul." Believing in the Stoic principle that the soul of a child is derived from the soul of his father, like a shoot *(tradux)* from the parent stock of a tree, it followed that every soul is ultimately a branch *(surculus)* of Adam's soul. And inasmuch as the soul inherits from its parents their spiritual characteristics and qualities, those of Adam were unfortunately transmitted to all his descendents.[13]

This teaching, known as traducianism, became accepted in the Latin theology of St. Clement of Alexandria and St. Athanasius. However, it received its final modification by St. Augustine as a consequence of the Pelagian controversy.

Pelagius, a fifth-century British monk, held that man was basically good by nature and possessed the ability to merit salvation by his good works. In reaction to this, St. Augustine set forth the fully conceived notion of *originale paccatum*. In Adam, human nature was "changed and vitiated."[14] By inheriting this nature, every man is a slave to sin, a slave utterly reliant on God's grace for salvation. In *The City of God,* he spelled out for all Christians the terrible effects of the Fall of Adam:

> For we all existed in that one man who fell into sin through the woman who was made out of him before sin existed. Although the specific form by which each of us was to live was not yet created or assigned, our nature was already present in the seed from which we were to spring. And because this nature has been soiled by sin and doomed to death and justly condemned, no man was to be born in any other condition.
>
> Thus from a bad use of free choice, a sequence of misfortunes conducts the whole human race, excepting those redeemed by the grace of God, from the original canker in its root to the devestation of a second and endless death.[15]

St. Augustine's views were formalized as dogma by the Council of Trent in 1546. The Council taught that all men are guilty of the sin of Adam, that this sin is transmitted from generation to generation by procreation, and that baptism is necessary for its removal.[16]

19. *What is the Catholic meaning of the Incarnation?*

The Incarnation means the Word of God became flesh *(carnus)* as stated in John 1:14. "The Word became flesh and made his dwelling among us: and we have seen his glory; the glory of an only son coming from the father, filled with enduring love."

The dogma of the Incarnation was defined after centuries of bitter dispute over the human and divine natures of Christ. The debate reached a peak in 318 with the appearance of a theologian named Arius in the prestigious See of Alexandria in North Africa. Arius, a devotee of Neoplatonism, saw God as unbegotten, eternal, and immutable. Christ, he argued, could not be one with the Creator. He was rather the *Logos* or Word, the first born and highest of all created beings. Since He had been begotten, Arius continued, Christ must have been begotten in time and was, therefore, not co-eternal with the Father. What's more, since He was created, He must have been created out of nothing like the material world and not out of the substance of the Father and was, therefore, not "consubstantial" with God.[17]

To combat these arguments—especially the annoying notion that Christ was a creature—the first Ecumenical Council was held at Nicaea in 325. At the Council, Bishop Athanasius of Alexandria by clever questioning forced Arius to admit that if Christ were a creature and had a beginning in time, He could change like all created things, and could pass from virtue to vice. Moreover, Athanasius persisted, if Christ were not of the same substance as the Father, all Christians would be affirming a form of polytheism, since Christ at least must be perceived as a demi-god. Arius continued to provide answers that were honest, direct, and damning. He was condemned as a heretic and exiled.

Moreover, to solve forever the controversy regarding the nature of Christ, the Council published the following creed: "We believe in one God, the Father Almighty, maker of all things visible and invisible; and in one Lord Jesus Christ, the Son of God, begotten . . . not made, being of one essence homoousion with the Father, who for us men and for our salvation came down from heaven and was made man. . . ."

But the problem did not remain solved. It recurred again in 448, when Eutyches, head of a monastery in Constantinople, maintained that in Christ were not two natures—human and divine—but only a divine nature, since He was, as the Nicene Creed affirmed, "of one essence" with the Father. Flavian, the patriarch of Constantinople, egged on by Pope Leo I condemned this "Monophysite" or "one nature" position as heresy and excommunicated Eutyches. Eutyches, in turn, petitioned Dioscoras, Bishop of Alexandria, for a second hearing. Here the plot thickens. Dioscoras was a sworn enemy of

Flavian's, and, for personal political as well as religious reasons, managed to persuade Emperor Theodosius II to convoke the Second Council at Ephesus in 449. At this Council, Eutyches was exonerated and Flavian was assailed with such oratorical violence that he died. The Council then issued an anathema or formal ecclesiastical curse against anyone who divided Christ into two natures.

Pope Leo I, who had not attended the Council, sent several letters supporting Flavian's position. Hearing the results, the Pope refused to recognize its decrees and pronounced it a "Robber Council." Two years later, after much ecclesiastical intrigue, the Council of Constantinople nullified the decrees of the Second Council and upheld Pope Leo's position. Affirming the divine and human natures of Christ, the Council issued the following confession: "We confess one and the same Christ, Son, Lord Only-Begotten, made known in two natures [which exist] without confusion, without change, without division and without separation: the differences of the natures having been in no wise taken away by reason of the union, but rather the properties of each being preserved, and both occurring into one Person [*prosopon*] and one *hypostasis* [substance]."

20. *Why did God, according to the Catholic Church, become man?*

The first followers of Jesus came to the conclusion very early that Jesus had lived in order to die, that his death was not the interruption of his life but its ultimate purpose (". . . the son of Man came not to be served but to serve, and to give his life as a ransom for many . . ." Matt. 20:28).[18] For this reason, the Gospels offer information concerning less than a hundred days in the life of Jesus, but an hour-by-hour account of his Passion and Death. The Apostles' Creed and the Nicene Creed recognized this when they moved directly from "born of the Virgin Mary" to his crucifixion "under Pontius Pilate."[19]

Moreover, the New Testament writers (Matt. 8:17; Acts 8:26–39) saw in the suffering and death of Jesus the fulfillment of the prophecy of the Suffering Servant as set forth in the following passage from the Book of Isaiah (53:4–12):

It was our infirmities that he bore,
Our sufferings that he endured,
While we thought of him as stricken,
As one smitten by God and afflicted.
But he was pierced for our offenses,
Crushed for our sins;
Upon him was the chastisement that makes us white,
By his stripes we were healed. . . .

Like a lamb to the slaughter,
Or a sheep before the shearers,
He was silent and opened not his mouth. . . .

Therefore, I will give him his portion among the great. . . .

And he shall take away the sins of many
And win pardon for their offenses. . . .

This depiction of Jesus as the sacrificial "lamb" (John 1:29), "our Passover" (1 Cor. 5:7), "whom God put forward as an expiation by his blood to be received by faith" (Rom. 3:25) was the dominant conception of Christ in the first Christian centuries.

By the end of the second century, Tertullian, who was a lawyer by profession, began to cast this sacrificial image into a legalistic mold by speaking of Christ's death as a *satisfaction* for the sins of mankind.[20] This notion of satisfaction had its roots in the primitive rite of penance. The early Church Fathers believed that a sinner who was truly contrite for his or her sin and who confessed that sin and was truly absolved of its guilt, nevertheless, had to make some kind of restitution or penance for the offense in order to restore the moral balance of his or her life. Naturally, this restitution was determined by the severity of the sin. A really grievous sin—such as a homosexual act—required years of fasting, prayer, and acts of communal charity before proper reparation for the moral damage of the offense could be met.[21]

In 1097, while discussing the work of Jesus, St. Anselm of Canterbury placed this notion of satisfaction on a cosmic scale. By turning from God, Adam withdrew his due measure of honor to God and disrupted the moral rightness *(rectitudo)* of the universe. To make matters worse, he could not make proper restitution for this infinite offense since he already owed everything to God. Moreover, by his continued offenses, man persisted to place himself deeper and deeper in debt with absolutely no way of restoring what he took from the original rightness of things.

Since God is just and abides by the moral rightness which He established to govern the universe, He could not simply overlook Adam's offense or forgive his transgression by fiat. This would undermine the rightness of His order. Hence, reparation must be made. But God is also a God of mercy, the God who declares, "I have no pleasure in the death of the wicked, but that the wicked turn from his way and live" (Ezek. 33:11).

Such, for St. Anselm, was the divine dilemma to which the wisdom of the cross provided the only solution. Only a being responsible for making restitution or satisfaction (by being man) but capable of making this reparation (by being God) could simultaneously carry out the imperatives of divine justice and divine mercy. Thus it was necessary for the Son of God to become man, assuming a divine and human nature in one person, to pay the debt he did not owe. It is a testimony to St. Anselm's genius that he managed not only to be scriptural in developing this doctrine but also to uphold as necessity the Chalcedonian formula.

St. Anselm's doctrine also accounted for the necessity of Christ to be born of a virgin, since the sin of Adam was passed on from generation to generation (as St. Augustine had argued) by procreation.

Though Christ was born primarily to die, St. Anselm also found profound meaning in Christ's works and ministry, since His exemplary sinless life showed men how they should never turn away from "the justice they owed God."[22]

By the cross, therefore, Christ achieved the ends of divine mercy by laying down His life for the honor of God, thereby rendering satisfaction to divine justice.

The emphasis in this so-called Latin view of the Atonement is on the sacrificial death of Jesus and the terrible price that had to be paid for man's redemption. St. Anselm answered his student's objections to the severity of his doctrine with the words: *"Nondum considerati quandi ponderis sit peccatum"* (Not yet have you considered the seriousness of sin).[23] These words serve as a refrain throughout much of Catholic Christology and underscore the sacred mystery of the Mass.

At the Council of Trent (1546), St. Anselm's view became the official doctrine of Christ's work. The Council proclaimed the following: "The tragic consequences of Adam's sin had no other remedy than the merit of one Mediator, our Lord Jesus Christ, who reconciled us to God in His blood. . . . Jesus merited for us justification by His most holy passion on the wood of the Cross, and made satisfaction for us to God the Father."[24]

21. *Must Catholics believe in the Virgin Birth of Jesus?*

Yes. This is a teaching which Catholics are not allowed to question or debate. Not only must they accept the Virgin Birth of Jesus but also the Immaculate Conception of Mary, as pronounced by Pope Pius XII in 1954, and the perpetual virginity of Mary, as decreed by the Second General Council of Constantinople in 553.

The Virgin Birth is upheld by two scriptural passages. Matthew 1:18–20 states the following:

"Now the birth of Jesus Christ took place in this way. When his mother Mary had been betrothed to Joseph, before they came together she was found to be with child of the Holy Spirit; and her husband Joseph, being a just man and unwilling to put her to shame, resolved to divorce her quietly. But as he considered this, behold an angel of the Lord appeared to him in a dream, saying, 'Joseph, son of David, do not fear to take Mary your wife, for that which is conceived in her is of the Holy Spirit.' . . ."

Similarly, Luke 1:26–35 reads as follows:

"In the sixth month the angel Gabriel was sent from God to a city of Galilee named Nazareth to a virgin betrothed to a man whose name was Joseph of the house of David; and the virgin's name was Mary. And he said to her, 'Hail, O favored one, the Lord is with you.' But she was greatly troubled at the saying, and considered in her mind what sort of greeting this might be. And the angel said to her, 'Do not be afraid, Mary, for you have found favor with God. And behold you will conceive in your womb and bear a son, and you shall call him Jesus. . . .' And Mary said to the angel, 'How can this be, since I have no husband?' And the angel said to her, 'The Holy Spirit will come upon you, and the power of the Most High will overshadow you; therefore the child to be born will be called holy, the Son of God.' . . ."

While the virginity of Mary at the time of her conception *(in partu)* and afterward *(post partum)* is not a debatable matter among believing Catholics, the historicity of other matters surrounding the Nativity, including the Star of Bethlehem, the Stable, the Magi, and the flight into Egypt are matters of free study among Catholic historians and exegetes.

22. *Why do Catholics celebrate the birthday of Jesus Christ on December 25?*

The chosen date to celebrate the birth of Jesus is an example of the syncretism or the assimilation of pagan beliefs into the Christian faith. During the third century, Emperor Aurelian proclaimed December 25 as the birthday of the sun god Sol, whose cult was very strong in Rome at that time. In the fourth century, after Constantine became converted to Christianity, he developed an unfortunate tendency of confusing Christ with the Sun God. To commemorate the Edict of Milan (313), which led to Christianity becoming the official religion of the Empire, Constantine had coins struck which bore the symbols of Sol (the sun). These same symbols were engraved on the Arch of Constantine. Perhaps, because this confusion was becoming widespread, Bishop Liberius of Constantinople in 354 ordered all Christians to celebrate the annual holiday for Sol as the birthday of their Savior.[25]

23. *Must Catholics accept Christ's miracles as historical facts?*

Yes. The Church abhors rational and mythological explanations of the supernatural works of Jesus, such as those provided by the so-called Liberal Lives of Jesus, which were written during the nineteenth century (David Struass, Joseph Ernest Renan, *et alia*). Largely in reaction to such works, the First Vatican Council decreed the following: "If anyone shall say that miracles are impossible, and therefore that all accounts regarding them, even those contained in the Holy Scripture, are to be dismissed as fabulous or mythical; or that miracles can never be known with certainty, and that the divine origin of Christianity is not rightly proved by them, let him be anathema."[26]

24. *How do Catholics interpret Christ's message of the Kingdom of God?*

The Church decrees that it is the Kingdom of God in the making. Vatican II's "Document on the Church" *(Lumen Gentium, 5)* speaks of Christ's inaugurating the Church by His preaching of the coming of the Kingdom of God, the final fulfillment of which will be in eternity.

25. *According to the Church, was Jesus really human? Did he really grow in "wisdom and grace" (Luke 2:40)?*

Yes. Catholic doctrine, in accordance with the pronouncements of the Fourth Lateran Council (1215) which upheld the creeds of Nicaea and Chalcedon, maintains the full humanity of Jesus. It teaches that he grew in "wisdom and strength" (Luke 2:40), that he wearied (John 4:6), that he experienced hunger and thirst (Luke 4:2), that he underwent temptation (Matt. 5:1–11, Mark 1:12–13, Luke 4:1–3), that he wept (Luke 19:42), that he struggled with weakness and fear (Matt. 26:36–46; Mark 14:32–42; Luke 22:39–46), and that he truly suffered and died on the cross (Matt. 27:27–61; Mark 15:16–47; Luke 23:32–56; John 19:17–42).

From its primitive beginnings, the Church upheld the humanity of Jesus in opposition to Docetic and Gnostic depictions of Jesus as a spirit whose body was merely an illusion. Gnosticism and Doceticism, which arose in the early Hellenistic Christian congregations, were the results of a Greek conceptualization about the nature of Jesus Christ. The Hellenistic mind could not conceive how God, being a Spirit, could "pass" into matter. Therefore, several groups of Greek Christians came to believe that Jesus did not have a real but merely an illusionary body. As such, he could not suffer and die. His agony on the cross, therefore, represented a kind of divine play-acting.[27]

26. *How do Catholics explain that Jesus, the purported Second Person of the Trinity, said he did not know the hour of the passing of heaven and earth (Mark 13:32)?*

Throughout Church history, passages such as this have been interpreted as statements made by Jesus solely within the context of his human nature.

27. *What, according to Catholicism, is the unpardonable sin mentioned in Matthew 12:31?*

The unpardonable sin, according to St. Cyprian, was a third century heresy known as Novatianism, after the name of its proponent, a presbyter named Novatian. According to this heresy, anyone who renounced the Christian faith in time of persecution was, in turn, forever renounced by God and left to eternal damnation. The Church rejected this rigorist teaching and insisted that repentance is always possible and that the most heinous sin is the insistence that the Holy Spirit cannot forgive any sin.[28]

St. Augustine and St. Thomas Aquinas, however, held that the unpardonable sin was the sin of final unrepentance, i.e., the refusal to repent of one's sins even at the hour of death.

28. *Did Jesus, according to the Church, despair on the cross?*

Scripture teaches that Jesus at the moment of his death cried out, "Eli, Eli, lama sabachthani?" (My God, my God, why hast thou forsaken me?) (Matt. 27:46). These words cannot be accepted by Catholics as a statement of final despair, since despair is one of the seven deadly sins. Rather, they must accept the cry as a reference by Jesus to the following words of David in Psalm 22:

My God, my God, why hast thou forsaken me?
Why art thou so far from helping me, from the words of my
    groaning?

O my God, I cry by day, but thou dost not answer;
and by night, but find no rest.

Yet thou art holy,
enthroned on the praises of Israel.
In thee our fathers trusted;
they trusted, and thou didst deliver them.
To thee, they cried and were saved;
in thee they trusted and were not disappointed [1–5].

29. *What do Catholics mean by teaching that Christ descended into hell?*

This doctrine is related to the medieval notion of Limbo. Since the thirteenth century, Limbo (from the Latin *limbus* meaning "border" or "hem") had been used to designate the place for the souls of children who had died before receiving sanctifying grace through infant baptism. It also came to serve as a painless place in eternity for the Hebrew prophets and ancient Greek philosophers who had lived exemplary lives but died before the birth of Christ and never received sacramental remission for the sin of Adam. Thus it came about that there were in Catholic thought two Limbos: the Limbo of Children and the Limbo of the Fathers.

Based on the exegesis of such scriptural passages as Ephesians 4:9 ("In saying, 'He ascended,' what does it mean but that he had also descended into the lower parts of the earth?"), late medieval thinkers held that Jesus after his death descended not into hell (from which no soul can be saved) but into the Limbo of the Fathers. They interpreted this Limbo to be the Sheol or place of the dead mentioned in Christ's parable of the rich man and Lazarus (Luke 16:19–31). This teaching was stated as follows in the *Catechism of the Council of Trent:* "We profess that immediately after the death of Christ His soul descended into hell and dwelt there as long as His body remained in the tomb; and also that the one Person of Christ was at the same time in hell and in the sepulchre. . . . Hell here signifies those secret abodes in which are detained the souls that have not obtained the happiness of heaven."[29]

30. *How can Catholics believe this since Christ told the penitent thief,*
"This day you will be with me in paradise" (Luke 23:43)?

To address this complication, the Catechism of Trent maintained
that the soul of the penitent thief did not ascend into heaven but fell
into the Limbo of the Fathers or Sheol with his ancestors. Once Jesus
appeared, the just souls, including the soul of the thief, began to enjoy
the Beatific Vision and Sheol became immediately transformed into
Paradise.

31. *Why is the celebration of Christ's Resurrection called Easter?*

The word *Easter,* according to the Venerable Bede (673–735), came
from the name of the Teutonic goddess of spring, Eostre, who rose
flowering from the frozen earth each year.[30]

32. *Why does Easter occur on different dates each year?*

The Council of Nicaea set the date for the celebration of the Resurrection of Jesus on the first Sunday after the first full moon following the vernal equinox (March 21). The earliest possible date for
Easter is March 22; the latest, April 25.

33. *What does the Church teach about the Resurrection?*

"On the third day after His death, Christ rose gloriously from the
dead" is the earliest *kerygma* or proclamation of primitive Christianity
and has been taught as an infallible doctrine by the Church throughout the ages.

The Resurrection represents for Catholicism the greatest of Christ's
miracles, the fulfillment of all prophecy about Him, and the strongest
truth of his teaching. St. Paul saw this point clearly by writing: "If
Christ has not been raised, our preaching is void of content and your
faith is empty too" (1 Cor. 15:14). From the very beginning of the
Christian movement, the Resurrection has been known as "the Lord's
day." Vatican II, in discussing the Liturgy (106) summarized the
Church's view as follows: "By a tradition handed down from the
apostles which took its origin from the very day of Christ's Resurrec-

tion, the Church celebrates the paschal mystery every seventh day, which is appropriately called the Lord's Day."

34. *Have not several Catholic scholars denied the historicity of the Resurrection in recent years?*

Yes. What is surprising, perhaps, is that until recently the Church has had little need to explain apologetically its teaching on the Resurrection or to condemn those who denied its truth. In fact the Easter event was taken, by and large, as the given of Christianity.

In modern times, however, theologians' skepticism, often the end result of the historical-critical exegesis of the sacred writings, has led several Catholic theologians to question or deny the Resurrection of Jesus. They find discrepancy between the Easter kerygma of St. Paul in 1 Corinthians 15:3–8 and the Easter narratives in the Gospels. Moreover, they argue that the Gospel accounts of the Resurrection, unlike the rather straightforward accounts of the Passion, present no coherent sequence of events and, besides, manifest numerous discrepancies and inconsistencies. The Scriptures, they say, do not agree on such central details as to whom Jesus first appeared, the place of his first appearance, and the number of people who were the first witnesses of this monumental event.

With this as the prevailing mind-set, scholars such as Xavier Léon-Dufour, Edward Schillibeeckx, and Rudolf Pesch have sought to develop what to them is a more acceptable interpretation of the Resurrection. Léon-Dufour speaks of it as the spiritual experience of the Presence of Jesus in the early Christian gatherings. Schillibeeckx describes it as an experience of conversion based on the disciples' realization of God's continuing offer of forgiveness and acceptance. And Pesch maintains that the Resurrection is a concept meant to confirm the continuing faith of the apostles in Jesus as the prophetic Messiah.[31]

35. *Are such modern scholars heretics?*

The only one entitled to pronounce anyone guilty of heresy is a bishop, including the Bishop of Rome, after a formal hearing.

However, by separating themselves from the doctrines which the Church teaches as true, they cannot be called authentic voices of the

Church and, perhaps, fall into the category of Hans Küng and Charles Curran, neither of whom is considered by the Holy See to be a Catholic theologian.

36. Do Catholics believe that Jesus will come again to establish His Kingdom on earth as it says in the Scriptures (2 Peter 3:10; Rev. 20:4–5)?

No. Because the Church has identified itself with the forthcoming Kingdom of God as proclaimed by Jesus, Pope Pius XII in a *Decree of Holy Office* condemned as "naïve literalism" the faulty interpretation of certain scriptural passages (such as the ones mentioned in this question) which lead people to believe that Christ, together with His saints, will establish a temporal Kingdom of God on earth that will last for a thousand years.[32] While opposed to such millennianism, the Church, nevertheless, affirms its belief in the *Parousia,* the day when Christ will come again in glory to judge the living and the dead (Matt. 16:27, 26:64).

37. Why do Catholics call Jesus of Nazareth Jesus Christ?

Christ is the Greek word for "Messiah."

NOTES

1. Ronald Lawler, O.F.M. Cap.; Donald W. Wuerl; and Thomas Comerford Lawler, eds., *The Teaching of Christ: A Catholic Catechism for Adults* (Huntington, Indiana: Our Sunday Visitor, 1983), p. 210.

2. Henry Chadwick, *The Early Church* (Baltimore: Penguin Books, 1969), p. 39.

3. Robert Coughlin, "Who Was This Man Jesus," in *Life,* Vol. 52, No. 26 (December 25, 1964), p. 99.

4. Pope Pius XII, *Divino afflante Spiritu,* in *The Encyclicals of Pope Pius XII* (Washington, D.C.: National Catholic Welfare Conference, 1943), p. 4.

5. St. Augustine, *De Genesi ad Litteram (The Literal Meaning of Genesis),* translated by John Hammond Taylor, S.J., Vol. 41, in *Ancient Christian Writers,* edited by Johannes Quasten, Walter J. Burghardt, and Thomas Comerford Lawler (New York: Newman Press, 1982), p. 144.

6. Ronald Lawler, et al., *loc. cit.*

7. Joseph Cardinal Ratzinger, "Foundations and Approaches to Biblical Exegesis," in *Origins,* 17 (February 11, 1988), p. 596.

8. *Ibid.*

9. Thomas Bokenkotter, *Essential Catholicism: Dynamics of Faith and Belief* (Garden City, New York: Image Books, 1986), p. 21.

10. Chadwick, *op. cit.,* p. 89.

11. Pope Pius XII, *Humani generis,* in *The Papal Encyclicals in Their Historical Context,* edited by Anne Freemantle (New York: G. P. Putnam's Sons, 1956), p. 287.

12. F. R. Tennant, *The Sources of the Doctrines of the Fall and Original Sin* (New York: Schocken Books, 1968), p. 285.

13. *Ibid.,* p. 279.

14. St. Augustine, *The City of God,* translated by Gerald Walsh et al. (Garden City, New York: Image Books, 1958), p. 272.

15. *Ibid.,* p. 279.

16. Bokenkotter, *op. cit.,* pp. 199–300.

17. W.H.C. Frend, *The Early Church* (Philadelphia: J. B. Lippincott Company, 1966), p. 148.

18. Jaroslav Pelikan, *Jesus Through the Centuries* (New Haven: Yale University Press, 1985), p. 95.

19. *Ibid.*

20. Gustaf Aulen, *Christus Victor,* translated by A. G. Herbert (New York: Macmillian Company, 1972), p. 81.

21. Reay Tannahill, *Sex in History* (New York: Stein and Day, 1981), pp. 158–59.

22. St. Anselm of Canterbury, *Why God Became Man,* translated by Joseph M. Colleran (New York: Magi Books, 1969), p. 156.

23. *Ibid.,* pp. 106–7.

24. The Council of Trent, Session VI, Chapter 7, quoted in Fr. Bretrand L. Conway's *The Question Box* (New York: Paulist Press, 1929), p. 60.

25. Chadwick, *op. cit.,* p. 126.

26. Vatican I's Decree "Of Revelation," in *Dogmatic Canons and Decrees* (New York: Devin-Adair, 1912), p. 234.

27. Coughlin, *loc. cit.*

28. St. Cyprian, "Letter 69," in *Early Latin Theology,* translated by S. L. Greenslade, Vol. V, *The Library of Christian Classics,* edited by John Baillie, John T. McNeill, and Henry P. Van Dusen (Philadelphia: Westminster Press, 1956), pp. 150–54.

29. Ronald Lawler, et al., *op. cit.,* p. 519.

30. Will Durant, *The Age of Faith* (New York: Simon and Schuster, 1950), p. 745.

31. Bokenkotter, *op. cit.,* pp. 65–66.

32. Pope Pius XII, cited in Ronald Lawyer, et al., *op. cit.,* p. 531.

THREE

The Cult

of the Virgin Mary

It was fitting, certainly, that this Virgin should shine with that purity than which no greater, under God, can be thought of. For to her God the Father was disposed to give His only Son, begotten equal to Himself, whom from His heart He loved as Himself, with the result that this One would naturally be, singly and identically, the Son equally of God the Father and the Virgin. It is she whose very being the Son Himself chose to make a mother for Himself, and of whom the Holy Spirit willed and brought about that the One from whom He Himself proceeded should be conceived and born.

St. Anselm of Canterbury, "The Virgin Conception," Chapter 18

1. *What is a cult?*

Cult comes from the Latin word *cultus,* meaning "worship" and "veneration." Catholicism maintains a sharp distinction between these two meanings.

Worship or *latria* refers to supreme homage or the adoration that is due to God alone. For this reason, the Cult of the Sacred Heart of Jesus implies latria.

Veneration or *dulia* is the reverence or respect that is due to the saints and angels because of their special spiritual excellence and closeness to God. Thus, the cult of the saints implies dulia.

In this scheme of worship and respect, Mary is accorded a special place of honor. As the Mother of God, she is deemed worthy of *hyperdulia* or extreme veneration.

2. *Why do Catholics call Mary the Mother of God rather than the mother of Christ?*

The elevation of Mary to the exalted position of *theotokos* or "God-bearer" came about as a result of a fifth-century controversy between Bishop Cyril of Alexandria and Bishop Nestorius of Constantinople. When Nestorius came to Constantinople, he found the city deeply embroiled in a controversy concerning the veneration of Mary. The controversy centered on the question: How should one speak of Mary? Was she the bearer of God or the bearer of Jesus? For Nestorius the matter was clear. Mary, he said, had given birth to a man, for the mere thought of a woman bringing forth God Himself was absurd, if not blasphemous. Cyril, in turn, viewed the matter differently. By saying that only the human nature of Jesus was born of the Virgin, Nestorius had divided Christ into a being of two divided natures: a finite, human nature that grew in wisdom, suffered, and died; and a divine nature that performed miracles, imparted divine truth, and rose from the grave. No, said Cyril, the divine and human natures in Christ constitute a single entity *(hypostasis)*. Because of this hypostatic union, he continued, one can say as strict theology that God was born at Bethlehem and that the impassable and eternal Word suffered and died. In a sermon preached at Easter in 429, Cyril announced the position that two years later would be adopted by the Church: Mary is the true mother not of the Godhead Itself, but of the incarnate *Logos* or Word of God, containing both the human and divine natures of Christ.[1]

The dispute between the two bishops continued until 430, when Pope Celestine I, stirred by Cyril's pleas, called a Council at Rome. The Council demanded that Nestorius retract his "heretical" position. When Nestorius refused, an Ecumenical Council was called at Ephesus in 431 which not only deposed but excommunicated the recalcitrant bishop.

By bestowing upon Mary the sacred title of *theotokos,* the Council of Ephesus gave much impetus to the growing cult of the Virgin. Indeed, this cult soon would expand to such proportions that, within the popular piety of medievel art, the Virgin would come to assume a position for the purposes of veneration second only to the adoration given by believers to God the Father, Son, or Holy Spirit.

3. *What is the scriptural basis for the veneration of Mary?*

The scriptural basis comes primarily from the accounts of the Annunciation, the Visitation to Elizabeth and the Nativity in the Gospel of Luke. Luke's Gospel begins with the story of the conception of John the Baptist. Zechariah, a priest, is married to the barren Elizabeth. While performing his temple duties, an angel appears to tell him that a son will be born to him who will be called John. Zechariah, in turn, asks for a sign that this wondrous prophecy is true. The angel, after identifying himself as Gabriel, delivers a sign by striking the doubtful priest dumb. The suddenly mute Zechariah returns home and, shortly thereafter, his wife conceives.

Luke turns from this account to the story of the conception of Jesus. In the sixth month of Elizabeth's pregnancy, Gabriel ". . . was sent from God to a virgin betrothed to a man named Joseph of the house of David; and the Virgin's name was Mary" (Luke 1:26–27). Gabriel greets Mary with the words: "Hail, O favored one, the Lord is with thee, and blessed art thou amongst women." This angelic pronouncement that Mary is a chosen vehicle of God's grace and is "blessed" among women clearly shows that Mary is worthy of veneration and reverence, a fact too often overlooked by Protestant reactionaries.

After giving Mary words of assurance, Gabriel informs her of her destiny, stating the name of her divine son who is to be called Jesus. Mary responds to this with the most precious question in Mariology: "How can this be since I do not know man?" (Luke 1:34). The angel responds by saying: "The Holy Spirit will come upon you and the power of the Most High will overshadow you; hence, the holy off-spring to be born will be called the Son of God" (Luke 1:35). Gabriel next reveals to Mary that, as a sign of God's power, her barren cousin Elizabeth has also conceived a son. Hearing this, Mary accepts her destiny with the famous words, her fiat: "Behold the handmaid of the Lord. Let it be done to me as you say" (Luke 1:38).[2]

When the angel departs, Mary immediately makes her way to Elizabeth's house. She greets her cousin; and Elizabeth, hearing her greeting and feeling her baby "leap with joy" in her womb, is inspired by the Holy Spirit to say: "Blessed art thou among women and blessed is the fruit of thy womb" (Luke 1:42).

Elizabeth proceeds to call Mary "mother of my Lord" (Luke 1:43) and prophesizes the fulfillment of the Lord's promise to Mary. This pronouncement to Mary as "mother of my Lord" is the scriptural source of the Catholic doctrine of Mary as Mother of God and Queen of Heaven.

Mary answers her cousin with the so-called *Magnificat,* her longest speech in the Bible:

> My soul magnifies the Lord,
> and my spirit rejoices in God, my Savior,
> for he has regarded the low estate of his handmaiden.

For behold, henceforth all generations will call me blessed;
for he who is mighty has done great things for me,
and holy is his name.
And his mercy is on those who fear him
from generation to generation.
He has shown strength with his arm,
he has scattered the proud in the imagination of their hearts,
he has put down the mighty from their thrones,
and exalted those of low degree;
he has filled the hungry with good things,
and the rich he has sent away empty.
He has helped his servant Israel,
in remembrance of his mercy,
as he spoke to our fathers,
to Abraham and to his posterity forever.

In the second chapter of his Gospel, Luke tells of the Nativity of Jesus. The emperor Augustus issued a decree that each man was to be taxed in the city of his birth. So Joseph left for Bethlehem with Mary "who was great with child" (2:5). At Bethlehem, she gave birth to her son in a manger "because there was no room for them at an inn" (2:7). That night the shepherds in their fields were told of the birth of the Son of God and visit him in adoration. They proceeded to tell everyone what they have seen and heard, but Mary "kept all these things, and pondered them in her heart" (2:19).

The Lucan depiction of Mary is further enhanced by the account of the Presentation of the infant Jesus at the temple for purification and dedication. After Mary and Joseph offer two turtle doves to the temple, Simeon, an old priest, is inspired to recite the third canticle in this Gospel—the so-called *Nunc dimittis:*

Lord, now lettest thou thy servant depart in peace,
according to thy word;
for mine eyes have seen thy salvation
which thou hast prepared in the presence of all peoples,

a light for revelation to the Gentiles,
and glory to thy people Israel.

(2:29–32)

After reciting these words, Simeon turns to Mary and says: "This child is destined to be the downfall of many in Israel, a sign that will be opposed—and you yourself shall be pierced with a sword—so that the thoughts of many hearts may be laid bare" (2:34–35). This prophecy, which has puzzled Christians throughout the ages, eventually became the source for the Catholic devotion to the Virgin's Sorrows, a devotion represented by a sword transfixing her breast.

This scriptural material from Luke is the primary source from the synoptic Gospels for the veneration of Mary.

4. Isn't Mary rebuked in the Gospels?

In his Gospel, Mark states that Jesus early in his ministry was informed by a crowd that his "mother and brothers" were "standing outside" and were "calling to him" (Mark 3:31). Jesus replied by asking, " 'Who are my mother and my brothers?' and looking around on those who sat before him, he said, " 'Here are my mother and my brothers! Whoever does the will of God is my brother, and sister, and mother' " (3:32–35). Many exegetes, including some Catholics, interpret this as a denigration of Mary and her role in the life of Jesus. This, however, is reading into Scripture something that is not stated in the text. Jesus is merely directing his followers to the nature of his mission. The point made has nothing to do with his family at all.

Similar readings have been made into Luke's Gospel when a woman is reported as crying out from a crowd: " 'Blessed is the womb that bore you and the breasts that nursed you.' " To which Jesus responds, " 'Rather, blessed are they who hear the Word of God and keep it.' " (Luke 11:27–28). Again, the response is missionary in character and not familial. What's more, the Church, far from seeing a rebuke in this passage, interprets it as an example of the honor accorded to Mary in the Gospels. On the Feast of the Immaculate Conception in 1974, Pope Paul VI urged all Christians to follow the woman's example in this Lucan passage of praising Mary as the Mother of God. The response of Jesus to the woman, the Pope contended, did not contradict or deny the woman's accolade, but rather rephrased it in a loftier manner to emphasize the spiritual motherhood of the Church, which is prefigured in Mary.[3]

5. Does the Gospel of John justify Mary's position as Universal Mother?

The Church says yes. John, however, does not repeat any of the incidents concerning Mary in the synoptic Gospels nor does he mention Mary by name. However, she is a central figure in his account of Jesus' first miracle at the wedding in Cana, where, following his mother's wishes, he changed water into wine (2:3–5). In this passage, Jesus addresses Mary by the generic term *woman,* which was not a curt but courteous form of address in ancient Hebrew. Moreover, this form of address, according to some Catholic exegetes, implies the union of Mary with all believers.

Toward the close of his Gospel, John locates Mary at the foot of the Cross, where the dying Jesus upon seeing his mother with his beloved disciple says to her: "Mother, behold thy son." Then, turning to the beloved disciple, adds: "Son, behold thy mother." From that day on, the Gospel records, the disciple "took her into his care" (John 19:26–27). This scene at Calvary is the primary source for the Church's affirmation of Mary as Universal Mother.[4] As the Dogmatic Constitution of the Second Vatican Council *(Lumen Gentium,* 61) says: "She . . . shared her Son's sufferings as he died on the cross. Thus in a wholly singular way she cooperated by her obedience, faith, hope and burning charity in the work of the Savior in restoring supernatural life to souls. For this reason she is mother to us in the order of grace. . . ."

6. Is there mention of Mary in other New Testament writing?

Although Mary is not mentioned in the Epistles, she appears in Acts 1:12–14, where Luke writes that "Mary, the mother of Jesus, and his brothers" were present in the "upper room" in Jerusalem, when the disciples had gathered after the Ascension. Her presence with the disciples on this occasion is the basis for the belief that she also must have been present at the Ascension and on Pentecost, when the disciples received the gift of tongues. Often, in the iconography of medieval art, Mary is depicted at center stage on both events.

7. What is the dogma of Mary's perpetual virginity?

In 649, Pope Martin I at the Fourth Lateran Council declared Mary's perpetual virginity to be a dogma of the Church.[5] Her virginity was affirmed at the conception *(in partu)* and afterward *(post partum)*, meriting for her the title of *Aeriparthenos* (the Ever-Virgin).

8. How can Catholics assert this to be true when the New Testamnent speaks often of the brothers and sisters of Jesus (Matt. 12:46–50; Mark 3:31–35; Luke 8:19–21; John 7:3–10; Acts 1:14)?

In spite of these references and preeminence of "James, the brother of the Lord" in the early Church in Jerusalem (Gal. 1:19), the doctrine of Mary's perpetual virginity was championed by the early Fathers of the Church. Greek Church leaders such as Origen (d. 254) and Gregory of Nyssa (d. 394) maintained that these brethren were Joseph's children by a former marriage.[6] By the acceptance of this teaching into popular piety, Joseph was transformed into the hoary-headed old widower leaning on a staff so familiar in Christian paintings.[7] St. Jerome (d. 420), however, objected to this depiction of Joseph. In his work "Against Helvidius," he said: "He who was worthy to be called the father of the Lord remained a virgin." The brethren, according to St. Jerome, were "brethren in point of kinship" but "not by nature." The Jews, he continued, had a limited vocabulary for close relationships—brothers, cousins, friends were all "brethren."[8] This teaching was accepted by the Council of Constantinople in 553, and was crystallized into dogma by the Lateran Council in 649.

9. What is the dogma of the Immaculate Conception?

On December 8, 1854, Pope Pius IX in his bull, *Ineffabilis Deus,* declared it mandatory for all Catholics to believe that Mary was the Immaculate Conception, i.e., the only human being ever conceived without original sin, or, to state it more positively, "full of grace" from the moment of her being. By this same bull, Catholics are required to believe that Mary was wholly free from "concupiscence" or the "incentive to sin." Therefore, Mary in holiness surpassed the beatitude of Adam and Eve and the angels, who were capable of sin, while Mary was not.

10. Who is St. Anne?

St. Anne, according to tradition, was the mother of Mary.

11. What is the scriptural basis for belief in St. Anne?

There is no scriptural basis for belief in St. Anne. The tradition of St. Anne springs from several ancient Christian documents, including "The Apocryphal Gospel of the Nativity of Mary" (circa 140). According to this source, the barren St. Anne was married to a rich merchant named Joachim. As a reward for their godliness, an angel appeared separately to St. Joachim and St. Anne, telling them that the womb of St. Anne would be miraculously opened ". . . so that that which is born may be acknowledged to be not of lust, but of the gift of God. . . ."[9] The angel said that the child shall be called Mary and shall be consecrated to the Lord to be raised in the Holy Temple from the time of her infancy. "Therefore," the angel affirmed, "when she has grown up, just as she herself shall be miraculously born of a barren woman, so in an incomparable manner she, a virgin, shall bring forth the Son of the Most High, who shall be called Jesus. . . ."[10]

12. What is the dogma of the Assumption of Mary?

On November 1, 1950, in his Apostolic Constitution *Munificentissimus Deus,* Pope Pius XII decreed the following: "We proclaim, declare and define it to be a dogma revealed by God that the immaculate Mother of God, Mary Ever-Virgin, was taken up body and soul into the glory of heaven."[11]

This belief in the Assumption of Mary has its roots in ancient apocalyptic literature that flourished during the second and third centuries. According to these sources, including the highly influential *Pseudo Melito,* Mary dies, thus affirming—in opposition to the tenets of Gnosticism—her humanity. Yet she is saved from the "impurity of death," i.e., the corruption of the flesh, by Jesus himself who carries her bodily into heaven where she is revived to the praise of the saints.[12] This story was told and retold throughout the Middle Ages in wood carvings, stained glass, embroideries, and paintings in the cathedrals of Western Europe. As early as the year 500, the Church of the East celebrated the feast of Mary's "dormition" or "falling asleep" on August 15. Indeed, the tradition was so strong that Martin Luther did not question the widespread belief in Mary's Assumption until his later years, at which time he struck August 15 from the Lutheran calendar.

13. *If the dogma of the Assumption is unscriptural, what was the necessity for defining this dogma?*

The dogma of the Assumption of Mary is a logical and inevitable result of the previously proclaimed dogma of the Immaculate Conception. Since Mary had been conceived without original sin and was the Mother of God, it was deemed fitting that salvation should be bestowed upon her without her body being subject to the corruption of death, which, according to the Church, is the penalty for sin and thus inapt for one who was graced by God's presence from the first moment of her being.

From the beginning of May in 1946, Pope Pius XII queried the world's bishops whether Mary's Assumption could be defined as a true statement of the Catholic faith and whether they desired such a definition. Receiving an affirmative endorsement from the episcopacy, Pius proceeded accordingly.

14. *Do Catholics pray to Mary?*

Yes. However, according to Vatican II's "Dogmatic Constitution on the Church" *(Lumen Gentium,* 66), Mary, in spite of her unique prerogatives, is not to be regarded as some kind of semi-divine being exalted above humanity, but as a fellow member of the Church. Catholics ask Mary as a fellow Christian to pray for them. They seek her intercession, in much the same fashion as Christians from the earliest days petitioned the help of the holy martyrs.

15. *What is the Hail Mary and how did it originate?*

Gabriel's greeting, "Hail Mary, full of grace, the Lord is with thee," combined with Elizabeth's cry of praise, "Blessed are thou among women and blessed is the fruit of thy womb," turned up in the ancient Eastern liturgies of James and Mark and in the seventh century Offertory for the Feast of the Annunciation. As a prayer, however, it was not widespread until St. Peter Damian (d. 1072) called it the "angelic versicle" and recommended its recitation. By the twelfth century, a Church synod instructed the clergy to say the Ave Maria along with the Pater Noster (Our Father) and the Apostles' Creed. The Franciscans and the Dominicans spread the Hail Mary's use and encouraged the uneducated laity to recite it as often as possible. By the sixteenth century, Catholics began to close the prayer with the phrase: "Holy Mary, Mother of God, pray for us sinners now and at the hour of our death."[13] This formula was officially recognized by Pope Pius V in 1568 when he included the Hail Mary in the revised *breviary* or book of prayers for priests.

16. *What is the Rosary?*

The complete Rosary, normally recited on prayer beads, consists of one hundred and fifty Hail Marys arranged in groupings called "decades," i.e., ten Hail Marys in each grouping. For every ten Hail Mary's, Catholics meditate on one mystery of the life of Jesus and Mary, recite one Our Father, and close with a doxology ("Glory be to the Father, the Son, and the Holy Ghost"). Since the complete Rosary is so time-consuming to recite, one cycle (fifty prayers) with meditations on either the Joyful, Sorrowful, or Glorious Mysteries is considered adequate.

17. *Where did the Rosary come from?*

Secular scholars argue that the chain of prayer beads originated in Brahmanic India, where it is still used in the worship of Bishu and Shiva. Through Hinduism its use spread to Buddhism and, as early as the ninth century, to Islam. Through the Crusades, these scholars continue, the prayer chain or Rosary eventually entered Western Christendom.[14]

This argument is somewhat negated by the fact that Lady Godiva of Coventry in 1041 left in her will a circlet of gems on which she used to say her prayers. This circlet, she specified, was to be draped around a statue of the Virgin.[15]

Officially, however, the Church maintains that the Rosary originated with a thirteenth-century visit by the Virgin to St. Dominic. At that time, Mary gave St. Dominic the ring of beads and told him that Catholics should invoke her aid through its usage.

18. *What about the various appearances of Mary?*

Aside from St. Dominic's encounter, visitations by Mary were uncommon during the Middle Ages. St. Teresa of Avila (1515–1582) spoke of a vision of the Virgin that she experienced during Mass, when Mary with St. Joseph appeared to her "through the eyes of faith." St. Teresa described the Virgin in the following manner: "The beauty which I saw in Our Lady was wonderful, though I could discern in her no particularly beautiful detail of form: it was her face as a whole that was so lovely and the whiteness and the amazing splendor of her vestments, though the light was not dazzling, but quite soft . . . Our Lady looked to me quite like a child. . . ."[16]

A more tangible vision of Mary came in 1531 to a converted Indian named Juan Diego on a mountain near Tepejiac, outside of Mexico City. In this vision, Mary appeared as one of "exceeding great beauty, her garments shining like the sun," and told the awestruck Indian to instruct the local Bishop Zumarraga to build a Church in her honor. The dutiful Juan complied with this request. Bishop Zumarraga, however, refused to give credence to the peasant's story and rudely dismissed him. Some time later, the Virgin again materialized before Juan, this time calling upon him to gather roses from a bush on top of a nearby mountain. Though it was December, the faithful peasant climbed the mountain and, to his astonishment, found a rose bush in full bloom. Gathering the roses, he returned to the skeptical bishop and let the roses fall to the floor from his cloak. As soon as he did this, the image of the Virgin appeared on the humble cloak where the roses had been carried. This sign, at last, was sufficient to impel Bishop Zumarraga to build a Church, as the Virgin had demanded, in honor of Our Lady of Guadalupe.[17] In commemoration of this visitation, Mary was named patroness of Mexico in 1754 by Pope Benedict XIV, of Latin America in 1910 by Pope Pius X, and of all the Americas in 1945 by Pope Pius XII. As patroness of all Americas, her image, dark-complexioned like an Indian and with lustrous black eyes, appears as a magnetized ornament for the dashboards of cars, in amulets, statues, and portable shrines of every kind.

Three hundred years after the appearance to Juan Diego, a fourteen-year-old girl named Bernadette Soubirous, who could neither read nor write, saw the Virgin eighteen times in a grotto by a river near her home in the southern French town of Lourdes. On one occasion, Bernadette scraped the ground to uncover a spring, from which she drank the muddy water, and ate some grass, in obedience to a request of the Lady who had imposed the unusual acts on the child as a penance. As the visitations continued, the local bishop pressed Bernadette to ask the Lady for her name. On the Feast of the Annunciation, Bernadette raised the question, to which the vision replied: "I am the Immaculate Conception." This was in 1858, four years after the official definition of the Immaculate Conception was announced. The fundamental message of Mary to the world at this time was prayer and penance for the conversion of the world to Catholicism.[18] In 1987, approximately four million pilgrims traveled to Lourdes where the teenage daughter of a poor miller said the Rosary before her "shining lady." Since these pilgrimages began, the Church and the two medical committees at Lourdes have officially recognized sixty-one miraculous cures.

There have been other officially recognized visitations before and after Lourdes, three to Catherine Labourne in 1830, inaugurating the devotion to the miraculous medal; an appearance in Fatima in 1917, where Mary called herself Our Lady of the Rosary and sought the consecration of Russia; and an appearance to twelve-year-old Mariette Beco in 1933 at Banneux in Belgium. More than two hundred other appearances not authenticated by the Church have been reported in the past one hundred years, the most recent being in Medjurgorje, Yugoslavia.

The Medjurgorje appearances first occurred on two successive days to six children on June 24 and 25 of 1981. These incidents might have been forgotten, save the children—at that time aged ten through sixteen—continued (and continue) to have visions. The children described the Virgin as being about twenty years old with black hair and blue eyes. When she materializes, she hovers above the ground wearing a gray dress with a white veil and with a halo of bright stars around her head. The Virgin implores the children to pray for peace in the world by reciting the Rosary. From the time of the first appearance to 1987, approximately eight million pilgrims journeyed to this rocky mountain-top location in Yugoslavia, hoping to catch a glimpse of the Virgin during one of her visits. The local bishop, however, remains highly skeptical, despite hundreds of claims of miraculous cures.[19]

NOTES

1. Henry Chadwick, *The Early Church* (Baltimore: Penguin Books, 1969), pp. 194–99.

2. Marina Warner, *Alone of All Her Sex: The Myth and Cult of the Virgin Mary* (New York: Alfred A. Knopf, 1976), pp. 8–9.

3. Pope Paul VI, *Marialis Cultus* (Devotion to the Blessed Virgin Mary), Sec. 39 (Washington, D.C.: National Catholic Welfare Conference, 1974), pp. 28–29.

4. Warner, *op. cit.*, pp. 17–18. See also Raymond E. Brown, et al., eds., *Mary in the New Testament* (Philadelphia: Fortress Press, 1978), p. 215.

5. Warner, *op. cit.*, pp. 66–67.

6. *Ibid.*, p. 23.

7. *Ibid.*

8. J.N.D. Kelly, *Jerome* (New York: Harper and Row, 1975), pp. 105–6.

9. "The Apocryphal Gospel of the Nativity of Mary," in *Readings in Church History*, Vol. 1, edited by Colman J. Barry, O.S.B. (New York: The Newman Press, 1960), p. 9.

10. *Ibid.*, p. 10.

11. Pope Pius XII, *Munificentissimus Deus* (November 1, 1950), quoted in *The Teachings of Christ: A Catholic Catechism for Adults*, edited by Ronald Lawler, O.F.M.

Cap.; Donald W. Wuerl; and Thomas Comerford Lawler (Huntington, Indiana: Our Sunday Visitor, 1983), p. 233.

12. Warner, *op. cit.,* p. 85.

13. *Ibid.,* p. 306. See also Hilda Grael, *Mary: A History of Doctrine and Devotion* (New York: Sheed and Ward, 1963), p. 230.

14. Warner, *op. cit.,* p. 305.

15. *Ibid.*

16. *The Autobiography of St. Teresa of Avila,* translated by E. Allison Peers (Garden City, New York: Image Books, 1960), p. 317.

17. Ethel Cook Eliot, "Our Lady of Guadalupe in Mexico," in *A Woman Clothed with the Sun,* edited by John J. Delaney (Garden City, New York: Image Books, 1961), pp. 39–60.

18. Francis Parkinson Keyes, "Bernadette and the Beautiful Lady," in *Ibid.,* pp. 115–43.

19. Denis R. Janz, "Medjugorje's Miracles: Faith and Profit," in *The Christian Century,* Vol. 104, No. 24 (Aug. 26–Sept. 2, 1987), p. 724.

FOUR

The Sacraments:

An Overview

The sacraments are the primary and fundamental actions by which Jesus Christ constantly bestows his Spirit on the faithful, making them a holy people who, in him and with him, offer themselves as an acceptable offering to the Father. The sacraments are surely to be regarded as being of inestimable value to the Church, to which belongs the power to administer them. They must always however be referred to Christ, from whom their effectiveness derives. In fact, it is Christ who baptizes. It is not such a man who celebrates the Eucharist, as Christ himself; he offers himself by the ministry of priests in the sacrifice of the Mass. The sacramental action is, first and foremost, Christ's action and the Church's ministers are, as it were, his instruments.

Sacred Congregation for the Clergy, *Ad norman decreti,* 1971.

1. *What is a sacrament?*

St. Augustine spoke of a sacrament as a symbol of a sacred reality, a sign of a hidden *mysterium*.[1] The water poured over a new Christian at baptism, for example, is an outward sign of the inner cleansing of original sin. The pronouncement by a priest of the words of consecration over the elements on the altar is a verbal sign of the mysterious transformation of the bread and wine into the body and blood of Christ. The imposition of the bishop's hands on a candidate for the presbytery at ordination is a visible sign of the metaphysical change of the candidate into a sanctified priest. The anointing of the dying with oil is a tangible witness of an inner consecration to the Kingdom of God. These signs in Catholicism, therefore, are not merely spiritual metaphors. They are rather truly efficacious, i.e., means of imparting sanctifying grace, the grace that is necessary for human salvation.

2. *Whence comes the notion of sacraments?*

Christianity inherited its belief in sacred signs and symbols from Judaism. In traditional Judaism, the Ark of the Covenant, which contained the law of Moses on tablets inscribed by the hand of God, was a symbol of God's presence among the Israelites. Moreover, the Ark was an efficacious symbol, which accounts for the reason it was carried into battle to ensure victory against all opposing forces. Similarly, the ritual of the blessing of the eldest son, as dramatized in the story of Jacob and Esau, was an efficacious sign, which served to seal his inheritance. The Jewish people further celebrated a ritual meal of unleavened bread, wine, and bitter herbs at Passover as a symbol of their dedication to the Lord who had delivered them from slavery. There were many other ritualistic signs in ancient Judaism that served as models for the development of Catholic sacramentology: the rabbinic blessing of a marriage, the official confession of sins, the anointing of the sick with oil. Even baptism was first a rite in Judaism for the cleansing of sin and preparation for acceptance into the Kingdom of God.

3. Were the seven sacraments instituted by the New Testament?

The New Testament never employs the word *sacrament,* but it mentions numerous ritualistic actions that were efficacious signs of spiritual realities. The early Christians shared a common meal as a symbol of the death and resurrection of Christ. During such meals, they actually experienced the presence of Christ: "The cup of blessing which we bless, is it not participation in the blood of Christ? The bread which we break, is it not participation in the body of Christ?" (1 Cor. 10:16). Many of the post-Resurrection appearances of Christ occurred at such *agape* gatherings (Luke 24:13–43; John 20:19–23, 26–29). In baptism, the early Christians experienced their death to sin and the start of their new life in the Spirit. Baptism, for this reason, was not a mechanical ritual but an experience of actual participation in a divine mystery (Acts 8:12–13). One of the most dramatic rites was the laying on of hands, by which a believer received the gift of the Holy Spirit, a gift that was manifested in *glossolalia* or "speaking in tongues" (Acts 19:1–7). Moreover, upon undergoing this rite, the believer came to manifest what St. Paul called the "fruits of the Holy Spirit," i.e., love, joy, peace, patience, kindness, goodness, faithfulness, gentleness, and self-control (Gal. 5:22–23).

4. How did the pagan mystery religions impact the development of Catholic sacramentology?

The Roman world at the times of the first Christians was literally filled with so-called mystery religions, most of which were Oriental in origin and all of which celebrated a sacred ritual (called a *mysterion)* in which the secret meaning of the cult was revealed. These religions, with the singular exception of the cult of Mithras, centered on deities, associated with vegetation who died and rose again from the dead. The cult of the Great Goddess was based on the myth of Cybele, the mother of all gods and men, and her lover Attis, a semi-human hero who was born of a virgin. Attis committed an act of infidelity that sent Cybele into bitter mourning. To atone for his unfaithfulness, Attis castrated himself and died. Cybele restored him to life, deified him for his display of devotion to her, and made him immortal. Partakers in the mysteries of this religion underwent an initiation ceremony known as the *taurobolum* in which they were bathed in the blood of a castrated bull. The bull represented the dying Attis whose blood cleansed the bather from past guilt and sanctified his entrance into eternal life.[2]

In the Orphic religion, Zeus and Persephone gave birth to Dionysus Zagreus, who was captured by the Titans and eaten. Athena managed to save the heart of Dionysus Zagreus and brought it to Zeus, who ate it. Later, Zeus and Semele gave birth to Dionysus, who was looked upon as Zagreus reborn.[3] In a communal rite, the Orphic worshippers ate the raw flesh of a bull as a symbol of Dionysus to commemorate the slaying and eating of the god and to absorb his divine essence anew.

Other religions had other rituals. In the Eleusinian mysteries, initiates underwent a rite of purification of self-immersion in water to represent the death and rebirth of Demeter.[4] Like the rituals in primitive Christianity, these rites had a profound existential and moral effect upon the lives of the believers. Cicero wrote: "Nothing is higher than these mysteries. They have sweetened our character and softened our customs; they have made us pass from the condition of savages to true humanity. They have not only shown us the way to live joyfully but they have taught us how to die with a better hope."[5]

As Christianity spread through the Graeco-Roman world, Hellenistic converts, who were former adherents to mystery cults, began to speak of the rites of the Church as "mysteries." In communities comprised of such converts, Christian rituals were celebrated in the same manner as the clandestine ceremonies of the pagan cults. Just as outsiders were prohibited from observing the mysteries of Orpheus and Dionysus, nonbelievers, even catechumens, were prohibited from witnessing the consecration of the elements at the eucharistic gatherings. Just as the *taurobolum* permitted participation in the life and death of Attis, baptism permitted participation in the life and death of Christ.

Indeed, writers such as St. Clement of Alexandria employed the word *mysterion* to describe the rites of baptism and the eucharist, stating that they were mysteries concerning sacred realities that only the believing faithful could understand.[6]

5. Whence comes the word "sacrament?"

Sacrament comes from the Latin word *sacramentum*, which meant the pledge of allegiance to the Emperor that was administered to recruits when they entered the Roman Army. It was first applied to a Christian ritual by Tertullian, who spoke of baptism as a *sacramentum* since it represented entrance into Christian life and a statement of complete allegiance to the teachings of Christ.[7]

6. What is a sacramental seal?

The New Testament writers held that Christians are sealed with the Spirit as a sign of their heavenly inheritance (Eph. 1:13–14, 4:30). This seal marks them as different from others just as the divine seal on Christ identified Him as the Son of God (John 6:27, 10:36). Moreover, the seal will come to serve as a mark to distinguish the elect and thereby save them from the final tribulation (Rev. 5:1, 7:2–4).

Gradually, this doctrine of a seal came to be applied to the rites of the Church. After making their *sacramentum*, new recruits were often branded or tattooed to prevent them from deserting. Since baptism was referred to as a *sacramentum*, it was held that Christians, too, were branded with an identifying mark or seal (the Greek word used for seal was *sphragis*, which meant both the mark made by a branding iron and the instrument that made the mark).[8] St. Cyril of Jerusalem clearly understood this military meaning when he addressed candidates for baptism by saying: "Come for the mystical Seal, that ye may be easily recognized by the Master; be ye numbered among the holy and spiritual flock of Christ, to be set apart on His right hand, and inherit the life prepared for you."[9]

Like a brand or tattoo, the seal received at baptism (from the bishop's sign of the cross on the forehead) was permanent and un-removable.[10] St. Cyril spoke of it as "indelible throughout the ages,"[11] and St. Gregory Nazianzus said that the seal was more precious than gold since it could not be taken away even after one's death.[12] For this reason, there could be no possible need for a repetition of this sacramental rite.

7. Whence comes the notion of a total of seven sacraments?

Until the end of the twelfth century, there was no common consensus regarding the number of sacraments. In 420, St. Augustine listed numerous practices within the Church as sacraments, such as making the sign of the cross, reading the Scriptures, and reciting the Nicene Creed and the Lord's Prayer.[13] Two hundred years later, St. Isidore of Seville limited the total number to three—baptism, confirmation, and the Eucharist.[14] In 1130, Hugh of St. Victor voiced the scholastic opinion that St. Augustine's definition of a sacrament as a "sign of a spiritual reality" was too broad and proposed the following definition as being more precise: "A sacrament is a corporeal or material element set forth before the senses, representing by similitude and signifying by institution and containing by sanctification some invisible and spiritual grace."[15] From this, he listed not only baptism, confirmation, penance, holy communion, orders, matrimony, and extreme unction but also the incarnation of Christ, the Church, holy water, penitential ashes, the blessings of palms and foliage, the Psalms of David, and "the blowing of exorcization."[16]

At this same time, Hugh's contemporaries were busy attempting to unify all Christian doctrine into a single harmonious body of Catholic belief. This effort was originally undertaken by Peter Abelard in his monumental *Sic et Non* (1125). Thirty years later, Abelard's work came to be completed by his disciple Peter Lombard. In his so-called "Sentences," Lombard unified the various definitions of the sacraments into the following succinct statements: "For that is properly called a sacrament which is a sign of the grace of God and a form of invisible grace, so that it bears its image and exists as its cause. Sacraments were instituted, therefore, for the sake, not only of signifying, but also of sanctifying."[17] Moreover, he showed that the Church Fathers, on the basis of Scripture, commonly agreed that seven rituals were sanctifying, i.e., causes as well as signs of grace. This made them different from sacramentals, which were signs but not causes of grace. Among the sacraments, Lombard included statues and crucifixes, holy water and oils, blessings and prayers, religious promises and vows, and various ceremonies of the Church.[18] From the time of this work to the present, the Catholic Church has upheld baptism, confirmation, penance, holy communion, orders, matrimony, and extreme unction as its *sacramenta*. This teaching was sanctioned as dogma by the Council of Lyons in 1274.

8. *What further impact did scholasticism have on sacramentology?*

By the twelfth century, medieval theologians on the basis of St. Augustine's writings made an intricate threefold distinction in their discussion of the sacraments: the *sacramentum tantum* or sign or outward ceremony; the *sacramentum et res* or interior change or seal produced by the rite; and the *res tantum* or the spiritual benefit or grace which flowed from the *sacramentum et res*.[19] In the celebration of the Eucharist, for example, the words of consecration and the outward appearance of the bread and wine represented the outward ceremony and sign (the *sacramentum tantum*); the body and blood of Christ, which became truly present under this ceremony and sign, constituted both the change produced by the rite and the sign pointing to the spiritual nourishment to be received by the communicant (hence the *sacramentum et res*—the sign and the reality); and the sanctifying grace within the soul when the elements were received in faith was the *res tantum* (the final effect of the sacrament). All seven sacraments, according to this teaching, possessed these elements, albeit in some the stages were more difficult to trace than in others.

In the sacrament of baptism, the *sacramentum tantum* was held to be the rite of anointing the head with water; the *sacramentum et res* was the sacramental seal or character produced in the soul that made it possible for one to live in conformity with the teachings of Christ; and the *res tantum* was the Christian's life in keeping with this gift of faith. This system of precise intellectual distinctions permitted the Church to explain the widespread discrepancy between the reception of a sacrament *(sacramentum et res)* and its existential effect *(res tantum)*, that is, why those who were baptized could still sin, why those who were confirmed could deny the faith, and why those who were married could live in a loveless relationship.[20] The sacraments, the Church taught in accordance with its scholastic theology, were always efficacious—they always infused the soul with grace, but their effectiveness was contingent upon the individual's cooperation with this gift of grace.

9. What is meant by ex opere operato?

Ex opere operato was a scholastic expression that literally meant "by the work having been worked."[21] As applied to the sacraments by St. Thomas Aquinas and others, it meant that as long as a sacramental ritual was validly performed, that is, performed with the correct matter (water, bread, oil, and so on) and with the prescribed form (words, gestures, and the like) by a proper priest with the right intention, the sacramental reality *(sacramentum et res)* would be immediately conferred upon the recipient who had the full intention to receive it. This doctrine, in turn, gave rise to elaborate studies of what materials, gestures, and words truly constituted a valid sacramental rite. Could dirty water be used at baptism? How much of the Mass had to be recited in order to consecrate the elements? Could the altar bread still be transubstantiated (changed into the substance of Christ) if the priest forgot to make the sign of the cross over it?[22] The questions were seemingly endless and the answers filled a great many pages of canon law.

10. Why did Luther reject Catholic sacramentology?

By the time of the Reformation, the doctrine of *ex opere operato* and the distinction between *sacramentum et res* and *sacramentum tantum* became lost on much of the clergy (who, by and large, remained uneducated). *Ex opere operato* became used by some Churchmen to mean that the sacraments worked automatically. By pouring water on the head of an infant, the priest immediately saved the infant's soul from eternal perdition. Two people recited their wedding vows and were instantly joined as one flesh. The priest performed the rite of absolution and the most heinous sin was miraculously removed.[23]

Luther rejected Catholic sacramentology based on this misunderstanding of the threefold distinction. In his mind, the sacramental process of Roman Catholicism did not include the final stage of *res tantum* and thereby represented mechanical means of obtaining sanctifying grace.

Defining a sacrament as a testament or promise made by Christ for the forgiveness of sins, Luther maintained that on the basis of Scripture there were only two sacraments—baptism and the Lord's Supper. The efficacy of these sacraments, he continued, depended not on precise formulas and proper rituals but solely upon the faith of the recipient. He wrote: "For anyone readily understands that these two, promise and faith, are necessarily yoked together. No one can believe if there is no promise. If there is no faith, a promise is useless, because faith is its counterpart and its completion."[24]

11. *Did the Reformation alter Catholic doctrine on the sacraments?*

No. The Council of Trent (1545–63) solidified the traditional teachings of the Church. It held that there are seven, not two or three, divinely instituted sacraments. It maintained the threefold sacramental process of *sacramentum tantum, sacramentum et res,* and *res tantum.* It affirmed that the sacraments do more than offer a promise or nourish faith: they actually impart grace in the metaphysical, if not mechanical, manner of *ex opere operato.* This grace is not contingent upon the worthiness of the priest nor the faith of the recipient. However, the Council stressed, such grace is not sanctifying unless it is actualized by the cooperative faith of the receiver.[25]

12. *What changes did Vatican II effect on the sacramental life of the Church?*

Vatican II did not alter traditional dogma on the sacraments. It left intact the threefold distinction and the concept of *ex opere operato.* However, the Council in the name of *aggiornamento* or "updating" simplified many of the sacramental rites through the elimination of prayers, signs of the cross, genuflections, and so on. Moreover, the Council mandated that these rites were no longer to be celebrated exclusively in Latin but in the vernacular languages of the faithful.

13. *But were not these changes superficial?*

No. Cardinal John Henry Newman once described the importance of even accidental associations in the development of the conception of the divine:

> Nothing is so frivolous and so unphilosophical as the ridicule bestowed on the contest for retaining or surrendering a rite or an observance, such as the use of the Cross at Baptism or the posture of kneeling at the Lord's Table. As well might satire be directed against the manoeuvre of two generals concerning some small portion of ground. The Rubicon was a narrow stream. A slight advantage gained is often at once an omen and a measure of ultimate victory. Political parties, to look at the matter on the lowest ground, are held together by what are the veriest of trifles. An accidental badge, or an inconsistency, may embody the principle and be the seat of life of a party. A system must be looked at as a whole; and may as little admit of mending or altering as an individual.[26]

The accidental changes effected by Vatican II did not alter the essential teachings of the Church on the sacraments, but they produced an altered perspective of their meaning. Garry Wills dramatized this in his discussion of the changes in the sacrament of Holy Communion. Prior to Vatican II, the transformation of the elements into the body and blood of Christ (the *sacramentum et res)* was dramatized by the liturgical obeisance to the holiness of the Host. The Host could only be touched with the "canonical digits," the thumb and first finger. The priest had to keep these digits joined as he performed the other liturgical functions, the paten and the chalice, which were lifted with the third and fourth finger. Moreover, the Host could only be received by absolved penitents after a period of fasting, which began at midnight before the morning Mass. After Vatican II, communicants, after a mere hour of fasting, were permitted to do what was previously unthinkable. They were permitted to touch the Host, to *chew* it, and, in some congregations, even to drink from the chalice. The stress appeared to move from the *sacramentum et res* to the sacrament as symbol *(sacramentum tantum)*. For this reason, it was no longer viewed by many as necessary for salvation.[27] This contributed to the malaise within post-Vatican II Catholicism. Weekly attendance at Mass dropped from 82 percent in 1962 to 54 percent in 1987,[28] while 60 percent of those polled in 1987 said they went to confession less often then they used to.[29]

NOTES

1. St. Augustine, "The City of God," X, 5, in *The Writings of Saint Augustine,* translated by Gerard G. Walsh and Mother Grace Monahan, Vol. 7, *The Fathers of the Church,* edited by Roy Joseph Deferrari et al. (New York: Fathers of the Church, Inc., 1952), p. 123.

2. Rudolph Bultmann, *Primitive Christianity in its Contemporary Setting,* translated by R. H. Fuller (New York: World Publishing Company, 1972), pp. 158–59; Joseph Tyson, *A Study of Early Christianity* (New York: Macmillan Publishing Company, 1973), p. 84.

3. Tyson, *loc cit.*

4. Leonard J. Bialles, *Myths: Gods, Heroes and Saviors* (Mystic, Connecticut: Twenty-Third Publications, 1986), p. 270.

5. Cicero, quoted in Joseph Martos, *Doors to the Sacred* (Garden City, New York: Image Books, 1982), p. 35.

6. St. Clement of Alexandria, "*Stromata* (The Miscellanies)," IV, 22, translated by A. Cleveland Coxe, in *The Fathers of the Second Century,* Vol. II, *The Ante Nicene Fathers,* edited by Alexander Roberts and James Donaldson (Grand Rapids: William B. Eerdmans Publishing Company, 1983), p. 435. See also Martos, *op. cit.,* p. 41.

7. Martos, *op. cit.,* pp. 41–42.

8. *Ibid.,* p. 49.

9. St. Cyril of Jerusalem, "Catechetical Lecture," 1, 2, in *The Cathechetical Lectures of St. Cyril,* translated by Edwin Hamilton Gifford, Vol. VII, *The Nicene and Post Nicene Fathers,* Second Series, edited by Philip Schaff and Henry Wace (Grand Rapids: William B. Eerdmans Publishing Company, n.d.), p. 6. See also *ibid.,* p. 50.

10. Martos, *loc. cit.*

11. St. Cyril of Jerusalem, "Procatechesis," 17, in *The Catechetical Lectures of St. Cyril, op. cit.,* p. 5.

12. St. Gregory Nazianzen, "Oration on Holy Baptism," XV, in *Select Orations of Saint Gregory Nazianzen,* translated by Charles Gordon Browne and James Edward Swallow, Vol. VII, *The Nicene and Post Nicene Fathers, op. cit.,* p. 364.

13. Martos, *op. cit.,* p. 59.

14. Will Durant, *The Age of Faith* (New York: Simon and Schuster, 1950), p. 738.

15. Hugh of St. Victor, *On the Sacraments of the Christain Faith,* I, 9, translated by Roy Joseph Deferrari (Cambridge, Massachusetts: Medieval Academy of America, 1951), p. 153.

16. *Ibid.*, pp. 315–20.

17. Peter Lombard, "The Four Books of the Sentences," IV, II, translated by Eugene R. Fairweather, in *A Scholastic Miscellany: Anselm to Ockham*, Vol. X, *The Library of Christian Classics*, edited by John Baillie, John T. McNeill, and Henry P. Van Deusen (Philadelphia: The Westminster Press, 1956), p. 339.

18. Martos, *op. cit.*, p. 69.

19. *Ibid.*, pp. 71–72.

20. *Ibid.*, p. 73.

21. *Ibid.*, p. 84.

22. *Ibid.*, p. 89.

23. *Ibid.*, p. 96.

24. Martin Luther, "Pagan Servitude of the Church," in *Martin Luther: Selections from His Writings*, edited by John Dillenberger (Garden City, New York: Anchor Books, 1961), p. 277.

25. "Council of Trent," Seventh Session, in *Canons and Decrees of the Council of Trent*, translated by H. J. Schroeder (St. Louis: B. Herder Book Company, 1955), pp. 51–53.

26. Garry Wills, *Bare Ruined Choirs* (Garden City, New York: Doubleday and Company, 1971), pp. 64–65.

27. *Ibid.*, pp. 65–67.

28. *Time*, Vol. 130, No. 2, September 7, 1987, p. 48.

29. *Ibid.*

FIVE

The First Commandment

---

and the Community of Saints

The blood of the martyrs is the seed of the Church.

Tertullian, *De Apologeticus,* 13

At the same time, let the faithful be instructed that our communion with those in heaven, provided that it is understood in the more adequate light of faith, in no way weakens, but rather . . . more thoroughly embraces, the supreme worship we give to God the Father, through Christ, in the Spirit.

Vatican II, *Lumen Gentium,* 51

1. *What is the difference between a doctrine and a dogma?*

While the terms are often used interchangeably, there is a real difference between the two. All the teachings of the Church on faith and morals (e.g., the Creed and the Commandments) are called "doctrines." The word *doctrina* in Latin simply means "teaching." *Dogma* is a stronger Greek term: it means a doctrine that has been formally defined by the Church. In the beginning, the apostles and their immediate successors simply taught what they understood to be the Gospel of Christ. Then came expressed doubts and denials by prominent Christians that Jesus was not really the Son of God, that God was not triune in nature, that Mary was not a virgin, and so on. From the fourth century onward, the Church authorities defined the relevant doctrines as truths revealed by God. They became known as dogmas. Once in modern times (1950), without anyone contesting the doctrine, Pope Pius XII solemnly proclaimed the following: "It is a truth of faith revealed by God that the immaculate, ever Virgin Mary, the Mother of God, was assumed body and soul into heavenly glory after the completion of her earthly life. By this declaration, the doctrine of the Assumption of Mary became a dogma.

All the moral teachings of the Church—on marriage and family life, for example—are doctrines. For the better part of two millenniums, few Christians have contested what the Church taught about indissoluble marriage, adultery, contraception, homosexuality, and abortion. Under such circumstances, the Church had no reason to define formally its teachings on sexuality. However, in view of the widespread sexual revolution in modern times, it would not surprise knowing Catholics, if in the twenty-first century or before, Pope John Paul II or one of his successors formally defined a moral doctrine, thus making a dogma of a moral demand.

2. *How does a Catholic know what he or she is expected to believe as a member of the Roman Church?*

Vatican II's "Declaration on Religious Liberty" *(Dignitatis humanae)*, 14, provides the following answer: "The Christian faithful in forming their consciences should give diligent attention to the sacred and certain doctrine of the Church. For by the will of Christ the Catholic Church is the teacher of truth and it is her task to proclaim and authentically teach the truth which is Christ, as well as to declare and confirm by her authority the principles of the moral order which flow from human nature itself."

3. *Does that mean a Catholic is required to believe everything the Church teaches?*

No. The Council statement speaks of the "sacred and certain doctrine of the Church," that is, the truth revealed by Christ and the moral principles "which flow from human nature itself."

4. *Where can one find these moral principles in black and white?*

The simplest way, according to traditional Catholic *catechetics* (religious instruction), is to look to the Ten Commandments as defined by the Council of Trent.

5. *What are the Ten Commandments as defined by the Council of Trent?*

   I.   I am the Lord, your God, you shall not have other gods beside me.
   II.   You shall not take the name of the Lord, your God, in vain.
   III. Remember to keep holy the Sabbath day.
   IV.   Honor your father and your mother.
   V.   You shall not kill.
   VI.   You shall not commit adultery.
   VII. You shall not steal.
   VIII. You shall not bear false witness against your neighbor.
   IX.   You shall not covet your neighbor's wife.

X.   You shall not covet anything that belongs to your neighbor.

6. *Are these Commandments found in the Bible?*

Yes. They represent a variation and synthesis of the laws given by God to Israel through Moses as listed in two places in the Old Testament: Exodus 20:2–17 and Deuteronomy 5:6–22.

7. *Do other Christian bodies uphold these same Commandments?*

Essentially yes, albeit mainline Protestants divide the first commandment while the Catholics divide the last. Therefore, the Catholic second commandment becomes the Protestant third and so on.

8. *How do Catholics interpret the first commandment?*

This commandment forbids false worship and idolatry. Sins against this commandment include heresy and the refusal to believe all that the Church upholds as articles of faith. Other offenses include faith in such occult sciences as chiromancy or palmistry, necromancy or black magic, astrology, crystal gazing, and spiritualism. *Lumen Gentium,* 51, mentions supernatural practices associated with the veneration of the saints. This has been interpreted to mean trust in a precise multiplicity of prayers, genuflections, and lighted candles.

9. *But aren't Catholics given to idolatry by worshipping their saints?*

Lumen Gentium, 51, draws a sharp distinction between the worship or adoration given to God through Christ in the Spirit and the veneration offered to the angels and saints. Worship is the acknowledgement of complete dependence on a divine Being, while veneration is reverential respect for some quality in a person. Only God may be worshipped, but the saints deserve to be venerated for "the example of their way of life, their fellowship in communion, and the help of their intercession."

10. *Do Catholics pray to the saints?*

Catholics believe in the communion of saints. The saints remain ever present before the throne of God and are receptive to the petitions of their fellow believers. Therefore, Catholics feel free to ask for the saints' intercession in prayer. This belief in the power of the saints to intercede arose at the turn of the third century. In 202–3, the martyred Potamiaena appeared after her death to the soldier Basileides, a disciple of Origen, who had escorted her to the stake, telling the soldier that she had "interceded" with Christ for him and had obtained the favor of his immediate martyrdom. Potamiaena was as good as her word. The next day Basileides was led into the imperial courtyard and promptly beheaded.[1]

Not only could dead believers intercede for the living in the early Church, but living Christians could intercede for the dead. St. Perpetua, for example, while in prison prayed for the fate of her young dead brother and received a vision which informed her that her prayer of intercession had been granted.[2]

11. *What is the scriptural basis for the "communion of saints"?*

The communion of saints, understood as a body of heavenly intercessors between God and man, has little basis in Scripture and springs primarily from tradition. Through the ages, however, the Church has attempted to ground its belief in such passages as 1 Corinthians 12:26–27 and, particularly in Hebrews 12:1, which speaks of a "cloud of witnesses" that surround those who are wayfarers.[3]

12. *What is the origin of the "communion of saints"?*

The veneration of the saints was first manifested in the cult of the martyrs.[4] During the periods of persecution, thousands of Christians were condemned to unspeakable deaths. Many were thrown to ravenous beasts; some were beheaded; others flayed alive. Their unswerving courage in the midst of such terrors was an inspiration to the early Christian congregations. For this reason, believers began to gather in memory of the martyrs and their inspirational deeds on the anniversaries of the martyrs' deaths. Throughout the third century, each church kept a list of such anniversaries and these became the first matryrologies.

After Christianity became an accepted religion with the Edict of Milan in 313, Christians were at last given free rein to demonstrate their veneration of the Christian heroes. Huge basilicas were built over or near their tombs. At times, their bones were transported for safe-keeping to various places of worship. And their feast days became celebrated with splendid processions and ornate liturgies.[5]

By the fourth century, bishops encouraged believers to call upon the holy martyrs to intercede for them in times of need. For example, St. John Chrysostom (344–407) instructed his congregation as follows: "When thou perceivest that God is chastening thee, fly not to His enemies . . . but to His friends, the martyrs, the saints, and those who are pleasing to Him, and who have great power."[6] Similarly, St. Cyril of Jerusalem (315–386) encouraged the veneration of the saints by writing: "We, then, commemorate those who have fallen asleep before us, patriarchs, prophets, apostles, and martyrs, in order that God, by their prayers and intercessions, may receive our petitions."[7]

And so, the concept of the communion of saints became a Christian reality. Abuses arose when pagan converts with their natural penchant toward polytheism began to see the saints as demi-gods and prayed directly to them. This problem was compounded when the calendar of the saints came to replace the Roman *fasti*. Suddenly, ancient deities dear to the pagans were revived as Christian saints: the Dea Victoria of the Basses-Alpes became St. Victoire, and Castor and Pollux were reborn in the legends of Sts. Cosmas and Damian.[8] For this reason, St. Claudius of Turin bitterly complained that many converts "have not abandoned their idols, but only changed their names."[9]

13. Who were the "confessors"?

After the persecutions ceased with the conversion of Constantine and the recognition of Christianity as a legitimate religion *(religio licita)*, believers, who could no longer shed their blood for Christ in the arena, sought out new means of gaining entrance into the communion of saints. One way was to follow the example of St. Antony who had set out to suffer a slow martyrdom of the flesh by leading a life of perfect chastity in the solitude of the Egyptian desert. "Antony," St. Athanasius wrote in his famous life of this celebrated monk, ". . . was daily a martyr to his conscience, and contending in the conflicts of faith. And his discipline was much severer, for he was ever fasting, and he had a garment of hair on the inside, while the outside was skin, which he kept until the end. And he neither bathed his body with water to free himself from filth, nor did he ever wash his feet, nor even endure so much as to put them into water, unless compelled by necessity."[10]

By the turn of the fourth century, thousands of Christians followed St. Antony's example and retreated to isolated cells in the deserts and mountains in search of a "white martyrdom." Here they performed many incredible feats of asceticism. An early monk named Pachomius didn't lay down to sleep for fifty years. Others, such as Simeon Stylites (390?–459), used to go without food through the forty days of Lent.

For witnessing their faith in this way, they became known as confessors. After Vatican II, the category of Masses venerating saint-confessors was dropped from the Roman calendar in favor of the designation "holy men and women."

14. *What were the criteria for sainthood in the early Church?*

By the end of the fifth century, validating a confessor's title to the designation "saint" began to involve a more formal process than popular acclamation. The Church, before officially recognizing a departed soul's entry into the heavenly community of intercessors, investigated the confessor's ascetic practices and personal holiness by the testimony of witnesses. Moreover, it required proof of the confessor's ability to perform miracles not only during his (or her) lifetime but after his death. This postmortem sign became the sine qua non for sainthood. Indeed, the acceptance of this criterion was already evident in "The Life of St. Martin of Tours" by Sulpicius Severus in 403, a work that became a model for Western hagiographies.[11] The work is filled with page after page of such mind-boggling testimony to St. Martin's wonder-working ability that the reader easily loses sight of the fact that, sanctity aside, St. Martin founded Gallic monasticism and was the Church's greatest missionary to rural France.

In the aftermath of the new canonization process, deceased saints were besieged with numberless requests from the living believers. So many requests that, in fact, a division of labor began to occur within the communion of saints. Certain saints became identified with special cures. St. Apollonia, for example, whose jaw had been smashed by her executioner, became the proper saint to approach with a toothache. Similarly, St. Blaise, who had been beheaded under the reign of Licinius, was seen as a good intercessor for sore throats. Other saints became looked upon as guardians of private interest groups. St. Bartholomew, who had been flayed alive, became the protector of tanners; St. John, who had been plunged into boiling oil, the patron of candlemakers; and Mary Magdalene, who had washed Christ's feet with aromatic oils, the patroness of perfumers.

15. *Did the new criteria limit the number of saints?*

Far from it. From the fifth to the thirteenth centuries, the cult of the saints grew to extraordinary proportions. Indeed, by the millennium, more than twenty-five thousand saints had been canonized. The staggering increase came about because local bishops were given the right on their own authority to proclaim any departed believer a saint after a mandatory investigation into the character of the person's life and proof of his/her wonder-working ability. For this reason, many saints were canonized on the basis of spurious evidence; some merely as a result of folklore.

16. *Was St. Christopher a product of folklore?*

To a great extent, yes. The real St. Christopher was an obscure martyr from Asia Minor who died during the reign of Diocletian. Medieval authors developed the scant facts of this martyr's life into a full-blown fiction concerning a cannibalistic giant named Reprobus who became converted to Christianity and labored for the rest of his days as a pious and mild-mannered ferryman. One day a child appeared at the stream, and when Reprobus hoisted him onto his shoulders to carry him across, he almost buckled under the child's tremendous weight. Later, it was revealed to the ferryman that the child was Christ Himself, burdened by the sins of the world. Hence, the name of Reprobus was changed to Christophorus or "Christ-bearer."[12] Another legend held that a drop of Christopher's blood healed the wound of a king who was attempting to execute him. This story gave rise to the belief that anyone who beheld the image of Christopher would be free from harm that day, and so Christopher became the patron saint of travelers.[13]

After researching such accounts, the Church authorities deemed them legendary and, in 1968, removed Christopher's feast day from the Christian calendar.

17. Is it true that Buddha was canonized as a Christian saint?

Yes. The story of Buddha was carried by Crusaders and merchants from the East and passed into the tradition of the medieval Church as the life of St. Josaphat (not to be confused with the seventeenth-century Polish bishop by that name who was canonized in 1867). The name of the medieval Josaphat, as Thomas Bokenkotter points out, is probably a corruption of *bodhisattva,* an attribute of a future Buddha.[14]

18. Who were the Bollandists?

In the seventeenth century, the Church commissioned a remarkable group of Jesuit scholars called the "Bollandists" to separate fact from fiction in the lives of saints. Due to their efforts—efforts which persist to this day—thousands of bogus saints, including most recently St. Philomena, were removed from official hagiographies.

19. Why was St. Philomena removed from the official litany of the saints?

The legend of Philomena actually dates from the early nineteenth century. A glass vial that was said to have contained the blood of a martyr was found in a catacomb. The vial bore the inscription: *"Lumena—paxte—Fi."* This was mistranslated to read: "Philomena, peace be with you." Almost overnight, an elaborate biography of this newly found saint was concocted out of thin air.[15] Devotion to St. Philomena ran high and her cult became extremely popular.

In 1968, Bollandist scholars, relying on the findings of archaeologists, were able to convince the Vatican that the word *lumena* did not refer to a person but was a conventional expression such as "beloved one" found on ordinary tombs. The vial, they argued, was also a commonplace object, used to adorn a final resting place.

20. *What is beatification?*

Beatification is a papal decree that permits Catholics to venerate a person after his/her death. It is a preliminary step to canonization, although it does not ensure sainthood. Such a decree permits the name of the departed soul to be prefixed by the title "Blessed."

21. *What is the present procedure for canonization?*

To avoid the excesses of the early medieval bishops, Pope Gregory IX in 1234 reserved the right of canonization to the papacy alone. This right was reinforced by a decree of Pope Urban VIII in 1642. In 1734, Prospero Lambertini, the future Pope Benedict XIV, produced the definitive treatise on canonization. Entitled "The Beatification of the Servants of God and the Canonization of the Beatified" *(De Servorum Dei Beatificatione et Beatorum Canizatione),* this four-volume work laid down the following requirements for sainthood, which remain in force to the present day: (1) doctrinal purity; (2) heroic virtue; and (3) miraculous intercession after death.[16]

22. *Why do paintings and statues of the saints often include haloes?*

A *halo* is a circle of light around the head of a saint. It is a symbol that Christians took over from pagans and presently is used only by artists to suggest holiness. It has no Church significance. Originally, it denoted the deceased person's association with the Sun God (Sol).

NOTES

1. Robin Lane Fox, *Pagans and Christians* (New York: Alfred A. Knopf, 1987), p. 447.

2. *Ibid.*

3. Thomas Bokenkotter, *Essential Catholicism: Dynamics of Faith and Belief* (Garden City, New York: Image Books, 1986), p. 146.

4. Peter Brown, *The Cult of the Saints* (Chicago: University of Chicago Press, 1985), p. 5.

5. Bokenkotter, *op. cit.,* pp. 147–48.

6. St. John Chrysostom, "Oration 8: To Justinian," quoted in Fr. Bertrand L. Conway's *The Question Box* (New York: Paulist Press, 1929), p. 370.

7. St. Cyril of Jerusalem, "Lecture 20: On the Mysteries," quoted in Conway, *loc. cit.*

8. Will Durant, *The Age of Faith* (New York: Simon and Schuster, 1950), p. 743.

9. *Ibid.*

10. St. Athanasius, "The Life of St. Antony," in *St. Athanasius: Select Works and Letters*, translated by Archibald Robinson, Vol. IV, *The Nicene and Post Nicene Fathers*, Second Series, edited by Philip Schaff and Henry Wace (Grand Rapids: William B. Eerdmans Publishing Company, 1957), p. 209.

11. Bokenkotter, *op. cit.*, p. 152.

12. Walter J. Burghardt, S. J., *Saints and Sanctity* (Englewood Cliffs, New Jersey: Prentice-Hall, 1965), p. 117.

13. Bokenkotter, *op. cit.*, p. 152.

14. *Ibid.*

15. *Ibid.*, pp. 152–53.

16. *Ibid.*, pp. 155–56.

SIX

The Veneration

---

of Relics

Hic conditus est sanctae memoriae Martinus episcopus
Cuius anima in manu Deus est, sed hic totus est
Prasesens manifestus omni gratia virtutem.

(Here lies Martin the bishop, of holy memory, whose soul is in the
hand of God; but he is fully here, present and made plain in miracles
of every kind.)

Inscription on the tomb of St. Martin of Tours

1. What is a relic?

A *relic* is the remains of a martyr or a saint. From the early days of the Church, the body, bones, or possessions of recognized saints, especially of martyrs, were venerated with the devotion customarily given to holy persons while they were alive. Relics, such as the bones of St. Polycarp or the blood of St. Januarius, were called "first class." The farther the "remains" were from the person of the deceased saint, the lower the class of relics ("second class," "third class," etcetera).

2. Why do Catholics venerate relics?

The Council of Trent maintained that since the bodies of the saints were "temples of the Holy Ghost," the saints' physical remains could be the source of "many benefits" from God. The Council further stated that those who affirm "that veneration and honor are not due to the relics of the saints, or that these and other sacred monuments are uselessly honored by the faithful, and that the places dedicated to the memory of the saints are in vain visited with a view of obtaining their aid, are wholly to be condemned."[1] This teaching was reaffirmed in a more subdued manner by the Vatican II document "On Sacred Liturgy" *(Sacrosanctum Concilium,* 5, 11), which says: "The saints have been traditionally honored in the Church, and their authentic relics and images held in veneration. For the feasts of the saints proclaim the wonderful works of Christ in his servants and display to the faithful fitting examples of their imitation."

3. What is the basis of this veneration?

Among pagans, the blood of executed criminals was credited with special potency, especially in spells to cure epilepsy. Therefore, the pagans were probably the first to seek the blood-soaked remains of the martyrs.[2] Eventually, the Christians themselves began to believe in the healing power of the blood and bones. This can be witnessed in the early third century document "Acts of Thomas," in which the son of a king in India is reported as being miraculously healed by the dust from the tomb of St. Thomas.[3]

This belief was closely associated with the religious awe with which the early Christians viewed the remains of the martyrs. Such awe is already evident in the account by early Church Fathers of the martyrdom of St. Polycarp (circa 156): ". . . we afterwards took up his bones, more precious than costly stones and more excellent than gold, and interred them in a decent place. . . ."[4]

4. Why did Catholics place relics in their altars?

Until very recently, every Catholic altar contained a relic. This practice was a continuation of primitive Christian worship. Since Christianity was condemned by the Roman officials as a "depraved religion" (religio deprava), Christians were forced to conduct their worship services in the catacombs where the bodies of the holy martyrs had been buried. Such tombs served as the first altars. When Christianity became a "legitimate religion" (religio licita) in 313, the tradition of establishing the centerpieces of worship on the remains of the saints continued. Moreover, as the new religion continued to expand throughout the Empire, more and more remains were sought to sanctify the new places of worship. For this reason, the precious remains were cut into pieces and "translated" throughout Christendom as "altar stones."[5]

5. What was the primary reason for medieval pilgrimages?

Because the relics were held to be endowed with supernatural power, the shrines that housed the remains of the more powerful saints were eagerly sought out by the faithful. The central shrine throughout the Middle Ages remained the basilica of St. Peter, which contained the bodies of Sts. Peter and Paul. Other popular shrines were the Cathedral of Amiens, which allegedly enshrined the head of St. John the Baptist in a silver cup; the Abbey of Saint-Denis, which housed the crown of thorns and the body of St. Dionysius the Areopagite;

and the Cathedral of Canterbury, which contained the bones of St. Thomas à Becket.

6. What is the present practice of the Church regarding relics?

The New Code of Canon Law, promulgated in 1983 (Canons 1186–90), recommends the veneration of saints as helpful to authentic devotion, but only those who are listed in the catalogue of the saints or otherwise blessed by the Church. Displaying sacred images is also to remain in force, although their number must be moderate "lest they bewilder the Christian people and give opportunity for questionable devotion." It is absolutely forbidden to sell relics. According to Canon 1237, 2, the ancient tradition of keeping relics under a fixed altar is to be preserved according to approved liturgical norms. Nothing is said, however, about placing relics in the altar itself.

7. What is the "most important relic" in the Church?

Before recent discoveries, according to a pronouncement by Pope Paul VI, the most important relic was held to be the Shroud of Turin. The Shroud is an ancient cloth, measuring fourteen feet by four feet, which is purported to have been the burial garment of Jesus. It is significant because it contains what is believed to be an image of Christ on the cloth. This image, many clergymen and scientists argue, offers positive proof that the body of Jesus radiated an incredible amount of energy after his death.

First mentioned by religious writers in the seventh century, the Shroud was discovered in the year 1204, during the course of the Fourth Crusade, when the Crusaders captured Constantinople. In connection with this event, the chronicler Robert de Clari reported that a Frenchman named Otto de la Roche came into possession of a linen shroud as part of the spoils. This cloth was held to be Christ's shroud and, indeed, bore marks made by sweat and blood. On closer inspection, the chronicler noted that it also appeared to bear the almost indistinct outlines of a human body.[6]

In 1357, the Shroud appeared in Europe, when a noble named Geoffrey de Charney, who had purchased it under mysterious circumstances, displayed it to the public in Lirey, France.

Three years later, Margaret de Charney sold the Shroud for a handsome sum to the Duke of Savoy. In 1532, it was slightly damaged by a fire in the Sainte Chapelle of Chambéry.

In 1889, the first photograph was taken of the Shroud and something extraordinary happened. The photographic plate converted the impressions on cloth into the black and white image of a man who had been crowned with thorns, whipped, crucified, and lanced with a spear.

Moreover, the image, when submitted to art experts, was ruled not to be a forgery. Such experts noted that the image was amazingly natural and anatomically correct since, as with every human being, the features are not the same on both sides of the face. Medieval artists didn't heed such dissimilarity. Even more conclusive proof of the image's authenticity came from the fact that no artist, modern or ancient, has been able to convert a human face by the processes of the mind into a negative image and paint it.[7] Later studies explained the appearance of the image on the theory that the cloth must have come into contact with radiation shortly after the man's death.

The issue of the Shroud is clouded by the absence of any reference to a cloth with the image of Jesus either in the New Testament or in the writings of the early Church Fathers. Furthermore, in the wake of the Crusades, at least forty Shrouds of Jesus were circulated throughout the Western world, all with claims of authenticity.

In recent years the Shroud has been subjected to numerous methods of scientific analysis, including chemical tests, X rays, gamma rays, and even computer analysis. Such research has affirmed that the cloth contains particles of ancient Near Eastern origin and probably dates from the time of Christ. What's more, the corpse appears to have been powdered and anointed with oil in the manner described in John 19:38–40.

In 1988, the Church consented to have a swatch removed from the relic for carbon dating. The results of these tests conducted at independent laboratories in Oxford, England; Arizona; and Zurich determined that the cloth was made between A.D. 1000 and 1500.

NOTES

1. "The Council of Trent, Session 25," quoted in Fr. Bertrand L. Conway's *The Question Box* (New York: Paulist Press, 1929), p. 372.

2. Robin Lane Fox, *Pagans and Christians* (New York: Alfred A. Knopf, 1987), p. 446.

3. *Ibid.*

4. "The Martyrdom of Polycarp, Bishop of Smyrna," translated by James A. Kleist, S. J., in *Readings in Church History,* Vol. I, edited by Colman J. Barry, O.S.B. (New York: Newman Press, 1960), p. 74.

5. Thomas Bokenkotter, *Essential Catholicism: Dynamics of Faith and Belief* (Garden City, New York: Doubleday-Image Books, 1986), p. 148.

6. Werner Keller, *The Bible as History,* 2d. rev. ed. (New York: William Morrow and Company, 1981), p. 354.

7. *Ibid.,* p. 355.

SEVEN

The Church

Fathers

The mission of teaching that belonged to the Apostles and their first fellow workers was continued by the Church. Making herself day after day a disciple of the Lord, she earned the title of "Mother and Teacher." From Clement of Rome to Origen, the post-apostolic age saw the birth of remarkable works. Next we see a striking fact: some of the most impressive Bishops and pastors, especially in the third and fourth centuries, considered it an important part of their episcopal ministry to deliver catechetical instructions and write treatises. It was the age of Cyril of Jerusalem and John Chrysostom, of Ambrose and Augustine, the age that saw the flowering, from the pen of numerous Fathers of the Church, of works that are still models for us.

Pope John Paul II, *Catechesi tradendae*, October 16, 1979, 12

1. *Why are some saints known as the Fathers of the Church?*

From a very early date, the title "Father" was applied to bishops as witnesses of the Christian tradition. Teaching bishops were known as "fathers" of their students. St. Paul, in his letter to the Corinthians, applied this title to himself by writing: "For though you have countless guides in Christ, you do not have many fathers. For I became your father in Christ Jesus through the Gospel" (1 Cor. 4:15). By the fifth century, the term came to be used in a more comprehensive manner to include ecclesiastical writers who were not bishops but who were acknowledged for their doctrinal purity and personal holiness. St. Jerome, for example, was not a bishop, but he was listed among the Fathers by St. Augustine. By the thirteenth century, the title "Apostolic Father" became reserved for the Christian Apologists who wrote before the reign of Constantine. The list includes St. Clement of Rome, The Shepherd of Hermas, Papias of Hierapolis, St. Ignatius of Antioch, St. Polycarp of Smyrna, St. Clement of Alexandria, and St. Cyprian of Carthage. The expositors and defenders of the father who lived after the time of Constantine became known as the Dogmatic Fathers.[1]

2. *Who are the "Doctors of the Church"?*

In 1295, Pope Boniface VIII declared that Sts. Ambrose, Jerome, Augustine, and Gregory the Great should be known as the outstanding teachers of the Church *(egregii doctores ecclesiae)*. Similarly, Pope Pius V in 1568 named Sts. Basil the Great, Gregory of Nazianzus, John Chrysostom, and Athanasius as the "great Fathers of the East."[2]

The number of Doctors of the Church presently stands at thirty-two. The latest saints to receive this honor were Sts. Teresa of Avila and Catherine of Siena, both of whom were pronounced Doctors by Pope Paul VI in 1970.

The list of Doctors (with the dates of their designation and the name of the presiding pontiff) is as follows:

St. Albert the Great (1932, by Pope Pius XI)
St. Alphonsus Liguori (1871, by Pope Pius IX)
St. Ambrose (1295, by Pope Boniface VIII)
St. Anselm of Canterbury (1720, by Pope Clement XI)
St. Anthony of Padua (1946, by Pope Pius XII)
St. Athanasius (1568, by Pope Pius V)
St. Augustine (1295, by Pope Boniface VIII)
St. Basil the Great (1568, by Pope Pius V)
St. Bede the Venerable (1899, by Pope Leo XIII)
St. Bernard of Clairvaux (1830, by Pope Pius VIII)
St. Bonaventure (1588, by Pope Sixtus V)
St. Catherine of Siena (1970, by Pope Paul VI)
St. Cyril of Alexandria (1882, by Pope Leo XIII)
St. Cyril of Jerusalem (1882, by Pope Leo XIII)
St. Ephraem the Syrian (1920, by Pope Benedict XV)
St. Francis de Sales (1877, by Pope Pius IX)
St. Gregory the Great (1295, by Pope Boniface VIII)
St. Gregory of Nazianzus (1568, by Pope Pius V)
St. Hilary of Poitiers (1851, by Pope Pius IX)
St. Isidore of Seville (1722, by Pope Innocent XIII)
St. Jerome (1295, by Pope Boniface VIII)
St. John Chrysostom (1568, by Pope Pius V)
St. John of Damascus (1890, by Pope Leo XIII)
St. John of the Cross (1926, by Pope Pius XI)
St. Lawrence of Brindisi (1959, by Pope John XXIII)
St. Leo the Great (1754, by Pope Benedict XIV)
St. Peter Canisius (1925, by Pope Pius XI)
St. Peter Chrysologus (1729, by Pope Benedict XIII)
St. Peter Damian (1828, by Pope Leo XII)
St. Robert Bellarmine (1931, by Pope Pius XI)

St. Teresa of Avila (1970, by Pope Paul VI)

St. Thomas Aquinas (1567, by Pope Pius V)

3. *Why wasn't Tertullian, the "father of Latin theology," named a Father of the Church?*

Tertullian (160–240), despite the fact that he was highly instrumental in the formation of the doctrines of original sin, the Atonement, and the Trinity and who gave the word *sacramentum* to several sacred mysteries of the Church, ended his days as a Montanist—a third-century "pentecostal" sect which espoused belief in the impending end of the world—decrying all moral laxity within the Church. Tertullian could not understand any relations between the Church and the world. For this reason, he condemned all Christians who became soldiers, artists, or state officials; all parents who did not veil their daughters; all bishops who restored repentant sinners to communion (the only repentance Tertullian would allow for baptized Christians was the "second baptism" of martyrdom); and finally the Supreme Pontiff whom he labeled *pastor moechorum*, "shepherd of adulterers." The reason for his attack on the Bishop of Rome is evident in the following passage from *De Pudicitia* (circa 220):

> I hear an edict has been issued, and that a peremptory one. The Supreme Pontiff, indeed, the bishop of bishops, puts forth his edict: "To those who have done penance, I remit the sins of adultery and fornication." What an edict! Who is going to endorse that with a "Well done?" And where will this bounteous gift be posted up? On the spot, I suppose, on the very doors of the brothels, just by the advertisements of lust. Penance like that must surely be promulgated exactly where the offense is going to be committed. We must read about the pardon where we are hoping for it. But this is read in the Church, proclaimed in the Church—and the Church is a virgin![3]

For such ferocious attacks on the Pope, Tertullian and his fellow Montanists were condemned as heretics by the Council of Constantinople in 381.[4]

4. *Why wasn't Origen, the "father of Greek theology," named a Father of the Church?*

Ironically, Origen (185–253), who interpreted Matthew 19:12 in such a literal sense that he castrated himself, spent his days allegorizing the Scriptures from a Neoplatonic perspective. The literal meaning of the Old and New Testaments, he maintained, overlay two deeper layers of meaning—the moral and the spiritual—to which only the esoteric and educated few could penetrate.[5] He questioned the truth of Genesis as literally understood, explained away as symbols many aspects of God's dealings with Israel, and dismissed as pious legends such stories as that of Satan taking Jesus up to a high mountain and tempting him with the riches and kingdoms of the world. Sometimes, Origen insisted, scriptural narratives were invented to convey some spiritual sense.[6]

Such allegorizing led Origen to state that the soul passes through a succession of stages and embodiments before arriving at the Kingdom of God. This belief in reincarnation was coupled with Origen's insistence that after the "final conflagration," there will be another world with a long history, and then another, and another until the perfect status of God's creation is restored.[7]

Because of such statements, which entailed an implicit denial of hell and the resurrection of the body, Origen was condemned as a heretic by the Second Council of Constantinople in 553.[8]

5. *Who was the greatest of the early Dogmatic Fathers?*

St. Augustine (354–430). One of the most influential thinkers in the history of Western civilization, St. Augustine, apart from the concern of his See in Hippo, lived almost entirely in the country of the mind. As a theologian, he squared the existence of evil with the concept of God as the *Summum Bonum*. In *De Libero Arbitrio* (On Free Will), he articulated the Catholic position by stating that evil was the result of free will. God could not leave man free without granting him the possibility of doing wrong as well as right. The original man's choice to do wrong resulted in an evil inclination, which was passed on by generation to Adam's progeny. No amount of good works, St. Augustine argued, can enable a man to overcome this inclination and thereby achieve salvation. Man remains totally dependent on grace. In this way, St. Augustine set forth the dynamic between nature and grace that undergirds much of Catholic (and Protestant) theology. Grace is offered to all men, he wrote, but most refuse it. This refusal merely serves to affirm the complete moral freedom of man.[9]

Realizing man's infirmity as a result of original sin—a doctrine he was primarily responsible for defining—St. Augustine upheld the primacy of faith over reason in theological investigations. "Dispute not by excited argument," he wrote to a friend, "those things which you do not comprehend; or those which in Scripture appear to be incongruous and contradictory; meekly defer the day of your understanding."[10] In this way he set forth the formula of *Credo ut intelligam* ("I believe so that I might understand.") which characterises the traditional Catholic approach to theology.[11]

From this position of faith *(fides)* seeking understanding *(ratio),* St. Augustine presented the Catholic view of Scripture. The authority of Scripture, he said, is higher than all the efforts of human intelligence. Yet the Bible need not be taken literally; it was written to be intelligible to average minds, and, therefore, utilized symbolic or natural terms to explain spiritual realities.[12] When opinions differ, one must turn to the Church, which maintains the ultimate authority for the interpretation of God's Word.

Despite this reliance on faith, St. Augustine anticipated the scholastics by maintaining that God can be known through His creation by natural reason. Everything in the world, he said, is an infinite marvel in its organization and attests to a creative intelligence. He perceived this intelligence in Platonic terms as a Being in which Beauty, Truth, and Wisdom are one. Moreover, this wondrous Being calls men into fellowship. "You have made us for yourself," he wrote in his *Confessions,* and "our hearts are restless until they rest in you."[13]

Interpreting the Persons of the Trinity as exemplifying Being, Knowledge, and Love, St. Augustine found numerous signs pointing to the validity of this conception, including an image within the self. He wrote: "We are, and we know that we are, and we love to be and to know that we are." This image stands even against the skeptics, for even if he is mistaken he is, in order to be mistaken; and therefore correctly knows that he is, and loves this being and knowledge.[14]

As a philosopher, St. Augustine provided the Western world with the first clearly defined philosophy of history. In *The City of God,* he attempted to explain the events of recorded history from the fall of Adam to the sack of Rome in 410 as a tale of two cities. "In regard to mankind," he wrote, "I have made a division. On the one side are those who live according to man; on the other, those who live according to God. And I have said that, in a deeper sense, we may speak of two cities or two human societies, the destiny of the one being an eternal kingdom under God while the doom of the other is eternal punishment along with the Devil."[15] These two cities are characterized by two loves. The members of the heavenly City *(civitas Dei)* are motivated by a love of God, while the members of the earthly City *(civitas terrena)* are motivated by concupiscence or the lust of the flesh. Abel belonged to the City of God, Cain to the city of man. The followers of Cain make their home in the earthly kingdom; the followers of Abel remain pilgrims on their journey to their true home with God.

In several passages of his masterpiece, St. Augustine identified the City of God with the Catholic Church. This identification became an important factor in the development of medieval ecclesiology.

6. Who was the greatest of the Dogmatic Fathers?

St. Thomas Aquinas (1225–1274): considered the perennial and common universal Doctor of Catholicism, St. Thomas is also called the "Angelic Doctor" and has been officially proclaimed as the patron of Catholic theology.

His writings represent, to a large extent, a response to the rediscovery of Aristotle in the West and the masterful Arabic commentaries on this Greek philosopher by the prominent Mohammedan scholars Avicenna (d. 1037) and Averroës (d. 1198). Aristotle, to the dismay of medieval scholars, maintained that the world is eternal, that God is an impersonal Being with no knowledge of individual persons or particular events, and that the soul as the form of the body is not immortal. The Church initially responded to this challenge in 1210 by banning the reading of Aristotle's "metaphysics and natural philosophy" and all "comments" on his works. These prohibitions were modified by the Fourth Lateran Council, which permitted the reading of Aristotle's work on logic and ethics, but proscribed the rest.[16] In 1263, Pope Urban IV restated these prohibitions, while St. Thomas quietly labored to show that the claims of Aristotelianism can be made to congress with the declarations of faith.

This attempt at assimilation represents one of the most staggering achievements in Western thought and resulted in the creation of a new metaphysic: Thomism.

Thomism represents a synthesis of Aristotelian, Platonic, and Christian insights into a single system of thought. The basis of this system is a rational understanding of God as Creator and source of all being, goodness, and truth; present in all beings by His power and essence; the uncaused cause, in whom essence and existence are one.

The sheer audacity of the work of St. Thomas can be seen in his Christian psychology, which accepts the Aristotelian conception of man as a composite of body and soul, matter and form. Prior to St. Thomas, Christian thinkers, including St. Augustine and St. Bonaventure, depicted the soul as a prisoner within the body, and hence identified the soul with man. For Aquinas, however, the soul is the life-giving, form-creating energy that is indivisibly present in every part of the body. He managed to establish that the soul, as evident by its power to abstract, generalize, and reason, is a spiritual reality not related to the material world, but infused in man by the breath of God.[17]

Moreover, St. Thomas employed the Aristotelian equation of happiness with understanding and transformed it into the Christian ethic of the final fulfillment of happiness in the Beatific Vision.[18]

Of great importance for doctrinal development, St. Thomas established the concept of natural law *(ius naturale)* as the guide for morality. He viewed right action as action "which proceeds to its proper end" in accordance with its primary purpose as governed by natural law. This law, he maintained, has been implanted by God in man and is discernible by human reason.[19]

This concept of natural law undergirds the Church's teachings on sexuality and provides the philosophical basis for the dictates of Pope Paul VI's encyclical on birth control, *Humanae Vitae.*

NOTES

1. Ronald Lawler, O.F.M.; Donald W. Wuerl; Thomas Comerford Lawler, eds., *The Teaching of Christ: A Catholic Catechism for Adults* (Huntington, Indiana: Our Sunday Visitor, 1983), p. 57.

2. *Ibid.*

3. Tertullian, *De Pudicitia,* translated by S. L. Greenslade, in *Early Latin Theology,* Vol. V, *The Library of Christian Classics,* edited by John Baillie, John T. McNeill, and Henry P. Van Deusen (Philadelphia: Westminster Press, 1956), p. 74.

4. "Decrees of the Council of Constantinople" (381), Canon VII, in *The Seven Ecumenical Councils of the Undivided Church,* edited and translated by Henry R. Percival (New York: Edwin S. Gorham, 1901), pp. 185–86.

5. Origen, "First Principles," translated by G. W. Butterworth, in *Readings in Church History,* Vol. I, edited by Colman J. Barry, O.S.B. (Westminster, Maryland: Newman Press, 1960), p. 61.

6. *Ibid.*

7. Henry Chadwick, *The Early Church* (Baltimore: Penguin Books, 1969), pp. 104–7.

8. "Anathemas Against Origen," from "Decrees of the Second Council of Constantinople" (557), in *The Seven Ecumenical Councils of the Undivided Church, op. cit.,* pp. 318–19.

9. St. Augustine, *De Libero Arbitrio* (On Free Will), Book II, Chapters 1 and 2, in *Selections from Medieval Philosophers: Augustine to Albert the Great,* translated by Richard McKeon (New York: Charles Scribner's Sons, 1929), pp. 11–17.

10. St. Augustine, "Epistle 81 A," quoted in Will Durant, *The Age of Faith* (New York: Simon and Schuster, 1950), p. 70.

11. St. Augustine, "On the Gospel of John," Tractate XXIX, 6, in *St. Augustin: Homilies of the Gospel of John, Homilies on the First Epistle of John, and Soliloquies,* translated by Alexander Robertson, Vol. VIII in *Nicene and Post Nicene Fathers,* First Series, edited by Philip Schaff (Grand Rapids: William B. Eerdmans Publishing Company, 1956), p. 184.

12. St. Augustine, *De Genesi Ad Littteram* (The Literal Meaning of Genesis), translated by John Hammond Taylor, S. J.), Vol. 41, in *Ancient Christian Writers,* edited by

Johannes Quasten, Walter J. Burghardt, and Thomas Comerford Lawler (New York: Newman Press, 1982), pp. 144–45.

13. St. Augustine, *Confessions,* translated by John K. Ryan (Garden City, New York: Image Books, 1960), p. 43.

14. St. Augustine, *The City of God,* translated by Gerald G. Walsh, et al. (Garden City, New York: Image Books, 1958), pp. 235–36.

15. *Ibid.,* p. 323.

16. F. C. Copleston, *Aquinas* (Baltimore: Penguin Books, 1953), pp. 63–69.

17. St. Thomas Aquinas, *Summa Theologiae,* Part One, Question 75, Article 6, in *Introduction to St. Thomas Aquinas,* edited by Anton C. Pegis (New York: Random House, 1948), pp. 287–90.

18. St. Thomas Aquinas, *Summa Contra Gentiles,* Book III, Chapter 48, in *ibid.,* pp. 463–67.

19. St. Thomas Aquinas, *Summa Theologiae,* Part One of Book II, Question 91, Article 2, in *ibid.,* pp. 617–19.

EIGHT

The Church and

the "Separated Brethren"

The restoration of unity among all Christians is one of the principal concerns of the Second Vatican Council. Christ the Lord founded one Church and one Church only. However, many Christian communities present themselves to men as the true inheritors of Jesus Christ; all indeed profess to be followers of the Lord, but they differ in mind and go their different ways, as if Christ Himself were divided. Certainly, such division openly contradicts the will of Christ, scandalizes the world, and damages that most holy cause, the preaching of the Gospel to every creature.

Opening lines of Vatican II's *Decree on Ecumenism*

1. *Does the first commandment forbid Catholics to participate in non-Catholic worship services?*

The first commandment, according to catechists, includes all "sins against the faith," including apostasy, indifferentism, and heresy. Prior to Vatican II, such sins against the faith included participation in non-Catholic worship services, since such participation was held as profession of belief in a "false religion." Following Vatican II, outreach to those of other religious faiths called for new Church legislation, which was adopted by Pope Paul VI almost immediately.

2. *Does the Catholic Church maintain that it is the sole source of man's salvation?*

Yes. This teaching, which was originally stated by St. Cyprian, maintains that the Church is the Ark of Salvation outside of which there is no hope of deliverance from sin and damnation.[1] It was upheld by the fourth Lateran Council in 1215, the Council of Florence in 1431, the Council of Trent in 1545, and by the Dogmatic Constitution of Vatican II *(Lumen Gentium, 14)* which states that "the Church, a pilgrim now on earth, is necessary for salvation."

3. *Does this mean that non-Catholics will automatically go to hell?*

No. The exemplary lives of many pagan philosophers and the ancient Hebrew prophets prompted the important Church Fathers, including St. Augustine, to maintain that while such saintly figures were not united with the Church *in fact,* they were, nevertheless, united with the Church *in desire.* St. Thomas Aquinas restated this teaching and spoke of the possibility of salvation extra-sacramentally by a "baptism of desire."[2] This teaching was solemnly upheld by the Council of Trent. In accordance with this doctrine, Pope Pius IX in a papal allocution delivered on December 9, 1854, maintained that those who are "in invincible ignorance of the true religion" are not guilty of their ignorance before God and, therefore, will not suffer eternal damnation.[3] Vatican II's "Dogmatic Constitution on the Church" *(Lumen Gentium,* II, 14) ratified the excusability of the ignorant by stating: "He [Christ] himself explicitly asserted the necessity of faith and baptism (cf. Mk. 16:16; Jn. 3:5), and thereby affirmed at the same time the necessity of the Church which men enter through baptism as through a door. Hence they could not be saved who, knowing that the Catholic Church was founded as necessary by God through Christ, would refuse to enter it, or to remain in it."

4. Do Catholics consider Protestants heretics?

A heretic, according to Canon 751 of the New Code (1983) of Canon Law, is one who obstinately denies or doubts "some truth which must be believed with divine and Catholic faith." But such a person must willfully separate himself (or herself) from or break with the Church. With this understanding, St. Augustine wrote that those who were led into error by their parents were "by no means to be counted among the heretics."[4] This view underpins all Catholic doctrine on heresy. Luther and Calvin, therefore, were heretics along with the first members of their congregations, but not the children who were born and raised in their churches. Indeed, Vatican II's "Decree on Ecumenism" *(Unitatis Redintegratio,* 3) said that ". . . one cannot charge with the sin of separation those who at present are born into these communities and in them were brought up in the faith of Christ, and the Catholic Church accepts them with respect and affection as brothers. . . ."

5. What was the primary intention of the Decree on Ecumenism?

The "Decree on Ecumenism" attempted to open channels of communication with the "separated brethren" for the purpose of working toward a reunion of the Catholic family. In no way was this attempt at unity to involve a submergence of Catholic identity or suppression of Catholic truth.[5] Indeed, Catholics, by this conciliar document (3), held that ". . . it is through Christ's Catholic Church alone, which is the all-embracing means of salvation, that all fullness of the means of salvation can be obtained. . . ."

6. What does ecumenism mean in the practical order?

The Holy See outlined the following five stages to intercredal fellowship: (1) the removal of disagreeable words and actions between religious bodies and the perpetuation of mutual respect and friendly relations; (2) ongoing dialogues among Communions concerning doctrinal and sacramental differences; (3) cooperation in social projects that deal with the problems of peace and justice; (4) common prayers for God's help in effectuating the proper goals of ecumenism; and (5) the spiritual renewal of all Churches in the hope of the fulfillment of Christ's prayer that "they all might be one" (John 17:11).

7. Has this Decree brought about any difference in the relationship between the Catholic Church and the various other Christian churches?

Somewhat. Since the Eastern Orthodox churches already have (in the eyes of Rome) a valid priesthood, the major obstacle to reunion revolves around the jurisdictional power of the Pope. Such a reunion, therefore, would require only a profession of the Catholic faith by the Orthodox bishops and priests, although this is not a simple matter. Not only historical antagonism between East and West, but the entanglement of the Orthodox with the Greek and Russian governments, make reunion difficult.

Nonetheless, the Orthodox are permitted to receive Catholic sacraments, and Catholics may receive the sacraments from an Orthodox priest when their own priest is inaccessible, an unlikely event in the United States.

The situation vis-à-vis Protestants is different, largely because the belief systems of the various Protestant churches vary widely and because the Protestant priesthood (or ministry) is not accepted as valid by the Catholic Church. While the above-mentioned five ecumenical steps are recommended, full participation in Protestant liturgy is still prohibited, especially inter-Communion. In special cases, a Protestant who fully believes in the real presence of Christ in the Eucharist and has a special need (for example, danger of death or dire spiritual need) may receive Communion from a Catholic priest. Catholics may not reciprocate because of fundamental differences over the meaning of the Eucharist. Catholics may appear as official witnesses to Protestant baptisms and marriages, but not as sponsors.

8. Why have there been so few liturgical breakthroughs?

Pope John Paul II explained that pastoral problems between religious bodies cannot be solved if the participants in ecumenical dialogue gloss over the doctrinal differences that created those problems in the first place.[6]

9. Does the "Decree on Ecumenism" represent a mitigation of the traditional Catholic stance that the only true Church is the Catholic Church?

No. Pope Paul VI's statement that Catholics were guilty of sins against unity with non-Catholics for which they must repent does not radically alter what Vatican II reaffirmed about the Catholic Church: that it is the one, holy, apostolic, and unique Church founded by Christ, with a hierarchical constitution, whose bishops received their power from the apostles, whose visible head was Peter first and then succeeding bishops of Rome, a Church which infallibly teaches through bishops in union with the Pope revealed truths of faith and morals.

NOTES

1. St. Cyprian, "Epistle LXXIV," translated by Ernest Wallis, in *The Fathers of the Third Century,* Vol. V, *The Ante Nicene Fathers,* edited by Alexander Roberts and James Donaldson (Grand Rapids: William B. Eerdmans Publishing Company, 1981), p. 384.

2. St. Thomas Aquinas, *Summa Theologiae,* Part Three of Book I, Question 67, Article 2, Vol. 17, translated by the Fathers of the English Dominican Province (London: Burns, Oates and Washbourne, Ltd., 1923), pp. 143–45.

3. Pope Pius IX, quoted in Fr. Bertrand Conway's *The Question Box* (New York: Paulist Press, 1929), p. 216.

4. St. Augustine, "Epistula 43 (1)," quoted in *The Teachings of Christ: A Catholic*

Catechism for Adults, edited by Ronald Lawler, O.F.M. Cap.; Donald W. Wuerl; and Thomas Comerford Lawler (Huntington, Indiana: Our Sunday Visitor, 1983), p. 240.

5. *Ibid.,* pp. 245–46.

6. Pope John Paul II, Encyclical *Redemptor Hominis* (March 4, 1979), quoted in *Ibid.*

NINE

The Second Commandment:

Solemn Vows

---

and Priestly Promises

Say to them, "If any one of all your descendants throughout your generation approaches the holy things, which the people of Israel dedicate to the Lord, while he has an uncleanness, that person shall be cut off from my presence: I am the Lord. None of the line of Aaron who is a leper or suffers discharge may eat of the holy things unless he is clean. Whoever touches anything that is unclean through contact with the dead or a man who has had an emission of semen, and whoever touches a creeping thing by which he may be made unclean or a man from whom he may take uncleanness, whatever his uncleanness may be—the person who touches any such shall be unclean until the evening and shall not eat of the holy things unless he has bathed his body in water.

Leviticus 22:3–6

In the days of his flesh, Jesus offered up prayer and supplication with loud cries and tears to him who was able to save him from death, and he was heard for his godly fear. Although he was a Son, he learned obedience through what he suffered; and being made perfect he became the source of eternal salvation to all who obey him, being designated by God a high priest after the order of Melchizedek.

Hebrews 5:7–10

1. *How do Catholics interpret the second commandment: You shall not take the name of the Lord, your God, in vain?*

This commandment, an extension of the obligation to worship God, instructs Catholics to speak of God and His saints with respect and reverence. They violate this commandment by neglect of prayer, by taking God's name in vain, by blasphemy, by profanity, by breaking a solemn promise, and by not keeping a sacred vow.[1]

2. *What do Catholics mean by a vow?*

Vow comes from the Latin word *votum,* meaning "to be willed." It is a deliberate and free promise made to God concerning some good which must be fulfilled as a matter of religious obligation (Canon 1191).[2] It must involve a supererogative act, i.e., something over and above God's normal expectations of man.

Vows in the Catholic tradition are private and public. Private vows are made with the consent of confessors and usually involve such supererogative works of penance as making a religious retreat or a holy pilgrimage. Such vows only concern the spiritual welfare of the individuals who make them. Of far greater significance are public vows, which are made in the name of the Church and received by a legitimate ecclesiastical superior. Such vows are usually tied to sacramental rites, most specifically the rites of baptism, confirmation, penance, matrimony, and Holy Orders. Public vows may be solemn or simple, solemn if acknowledged by the Church (as in certain religious professions); otherwise, they are simple. Vows may be temporal (for a time) or perpetual (for life).

3. *What is the difference between a promise and a vow?*

A *promise* is a conscious and deliberate pledge to oneself or another person. To break a solemn promise without just and reasonable cause is a grievous sin. A *vow,* however, is infinitely more solemn. It represents a conscious and deliberate pledge to God. For this reason, any attempt to break a consecrated vow without just and reasonable cause constitutes an act of sacrilege, which incurs immediate excommunication.

4. *Who are the Catholics who live under vows?*

Such Catholics are, by and large, priests, brothers, and sisters who belong to a religious community (Franciscans, Dominicans, Carmelites, etcetera) and who live in a monastic setting. These "religious servants" vow themselves to a life of poverty, chastity, and obedience.

5. *Do parish priests assume vows?*

No. Parish or diocesan priests do not take vows. Rather, they make promises to a bishop at the time of their ordination. When a priest becomes a deacon, he is asked by a bishop: "Are you resolved to shape your way of life always according to the example of Christ, whose body and blood you will give to the people?" The candidate answers, "I am," binding himself to the rule of poverty.[3]

Similarly, the candidate is asked to kneel before the bishop and to place his hands between those of the bishop. The bishop asks him, "Do you promise respect and obedience to me and my successors?" The candidate answers, "I do," binding himself to the rule of obedience.[4]

Finally, after the homily, the candidate stands before the bishop, who addresses the following to him: "By your own free choice you seek to enter the order of deacons. You shall exercise this ministry in the celibate state, for celibacy is both a sign and a motive of pastoral charity, and a special source of spiritual fruitfulness in the world. By living in this state with total dedication and moved by a sincere love for Christ the Lord, you are consecrated to Him in a new and special way. By this consecration you will adhere more easily to Christ with an undivided heart; you will be more freely at the service of God and mankind, and you will be untrammeled in the ministry of Christian conversion and rebirth. By your life and character you will give witness to your brothers and sisters in faith that God must be loved above all else, and that it is He whom you serve in others. Therefore, I ask you: In the presence of God and the Church, are you resolved as a sign of your interior dedication to Christ, to remain celibate for the sake of the Kingdom and in lifelong service to God and mankind." The candidate answers, "I am." The bishop then adds, "May the Lord preserve you in this commitment." The candidate answers, "Amen."[5] Thus is he bound to the rule of celibacy.

6. Whence comes the ideal of clerical celibacy?

The key scriptural text for the development of the doctrine of clerical celibacy is the following passage from the Gospel of Matthew:

> He [Jesus] said to them, "For your hardness of heart Moses allowed you to divorce your wives, but from the beginning it was not so. And I say to you: Whoever divorces his wife, except for unchastity, and marries another, commits adultery. The disciples said to him, "If such is the case of a man with his wife, it is not expedient to marry." But he said to them, "Not all men can receive this precept, but only those to whom it is given. For there are eunuchs who have been so from birth, and there are eunuchs who have been made eunuchs by men, and there are eunuchs who have made themselves eunuchs for the sake of the Kingdom of heaven. He who is able to receive this, let him receive it" (19:8–12).

This stress on a sexless existence as a statement of complete dedication to the Kingdom of God was fortified by Christ's own example. Jesus never married, despite the Jewish injunction for men to "be fruitful and multiply."[6] Moreover, he enjoined his disciples to set aside their wives and families in order to follow him without encumbrance (Luke 14:26).

St. Paul, in his letter to the Corinthians, further advanced the prevailing teaching of the spiritual advantage of the celibate state: "I want you to be free from anxieties. The unmarried man is anxious about the affairs of the Lord, how to please the Lord; but the married man is anxious about worldly affairs, how to please his wife, and his interests are divided" (1 Cor. 7:32–34).

The New Testament exaltation of the ideal of chastity is climaxed by St. John's vision of heaven in which he sees 144,000 men who remain the true followers of the Lamb of God. These men are "chaste," since they have never "defiled themselves with women" (Rev. 14:1–4).

Based on such teachings, many groups within the early Church forbade marriage after ordination to the ministry. There was, however, a common consensus that marriage before ordination did not necessarily constitute an impediment to Holy Orders; but the matter of whether or not such married ministers could continue to partake of the conjugal right with their wives remained a subject of widespread debate. In 300, the Synod of Elvira denied such married clergymen this right and forbade them to live with any woman but a mother, sister, or virgin daughter who was consecrated to the Lord.[7] At the Council of Nicaea in 325, the Western bishops attempted to press a rule of clerical celibacy on the universal Church, but this attempt was thwarted by the Eastern bishops, who upheld a more tolerant view of marital sex.[8]

Despite the ruling at Nicaea, demands increased for a rule of clerical celibacy in the Church of the West. Such demands were intensified as the role of Christian ministers began to center solely on the celebration of the Eucharists. Theologians, including St. Jerome and St. Augustine, viewed Christian ministers as the successors of the Jewish priesthood in the order of Melchizedek who had made a "perfect offering" unto the Lord of bread and wine (Gen. 14:18; Heb. 5:6–10; 7:1–2). Such priests of the Old Covenant were forbidden to engage in sexual congress with their wives during their service at the temple (Lev. 22:3–6). Since the priests of the New Covenant served at the altar everyday, it was only to be expected that they should live in a state of perpetual continence. By the end of the fourth century, St. Ambrose provided testimony that such continence was in general practice in all but the most remote areas of Christendom:

> But ye know that the ministerial office must be kept pure and unspotted, and must not be defiled by conjugal intercourse; ye know this, I say, who have received the gifts of the sacred ministry, with pure bodies, and unspoilt modesty, and without ever having enjoyed conjugal intercourse. I am mentioning this, because in some out-of-the-way places, when they enter on the ministry, or even when they become priests, they have begotten children. They defend this on the old custom, when, as it happened,

the sacrifice was offered up at long intervals. However, even the priests had to be purified two or three days beforehand, so as to come clean to the sacrifice, as we read in the Old Testament. They even used to wash their clothes. If such regard was paid in what was only the figure, how much ought it to be shown in the reality. Learn, then, priest and Levite, what it means to wash thy clothes. Thou must have a pure body wherewith to offer up the sacraments. If the priests were forbidden to approach their victim unless they washed their clothes, dost thou, while foul in heart and body, dare to make supplication for others? Dost thou dare to make an offering for them?[9]

7. But didn't the Church continue to permit married men to be ordained until the time of the Second Lateran Council in 1139?

Yes. But such clerics were obliged to abstain from all sexual activity with their wives. This rule was issued by Pope Siricius in 385 and was enforced by a succession of Church synods, including Carthage in 390, Toledo in 400, Turin in 401, and Rome in 402.[10] In 462, Pope Leo I extended the "law of continence" to sub-deacons and insisted that married clerics "have their wives as if they had them not."[11] These prohibitions remained in force throughout the Middle Ages. In 1059, Pope Nicholas II promulgated decrees which prohibited the faithful from attending Masses celebrated by priests who continued to live with their wives. In 1139, the Second Lateran Council laid down the law that holy orders constituted an impediment that automatically invalidated the marriage of clergymen.

In 1971, the question of celibacy was discussed at length at the Second General Assembly of the Synod of Bishops, which concluded that "the law of priestly celibacy existing in the Latin Church is to be kept in its entirety."[12]

8. Did the early apostles see themselves as priests?

Traditional Catholic doctrine states that the apostles were made priests at the Last Supper by Christ's injunction: "Do this in remembrance of me" (1 Cor. 11:23–26). Certainly the apostles complied with this injunction and celebrated the eucharistic meal in community gatherings. However, they did not view their position within the early

Church to be primarily sacerdotal. They were primarily concerned with spreading the News of the imminent coming of the Kingdom of God to a dying world (Luke 9:2; 1 Peter 4:7). What's more, the early apostles and their fellow "Nazarenes" remained devout Jews, who worshipped daily at the temple and accepted the legitimacy of the Jewish priesthood (Acts 2:46).

Gradually, however, the bond between primitive Christianity and traditional Judaism weakened. When the Nazarenes began to accept uncircumcised Gentiles into the fold, they were denounced and persecuted by Jewish officials as heretics (Acts 11:1–26). The final break with Judaism came with the destruction of the Great Temple in Jerusalem by the Roman Army in 70. Henceforth, there was no central place for ritual sacrifice.

Shortly after this cataclysmic event, the writer of the Letter to the Hebrews expressed the belief that ritual sacrifices for sin were no longer required to appease God since Christ had offered Himself as the perfect sacrifice (7:26–28). Since the apostles and their successors conducted the celebration of the Eucharist in commemoration of Christ's suffering and death, they came to be seen as serving in the priesthood of the New Covenant.

9. What forms did ministry take in the early Church?

There were varieties of ministries in primitive Christianity. The twelve disciples under Peter's leadership oversaw the material needs of the community (Acts 4:32–34), proclaimed the Gospel to all who would listen (Acts 6:2–4), and served as official spokesmen for the Christian movement before Jewish and Roman authorities (Acts 4:5–21; 18:12; 26:32). In addition, they supervised communal worship, healed the sick and pronounced forgiveness of sins on all who repented (Acts, 4–6, 9–15). As Christianity spread to the Greek world, the Twelve became known as *apostolai,* meaning "ambassadors" or "emissaries," and the work they performed was called *diakonia,* meaning "service."[13] This term was further applied to the ministry of those who distributed food and clothing to those in need. Other leaders of the movement, besides the Twelve, became known as *apostolai,* including St. Paul, St. Barnabas, and those mentioned in Acts 14:14 and

Romans 16:7. In each city, the apostles began to appoint new leaders to act in their stead, a leadership apparently established on the model of the ascetic Jewish community of Essenes, with a ruling elder or *episkopos* supervising a council of elders, known as *presbyteros*. The duties of the *episkopos* consisted of spreading the Gospel, guarding the community like "shepherds" (Acts 20:28–32), teaching sound doctrine, and refuting those in error (Titus 1:9–15). The *presbyteros* were to aid in such administrative and catechetical tasks.

Such ruling elders and presbyters were to be chosen on the basis of personal qualities and abilities (1 Tim. 3:1–7; Titus 1:6–9). They were to be even-tempered, sensible, moderate in habits, friendly, hospitable, and not overly fond of money. They were expected to be able administrators of their own households, with one wife and obedient children. Deacons, who served the internal needs of the community, were to have similar qualifications (1 Tim. 3:1–7).[14]

10. *Whence comes the title "bishop"?*

Bishop comes from the Greek word *episkopos* by the way of the Latin *episcopus,* which became shortened to the Anglo-Saxon term *biscop.*

11. *Did the bishops in the ante-Nicene Church exercise real authority over their congregations?*

Yes. This is confirmed by St. Ignatius in his "Letter to the Smyrnaeans," one of the earliest Christian documents (circa 110), in which he writes: "You should all follow the bishop as Jesus Christ did the Father. Follow, too, the presbytery as you would the apostles; and respect the deacons as you would God's law. Nobody must do anything that pertains to the Church without the bishop's approval.[15] Approximately seventy years later, St. Irenaeus maintained that it is incumbent upon the laity to obey the bishops, who stand as the successors of the apostles.[16] Similarly, circa 250, St. Cyprian said: ". . . the bishop is in the Church and the Church is in the bishop and if any one be not with the bishop, then he is not in the Church. . . ."[17]

12. *But was not the Eucharist a communal celebration in the early Church with no distinct priest or principal celebrant?*

In Acts 20:28, the *episkopos* was instructed to "feed the Church of the Lord." Catholic tradition has understood this injunction to mean what Vatican II summarized in many places: that bishops or priests are "ministers of sacred ministries, especially in the sacrifice of the Mass." This interpretation has been challenged by several scholars, including the Jesuit theologian Edward Schillebeeckx. In a work entitled *Ministry,* Schillebeeckx argues, on the basis of a passage from the *Didache* or "The Teachings of the Apostles" (circa 110–20), that prophets and not bishops or presbyters served the central liturgical task of breaking the bread at eucharistic gatherings.[18] This interpretation, in turn, is refuted by St. Ignatius in his "Letter to the Smyrnaeans," a work contemporaneous with the *Didache,* in which he writes: "You should regard that Eucharist as valid which is celebrated by the bishop or someone he authorizes. Where the bishop is present, there let the congregation gather, just as where Jesus Christ is, there is the Catholic Church."[19] The letter testifies that the Eucharist was celebrated in many communities in an invalid manner, i.e., either by a prophet or another member of the laity. But such celebrations were to be shunned by the faithful.

By the turn of the third century, bishops throughout the Western and Eastern Church served as the principal celebrants of the Christian liturgy. In 220, St. Hippolytus described the bishop as a "high priest" with the sole authority to render unto God the gifts of the Church.[20] Thirty years later, St. Cyprian spoke of the bishop as a person "honored by divine priesthood" and consecrated to the service "of the altar and sacrifice."[21] By the end of this century, Christians everywhere referred to bishops in their liturgical roles as priests (in Latin, *sacerdotos;* in Greek, *hierup),* albeit the distinct office of priesthood remained to be developed within Catholicism.[22]

13. *How were bishops and presbyters chosen?*

The first bishops were appointed by the apostles in a ceremony which consisted of prayer and the laying on of hands (Acts 6:1–16;

1 Tim. 4:14). By 220, St. Hippolytus testifies that bishops in some communities were elected by the people in conjunction with the presbyters and neighboring bishops. Upon election, they were anointed with oil and ordained by the visiting bishops through the laying on of hands, while the presbytery and the people looked on in silence. Presbyters, St. Hippolytus continues, were elected in the same manner, although in their ordination fellow presbyters joined with the bishop in laying hands upon new elders. Deacons, he concludes, were appointed by the bishop to be his servants and were ordained simply by the laying on of his hand.[23]

In other communities, bishops appear to have been appointed by their predecessors. This accounts for the appearance of ecclesiastical dynasties in the early Church. Polycrates of Ephesus is a chief witness to dynastic nepotism. Challenged to defend his faithfulness to the apostolic tradition, he stated the following: "I observe the traditions of those of my family in whose footsteps I follow: seven of my forbears were bishops and I am the eighth."[24]

14. *What was the role of deacons in the early Church?*

They acted as special assistants to the bishops in liturgical matters by reading the Scriptures, administering Communion, and leading *catechumens* (new converts) through the preparation for the rite of baptism. They also cared for the sick and distributed food and clothing to the poor. Though their ministry was one of service and not administration, many deacons performed duties as financial officers by supervising collections and disbursing Church funds.[25]

15. *Were women ever ordained in the Catholic Church?*

The evidence here is unclear. Canon XV of the Council of Chalcedon, however, states that they were ordained as deaconesses. The decree says: "A woman shall not receive the laying on of hands as a deaconess under forty years of age, and then only after searching examination. And if, after she has had hands laid on her and has continued for a long time to minister, she shall despise the grace of God and give herself in marriage, she shall be anathematized and the man with her."[26] Women, however, were not ordained in all Christian communities, especially not in the ante-Nicene Church (i.e., the Church as it existed before the Council of Nicaea in 325). St. Hippolytus, for example, states that deaconesses were not appointed but named and did not receive the imposition of hands.[27]

Ordained or not, in the ante- and post-Nicene Church, a deaconess did not have equal status with a deacon. "The Constitution of the Holy Apostles," a fourth-century document, testifies that a deacon possessed the power to excommunicate a deaconess for a breach of discipline. The same document further illuminates the clerical status of deaconesses in its discussion of the proper way to distribute the remains of an oblation: four parts to a bishop; three to the presbyters; two to the deacons; and one to the subdeacons, lectors, singers, and deaconesses.[28]

16. *What was the function of the deaconess?*

In a manner not unlike a deacon, a deaconess was delegated to a ministry of service. She provided for the needs of the poor, cared for sick women, instructed catechumens of her own sex, and guarded the church doors against intrusion by women who were not members of the fold. However, the primary responsibility of a deaconess consisted of assisting in the baptism of female converts. Since such rites required nakedness and total immersion, a deaconess held up a covering so that the women should not be seen by men.[29]

17. *Did they assist at the altar?*

No. In keeping with St. Paul's injunction (1 Cor. 14:33–35; 1 Tim. 2:11–12), women took no part in public worship. The *Didascalia* or "The Teachings of the Holy Apostles" (circa 325) carried prohibitions that forbade deaconesses and widows to preach in holy places, to enter into theological disputations, and to touch the sacred vessels at the altar.[30]

18. *But were not some women in the early Church called "priestesses"?*

Yes. But such titles were reserved not for women with sacerdotal authority but for the wives of ecclesiastics. In his *dialogus*, for example, St. Gregory the Great mentioned a certain priest from Norcia, who, from the time of his ordination, kept his priestess *(presbyterem suam)* at a distance, loving her as a sister, but fearing her company as a possible threat to his chastity.[31] Similarly, Canon 21 of the Council of Auxerre (570) held that it was unlawful for a priest after his ordination to sleep with his "priestess" for fear he might indulge in sexual congress.[32]

19. What happened to the office of deaconess?

The primary function of a deaconess, as stated above, was to assist in the baptism of female initiates. By the sixth century, however, whole nations of barbarians became converted overnight when their king or ruler formally accepted the faith. Mass baptisms of entire tribes were conducted with the result that the adult population of Western Europe became predominantly Christian. Thereafter, infant baptism was widely used and there was little need for deaconesses to assist in the administration of the sacrament.

At the Council of Orange in 533, the Church decreed that women could no longer be ordained to the deaconate, stating that they were too fickle to manage well.[33]

Upholding this ruling, St. Thomas Aquinas circa 1260 said that any attempt to ordain a woman would be invalid. The sacrament of Holy Orders, he argued, implies an elevation, a promotion to a place of prominence in the Christian community. But women, he concluded, have been placed by God in a position of dutiful submission.[34]

This decision has prevailed in the Church and was restated by the Sacred Congregation for Divine Worship in its "Third Instruction on the Correct Implementation of the Constitution on the Sacred Liturgy" *(Liturgiae Instaurationes)*, 7, as issued on September 5, 1970.

20. Whence comes the office of cultic priesthood in the Catholic Church?

After Constantine issued the Edict of Milan (313), Christianity soon became the favored religion of the Empire and the dramatic rise in the number of converts created a pressing demand for more liturgical ministers. Bishops were no longer able to officiate at all the liturgical celebrations within their jurisdiction. A temporary solution came with the appointment of auxiliary bishops.[35] However, the demand for such prelates continued to exceed the supply by far. Therefore, bishops began to delegate their authority to the presbyters, permitting them to preside over eucharistic services in their stead. As representatives of the bishop, they were completely reliant on his authority for their cultic function. The presbyters were assigned to specific congregations and could not serve elsewhere without the bishop's permission. They were (as priests still are) *incardinated* to their parish and diocese.

In Rome and other Western provinces, bishops kept symbolic union with their presbyters by sending them a piece of consecrated bread from their altars, which was to be dropped by the presbyters into their chalices during the celebration of the Mass.[36]

Since presbyters now assumed the role of celebrants in the liturgy, they, too, were looked upon as priests. By the fourth century, as Joseph Martos points out in *Doors to the Sacred,* the Latin words *presbyter* and *sacerdos* became interchangeable since all presbyters were priests and all bishops were chosen from the presbyters. Indeed, the English word *priest* comes from the Greek *presbyteros* through the Latin *presbyter* and the shortened Anglo-Saxon word *prester.*[37] The difference between the presbyter and the bishop was conceived of being a difference in authority and jurisdiction rather than a higher and lower degree of priesthood.[38] St. John Chrysostom, for example, came to this conclusion from his study of the Pauline Epistles:

> Discoursing of bishops, and having described their character, and the qualities which they ought to possess, and having passed over the order of presbyters, he [St. Paul] proceeds to the deacons. The reason for this omission was that between presbyters and bishops there was no great difference. Both had undertaken the office of teachers and presidents in the Church, and what he [St. Paul] has said concerning bishops is applicable to presbyters. For they [bishops] are only superior in having the power of ordination, and seem to have no other advantage over presbyters.[39]

21. *Are Catholic priests held to be metaphysically different from other men?*

Yes. This belief arose slowly in Christian tradition. In the first three Christian centuries, bishops and presbyters were not distinct from the laity in dress nor their way of life (since many were married with families). However, after Constantine came to power, Christian ministers were granted the same social privileges as pagan priests. They were exempt from military duty and excused from other civic obligations such as the payment of property taxes. Moreover, Constantine gave bishops the authority to act as magistrates in civil disputes since bishops were usually well-educated and held in high esteem by the populace. For this reason, bishops were accorded the attire of their new rank: a special cape, headgear, footwear, and a ring, which they wore in all public ceremonies, including the celebration of the Mass.[40] Moreover, they were greeted as imperial officials with such titles as "Your Excellency," "Your Grace," and "Your Eminence."

By the fifth century, presbyters along with the bishops began to wear long tunics (albs) as a sign of their priestly status. A cincture or sash with a white or colored rope was used to gird the alb, since a loose tunic remained a sign of effeminacy. By this time, priests in the West also were bound by the rule of celibacy and lived as solitary figures among their congregations.[41]

Priests eventually were viewed as being different not only in dress, manner, and way of life but also in nature. St. Gregory of Nyssa believed this difference was effected by the bishop's word of ordination over the priest, a word that transformed the priest into an extraordinary individual in the same manner that the word transformed the elements at the altar into the body and blood of Christ. St. Gregory wrote:

> This same power of the word also makes the priest venerable and honorable, separated, by the blessing bestowed on him, from his community with the mass of men. While but yesterday he was one of the mass, one of the people, he is suddenly rendered a guide, a president, a teacher of righteousness, an instructor in hidden mysteries; and this he does without being at all changed in body or in form; but, while continuing to be in all

appearances the man he was before, being, by some unseen power or grace, transformed in respect of his unseen soul to the higher condition.[42]

This teaching was reinforced by St. Thomas Aquinas in the thirteenth century. He wrote that the change which occurred in a priest at the time of his ordination was an ontological change, a change in the very depth of his being, that could never be reversed or redone. This transformation, St. Thomas contended, granted priests the divine power to do what Christ had done: to forgive sins and to consecrate the eucharistic meal.[43]

22. *Can priests lose this divine power by denying Christ or living dissolute lives?*

No. Catholicism teaches that once a priest becomes a priest he always remains a priest. This teaching came about as a result of St. Augustine's conflict with the Donatists. The Donatists were a heretical sect of Christians, who believed that once a bishop committed a mortal sin, he lost the gift of the Holy Spirit and therefore no longer could transmit the Spirit to others at ordination. For this reason, the Donatists claimed that priests ordained by sinful bishops had to be reordained by those who had never faltered from their holy orders. St. Augustine refuted this by insisting that priests received their spiritual authority not from the ordaining bishop but from Christ Himself, the purest of priests, who works through His ministers no matter how unworthy they might be.[44]

23. *Do Catholics believe that Martin Luther remained a priest even after he denounced many of the major tenets of Catholicism as demonic and labeled the Bishop of Rome the Antichrist?*

Yes. The soul of a priest at the time of his ordination is sealed with the indelible mark of priesthood—a mark that cannot be removed, no matter how grievous his sin or how heinous his heresy. St. Augustine wrote: "If a priest is degraded from his office because of some offense, the sacrament of the Lord which he once received will not be lost, though it may remain for his judgment."[45]

24. *Why did Luther reject the Catholic concept of priesthood?*

Luther rejected the belief that priests were metaphysically transformed into divine agents at their ordination as a "man-made fiction" that had no basis in Scripture.[46] Since they were not transformed, they bore no indelible mark or sacramental character on their souls. Christ, he argued, had made all men "priests and kings" (1 Peter 2:5). Therefore, any Christian could legitimately perform the liturgical functions that priests perform, and certain individuals should be singled out to perform these functions only for reasons of proper decorum and Church order.

Luther further dismissed the mandate for clerical celibacy as a "papal invention" that ran counter to the teachings of the New Testament: "The pope in making such a rule has no more power than if he were to forbid eating and drinking, or the performance of other functions, or growing fat. Hence it is no one's duty to obey this rule."[47] Luther dramatized his repudiation of this teaching in his personal life by marrying a nun.

25. *Didn't the Church at the Council of Trent (1545–63) alter its doctrines concerning the priesthood?*

No. The Council of Trent solidified the traditional teachings of the Church by upholding the following beliefs regarding the ministry:

1. Since the Eucharist was a sacrifice instituted by Christ, there had to be a new order of priesthood to replace the priests of the Old Testament.

2. The doctrine of ordination as a sacramental rite was firmly established by the Church Fathers, including St. Gregory of Nyssa and St. Augustine. This rite is the source of infused grace as Scripture affirms: "Hence I remind you to rekindle the gift of God that is within you through the the laying on of my hands; for God did not give us a spirit of timidity but a spirit of power and love and self-control" (2 Tim. 1:6–7).

3. At ordination, as St. Augustine affirmed, a Catholic minister receives the indelible character of priesthood, which separates him from other people.

4. Priests are equal to bishops in priestly dignity, even though they

do not possess the highest degree of priesthood and are dependent on bishops in the exercise of their power.[48]

26. *What effect did Vatican II have on the Catholic ministry?*

The Council upheld all the tenets of the ministry as set forth by the Council of Trent. But in its 1965 "Decree on the Ministry and Life of Priests" *(Presbyterium Ordines),* the Council also gave impetus to a broader understanding of ministry by exhorting priests to form Christian communities that make use of the talents and abilities of the laity: "Priests should also be confident in giving lay people charge of duties in the service of the Church, giving them freedom and opportunity for activity and even inviting them, when opportunity incurs, to take initiative in undertaking projects of their own" (9). It also encouraged priests to organize formal and informal associations with fellow priests and bishops for communication and support, as well as for a "safeguard from possible dangers arising from loneliness" (8). Moreover, the Council advised bishops not to act as mere authoritative figures but to regard their priests as "friends and brothers" and to take "the interest they are capable of in their welfare both temporal and spiritual" (7).

Subsequent Vatican documents called for the restoration of the permanent deaconate as a ministry of service to the sick and poor ("Apostolic Letter Containing Norms for the Order of Deaconate"—*Ad Pascendum*—August 15, 1972), the abolishment of the subdeaconate from Minor Orders, and the retention of the offices of lector and acolyte, not as steps to the priesthood, but as ministries for laypeople ("Apostolic Letter on First Tonsure, Minor Orders and the Subdeaconate"—*Ministeria Quaedam*—August 15, 1972). Of these lay ministries, lectors were permitted to serve by reading lessons from the Scriptures (but not the Gospel) at Mass, by announcing the intention of the prayer of the faithful when a deacon or cantor was not present, and to instruct the faithful in the proper means of receiving Holy Communion (5). Acolytes were granted the right to assist deacons and priests as extraordinary ministers in liturgical celebrations whenever a priest was not available to distribute the Eucharist because of sickness or old age (6).

27. *Did these reforms make the priesthood more attractive as a vocation?*

No. Between 1966 and 1974, 1 out of 7 priests in the United States (a total of 10,000 in all) left the priesthood. The decline by this time had been stabilized. In 1987, there were 57,183 priests in the United States, compared to 54,682 in 1960. Nonetheless, 44 percent were fifty-six or older, compared with 25 percent in 1970, and they were not being replaced.[49] In 1965, there was 1 priest to every 747 Catholic laypersons in the United States. Twenty years later, that ratio had risen to 1 priest to every 912 laypersons.[50] Even more telling of the severity of shortage of priests was the drop in enrollment in post-college seminaries from 8,887 in 1965 to 4,039 in 1985. One study predicts that by the year 2000, there will be half as many priests as there were in 1970.[51]

NOTES

1. John A. Hardon, S. J., *The Catholic Catechism* (Garden City, New York: Doubleday and Company, 1975), p. 305.

2. *Ibid.,* p. 306.

3. *The Rites of the Catholic Church as Revised by Decree of the Second Vatican Council* (New York: Pueblo Publishing Company, 1980), p. 54.

4. *Ibid.,* p. 52–53.

5. *Ibid.,* p. 54.

6. Robin Lane Fox, *Pagans and Christians* (New York: Alfred A. Knopf, 1987), p. 353.

7. Vern L. Bullough, "Chaste Marriage and Clerical Celibacy," in *Sexual Practices and the Medieval Church,* edited by Vern L. Bullough and James Brundage (Buffalo: Prometheus Books, 1982), p. 24.

8. *Ibid.*

9. St. Ambrose, "Duties of the Clergy," I, 258, in *The Principal Works of St. Ambrose,* translated by H. DeRomestin, Vol. X, *The Nicene and Post Nicene Fathers,* Second Series, edited by Philip Schaff and Henry Wace (Grand Rapids: William B. Eerdmans Publishing Company, 1955), p. 41.

10. Vern L. Bullough, "Formation of Medieval Ideals: Christian Theory and Christian Practice," in *Sexual Practices and the Medieval Church, op. cit.,* p. 15.

11. Pope Leo I, "Letter CLXVII," III, in *Leo the Great and Gregory the Great,* translated by Charles Lett Feltoe, Vol. XII, *The Nicene and Post Nicene Fathers,* Second

Series, edited by Philip Schaff and Henry Wace (Grand Rapids: William B. Eerdmans Publishing Company, 1958), p. 110. See also *Ibid.*

12. Ronald Lawler, O.F.M. Cap.; Donald Wuerl; and Thomas Comerford Lawler, eds., *The Teaching of Christ: A Catholic Catechism for Adults* (Huntington, Indiana: Our Sunday Visitor, 1983), p. 443.

13. Joseph Martos, *Doors to the Sacred* (Garden City, New York: Image Books, 1982), p. 461.

14. *Ibid.,* p. 462.

15. St. Ignatius, "Letter to the Smyrnaeans," 8, in *Early Christian Fathers,* translated by Cyril C. Richardson (New York: Macmillan Company, 1970), p. 115.

16. St. Irenaeus, "Against Heresies," XXVI, 2, *The Apostolic Fathers: Justin Martyr and Irenaeus,* translated by A. Cleveland Coxe, Vol. I, *The Ante Nicene Fathers,* edited by Alexander Roberts and James Donaldson (Grand Rapids: William B. Eerdmans Publishing Company, 1981), p. 497.

17. St. Cyprian, "Letter 68," 8, translated by Ernest Wallis, in *Fathers of the Third Century,* Vol. V, *The Ante Nicene Fathers,* edited by Alexander Roberts and James Donaldson (Grand Rapids: William B. Eerdmans Publishing Company, 1981), pp. 374–75.

18. Edward Schillebeeckx, *Ministry: Leadership in the Community of Jesus Christ* (New York: Crossroad Publishing, 1981), p. 27.

19. St. Ignatius, *loc. cit.*

20. St. Hippolytus, "The Apostolic Tradition," 3, translated by Gregory Dix, in *Readings in Church History,* Vol. I, edited by Colman J. Barry, O.S.B. (New York: Newman Press, 1960), p. 47.

21. St. Cyprian, "Letter 1," 1, cited in Martos, *op. cit.,* p. 471.

22. Martos, *loc. cit.*

23. St. Hippolytus, "The Apostolic Tradition," 4, in *Readings in Church History, op. cit.,* p. 49.

24. Charles R. Meyer, *Man of God: A Study of the Priesthood* (Garden City, New York: Doubleday and Company, 1974), p. 15.

25. Martos, *op. cit.,* pp. 462–63.

26. "The Canons of the Council of Chalcedon," Canon XV, in *The Seven Ecumenical Councils of the Undivided Church,* edited and translated by Henry R. Percival (New York: Edwin S. Gorham, 1901), p. 279.

27. St. Hippolytus, cited in Meyer, *op. cit.,* p. 63.

28. "Constitutions of the Holy Apostles," VIII, 12, in *Fathers of the Third and Fourth Centuries,* translated by James Donaldson, Vol. VII, *The Ante Nicene Fathers,* edited by Alexander Roberts and James Donaldson (Grand Rapids: William B. Eerdmans Publishing Company, 1951), p. 410.

29. Meyer, *op. cit.,* p. 64.

30. The *Didascalia,* cited in Meyer, *op. cit.,* p. 67.

31. St. Gregory the Great, "Dialogue Four," 12, in *Saint Gregory the Great: Dia-*

logues, translated by Odo John Zimmerman, O.S.B., Vol. 39, *The Fathers of the Church*, edited by Roy Joseph Deferrari et al. (New York: Fathers of the Church, Inc., 1959), p. 203.

32. Council of Auxerre, cited in Meyer, *op. cit.*, p. 71.

33. Council of Orange, in *Ibid.*, p. 75.

34. St. Thomas Aquinas, *Summa Theologiae*, III (Supplement), Question 39, Article 1, Vol. 19, translated by the Fathers of the English Dominican Province (London: Burns, Oates and Washbourne, 1922), p. 52.

35. Martos, *op. cit.*, p. 473.

36. *Ibid.*, p. 474.

37. *Ibid.*, p. 475.

38. *Ibid.*, p. 481.

39. St. John Chrysostom, "Homily XI" (On I Timothy 3:8–10), in *Saint John Chrysostom: Homilies*, translated by Philip Schaff, Vol. XIII, *The Nicene and Post Nicene Fathers*, First Series, edited by Philip Schaff (Grand Rapids: William B. Eerdmans Publishing Company, 1956), p. 44.

40. Martos, *op. cit.*, p. 250.

41. *Ibid.*, p. 493.

42. St. Gregory of Nyssa, "On the Baptism of Christ," in *Select Writings and Letters of Gregory, Bishop of Nyssa*, translated by William Moore and Henry Austin Wilson, Vol. V, *The Nicene and Post Nicene Fathers*, edited by Philip Schaff and Henry Wace (Grand Rapids: William B. Eerdmans Publishing Company, 1955), p. 519. See also Martos, *op. cit.*, pp. 479–80.

43. St. Thomas Aquinas, *Summa Theologiae*, Book III, Question 63, Article 4, Vol. 17, translated by the Fathers of the English Dominican Province (London: Burns, Oates and Washbourne, 1923), pp. 51–53.

44. St. Augustine, "Reply to Petilian the Donatist," CVI, 241, in *St. Augustin: Writings in Connection with the Donatist Heresy*, translated by Richard Stothert, Vol. IV, *The Nicene and Post Nicene Fathers*, First Series, edited by Philip Schaff (Grand Rapids: William B. Eerdmans Publishing Company, 1956), pp. 593–94.

45. St. Augustine, cited in Martos, *op. cit.*, p. 480.

46. Martin Luther, "Pagan Servitude of the Church," 6, in *Martin Luther: Selections from his Writings*, edited by John Dillenberger (Garden City, New York: Doubleday and Company, 1961), p. 340.

47. Martin Luther, "An Appeal to the Ruling Class," 14, in *Ibid.*, p. 450.

48. Martos, *op. cit.*, pp. 506–7.

49. *Time*, Vol., 130, No. 10, September 7, 1987, p. 50.

50. *U.S. News and World Report*, Vol. 101, No. 2, November 17, 1986, p. 70.

51. *Time, loc. cit.*

TEN

The Brides

of Christ

Join with the Lord, then, daughters, in begging the Father to let you have your Spouse today, so that, as long as you live, you may never find yourself in this world without Him. Let it suffice to temper your great joy that He should remain disguised beneath these accidents of bread and wine, which is real torture to those who have nothing else to love and no other consolation. Entreat Him not to fail you but to prepare you to receive Him worthily.

St. Teresa of Avila, "The Way to Perfection," 34

1. *What does the Church mean by the expression "religious life"?*

By this term, the Church customarily refers to those bands of men and women who live in monastic communities.

2. *Can the essential ingredients of religious life be summarized in such a way that its nature is distinguishable from all others?*

Yes. The essentials of religious life as contained in the documents of the Second Vatican Council (including "The Contemplative Dimension of Religious Life" or *La plenaria,* as issued by the Sacred Congregation for Religious and Secular Institutes in January 1981) are as follows:

1. The pursuit of holiness through the practice of poverty, chastity, and obedience.

2. Community life with community worship and prayer.

3. A permanent commitment by vow, simple or solemn, to a corporate apostolate of the Church under the direction of the local bishop or the law of the Pope.

4. Public witness of this commitment by wearing a distinctive habit.

5. Life under duly chosen superiors.

3. *What is meant by "religious profession"?*

According to Canon 654, religious profession occurs when members of a community take their vows—for a time (usually three years at first) or perpetually when after a period of time, at least three but not to exceed nine years, the religious commits himself or herself to monastic life for life.

4. *Can a religious be dispensed from these vows?*

Priests excepted, religious generally may be dispensed from vows, even perpetual ones, by a competent ecclesiastical superior. Temporal vows cease automatically when the term has elapsed.

5. *How many religious are there in the United States?*

There are approximately 138 communities of men with 26,000 adherents, and 419 communities of women numbering 113,000.

6. *How does the Church receive a nun into a community with solemn vows?*

Before consecration, a candidate for the vocation of a nun kneels before a bishop or priest who asks, "Are you resolved to perseve to the end of your days in the holy state of virginity and in the service of God and His Church?" The candidate answers, "I am." The bishop proceeds by saying, "Are you resolved to accept solemn consecration as a bride of our Lord Jesus Christ, the Son of God?" The candidate answers, "I am." The bishop and all present then exclaim, "Thanks be to God."[1]

After offering a prayer of consecration, the bishop reads the following words from the Song of Solomon: "Rise my love, my fair one, and come away . . ." In response, the initiate, holding a candle, kneels before the bishop to receive her veil and ring. The bishop says, "Dearest daughter, receive the veil and the ring that are the insignia of your fidelity to your Bridegroom, and never forget that you are bound to the service of Christ and of his body, the Church." The newly consecrated nun responds by saying, "Amen." After this ceremony, the new Bride of Christ embarks on a three-day retreat, known as her honeymoon. Then she sits down with her fellow nuns for the wedding feast.[2]

7. *Whence comes this idea of consecrated virginity?*

The primitive Christian community on the authority of St. Paul (1 Cor. 7:8–9) encouraged young woman to retain their virginity and widows to refrain from remarriage in order to achieve the "angelic state" of single-minded devotion to Christ.[3] Such women were accorded places of honor in the early Church. By the turn of the third century, virgins and widows assumed vows of sexual abstinence before the congregation. They were then consecrated by bishops, although, as St. Hippolytus testifies, the ceremony did not consist of a "laying on of hands."[4]

In some communities, Christian parents made vows before the altar in the name of their newly born daughters, committing them to lives of perpetual chastity. This may have been the Christian alternative to the Roman practice of female infanticide.[5] Tertullian condemned such practices in his treatise "On the Veiling of Virgins" (circa 220), arguing that such solemn vows were often later desecrated—in some cases even raising the scandal of pregnant virgins.[6] Despite this condemnation, the practice continued. Two hundred hears later, St. Augustine addressed the problem of a widow who made a solemn vow of virginity in the name of her infant daughter, only later to discover that her daughter was unable to persevere in this commitment. Faced with the terrible spiritual consequences of breaking this vow, the mother shunned remarriage and lived as a chaste widow for the rest of her life.[7]

8. *Were these virgins looked upon by the early Church as the Brides of Christ?*

Yes. Employing imagery from the Old Testament which spoke of Israel as God's chosen bride (Isa. 49:18; 61:10; 62:5), the early Church Fathers spoke of consecrated virgins as the "brides of Christ." Tertullian wrote to the virgins of Carthage: "You married Christ, to him you gave your flesh and to him you betrothed your maturity."[8] To lapse from this continency, St. Cyprian maintained, was to commit an adultery.[9] This injunction was taken literally and in several Christian principalities of the fourth and fifth centuries, adultery to Christ was punishable by death.[10]

By the fourth century, the ceremony in which a virgin became consecrated to her vows came to resemble a nuptial service. This is vividly illustrated in the story of Amoun, the founder of the monastic community of Nitria in Egypt. As a young man, he was fiercely desirous to retain his virginity, although his desire was frustrated by his parents' determination that he marry. On his wedding day, Amoun was able to convince his bride that consummation would be a sin since the priest had mistakenly performed the ritual for the consecration of virgins rather than the rite of blessing their marriage.[11]

In 384, St. Jerome in a letter to the virgin Eustochium, maintained that such marriage to Christ, the "supreme opener" of virgins, gave rise to spiritual ecstasies:

> Let the seclusion of your own chamber ever guard you; ever let the Bridegroom sport with you within. If you pray, you are speaking to your Spouse; if you read, He is speaking to you. When you fall asleep, He will come behind the wall and will put His hand through the hole in the door and will touch your flesh. And you will awake and rise and cry: "I am sick with love" (Song of Sol. 5:8).[12]

Such experiences of ecstasy pulsate the writings of the consecrated Brides of Christ. They, perhaps, were best described by St. Teresa of Avila (circa 1562) in her "Autobiography":

> This time . . . the Lord desired that I see the vision in the following way: the angel was not large but small; he was very beautiful, and his face was so aflame that he seemed to be one of those very sublime angels that appear to be all afire. . . . I saw in his hands a large golden dart and at the end of the iron tip there appeared to be a little flame. It seemed to me this angel plunged this dart several times into my heart and that it reached deep inside me. When he drew it out, I thought he was carrying off with him the deepest part of me; and he left me all on fire with a great love of God. The pain was so great that it made me moan, and the sweetness this greatest pain caused me was so superabundant that there is no desire capable of taking it away, nor is the soul content with less than God. The pain is not bodily but spiritual, although the body doesn't fail to share in some of it, and even a great deal. The loving exchange that takes place between the soul and God is so sweet that I beg Him in His goodness to give a taste of this love to anyone who thinks I am lying.[13]

9. Whence comes habits for nuns?

When they assumed their vows, virgins and widows in the early Church were told to avoid the dress and manners of the unchaste. For

Tertullian, this meant fine hairstyles, makeup, jewelry, and elegant shoes. They were to dress in the "full garb of woman," and to wear their veils in the Church and on the streets so that all would be aware of their "standing as virgins."[14] St. Cyprian was particularly vehement in his demands for the renunciation of any appearance of worldliness in dress or manner, claiming that if virgins continued to look and act like worldly women they would be unrecognizable to God at the time of the final resurrection:

> Are you not afraid, I entreat you, being such as you are, that when the day of resurrection comes, your Maker may not recognize you again and may turn you away when you come to his rewards and promises and may exclude you, rebuking you with the vigor of a Censor and Judge and say: "This is not my work, nor is this our image. You have polluted your skin with a false medicament; you have changed your hair with an adulterous color; your face is violently taken possession of by a lie; your figure is corrupted; your countenance is another's. You cannot see God since your eyes are not those which God has made, but those which the devil has spoiled. You have followed him [the devil]; you have imitated the red and painted eye of the serpent. As you are adorned in the fashion of your enemy, with him also you shall burn. . . ."[15]

This advice was well-heeded. In congregations throughout Egypt and Syria, virgins and widows began to crop their hair, a practice that spread to the West by the turn of the fourth century. They now dressed like the widows with whom they were seated in church, with dark clothes, no makeup, and long veils. Their appearance, in fact, led many pagans to comment on the unattractiveness of Christian women.[16] In 420, nuns of the Augustinian order shared a common habit (from the Latin *habitus,* meaning "appearance" or "dress"), which came to consist of a long black tuniclike dress, a cincture or belt to hold the dress in place, and a black veil.[17] Throughout the centuries, each new order of nuns developed its own habit.

10. *Didn't virgins in the early Church live with priests in a so-called spiritual marriage?*

Yes. Until the end of the fourth century, virgins and widows lived in private homes, not religious communities, and at times they lived in the dwelling places of celibate men. Tertullian in 210 commended such formations of "spiritual marriages" between celibates on the premise that virgins and widows might prove to be helpful consorts with the housework.[18] This practice soon spread throughout the Christian communities, as many celibate men, including bishops and presbyters, began to cohabit in a spirit of brotherly love *(agape)* with consecrated women (who became known as *agapetae).* This situation of domestic bliss soon gave rise to serious scandal, especially when several *agapetae* admitted to sharing the same bed with their chaste partners. Hearing of these incidents, St. Cyprian insisted (circa 250) that such women be examined to see if they lived up to their vows and that the men involved (even though acts of sexual congress may not have transpired) be excommunicated.[19]

Although condemned by the Council of Nicaea in 325, the practice of celibate cohabitation continued. In 385, St. Jerome expressed his disgust at such "spiritual marriages" by writing: "How has this pest of *agapetae* come into the Church? Whence (comes) this other name for 'wives' for the unmarried? Worse, whence this new kind of concubine? I will go further: whence these one-man prostitutes? They use one house, one bedroom, often even one bed, and they call us suspicious if we infer anything?"[20]

11. *Whence comes the notion of a religious community for women?*

Many of the virgins and widows in the early Church were wealthy and took fellow celibate sisters into their homes in the spirit of charity.[21] Constantine's daughter, for example, opened her palace in Rome to fellow virgins, as did the sister of St. Ambrose.[22] St. Jerome called these households *domestica ecclesia* (domestic churches) and noted with satisfaction the formation of such communities in the Roman households of his disciples Marcella and Principia.[23]

In such assemblies or *conventa,* religious women lived joint lives of prayer and fasting, and earned money by spinning, making cloth, and occasionally copying manuscripts.

But the formation of religious communities for women received its impetus from the rise of the monastic movement.

12. How did monasticism develop?

In the fourth century, many Christians set out to give their lives to Christ through complete renunciation of their fleshly existence. They justified this by Christ's command for His followers to abandon all possessions in order to follow Him (Matt. 19:21; Luke 18:22) and St. Paul's insistence on quelling the passions of the flesh (Col. 2:11). Following the example of St. Antony, thousands set out to live as solitaries or hermits in the deserts and mountainous regions of Egypt. In such places, they lived lives of perfect chastity, depriving themselves of food and sleep, and often performing mind-boggling feats of asceticism. Simeon Stylites lived for thirty years on a pillar sixty feet high from which he preached to large crowds and performed marvelous cures by his thunderous words.[24] Others like St. Pachomius never reclined when they slept.[25] These solitaries (most particularly, St. Antony and St. Pachomius) became the new Christian heroes to replace the holy martyrs and they drew followers who built cells near them and tried to imitate their exemplary lives. In time, these cells became enclosed to the outside world and were called "monasteries."

13. Why are ascetics called "monks"?

The term monk comes from the Latin monachus, meaning "one who lives alone." It came to apply to all those who sought to live apart from the world in an enclosed Christian community.

14. Why is the head of a monastery called an "abbot"?

When Jesus prayed in the Garden of Gethsemane during the night in which he was betrayed, he addressed God by using the Aramaic term Abba, meaning "father" (Mark 14:36). St. Paul urged all Christians to employ this same title for God in their prayer life (Rom. 8:15; Gal. 4:6). By the fifth century, it became employed as a means of address for the head or "father" of a monastery.

15. Why are female monks called "nuns"?

"Nun" comes from the Coptic (Egyptian) word for "good" or "beautiful." It was applied to the first convent for women established by St. Pachomius.

16. *When was the first monastery for nuns established?*

The first monastic convent for women was established circa 330 on the opposite side of a river near Tabennisi where St. Pachomius organized the first cenobitic or communal life for celibate men. The convent, under the direct of the sister of St. Pachomius, employed the same rule of disciple and order as the monastery for men. The four hundred women who became the first nuns divided their time between prayer (private and common) and manual labor. They raised their own food, cleaned and decorated the chapel, and spun flax and made clothes for the monks and themselves. They also engaged in spiritual exercises under their "Mother Superior" and were expected to memorize the Holy Scriptures, especially the Psalms, for the enrichment of their devotional life. St. Pachomius believed that there should be no time for idle thoughts in monastic life, since such thoughts could give rise to *accidia* or spiritual sloth.[26]

Whenever a virgin died, her spiritual sisters would prepare her for burial in a wedding gown and place her body on the riverbank. The monks, upon receiving a signal, would cross the river on a ferry "with palms and olive branches, and singing Psalms, they would bring her body to the opposite side, burying her in a common cemetery." Except for such occasions, religious "brothers," save the priest and his deacon for Sunday Mass, were not permitted to cross over to the convent.[27]

Other monasteries for women soon appeared. The sister of St. Antony organized a convent in Egypt, as did St. Basil with his sister St. Macrina. One of the most famous of these early convents was established by St. Augustine in his province of Hippo (circa 420–23). Governed by his sister, St. Augustine's Order of Nuns maintained a strict schedule of prayer and work. They shared all things in common, engaged in constant fasting, kept their hair completely covered at all times, and washed no more than once a month.[28]

17. *When was a uniform rule set forth for convent life?*

In 520, St. Scholastica established a monastery for women near Monte Cassino in Italy, which was organized under the rule set forth by her brother St. Benedict for community of monks. The Benedictine Rule henceforth would become the standard means of regulating all aspects of convent life. Later orders of nuns, such as the Cistercians and Carmelites of the twelfth and thirteenth centuries respectively, would be organized not to alter but to adhere to a literal interpretation of this rule.

The rule required women seeking admission to the community to serve a novitiate of several months in order to experience the austerities that would be required of them. Only after successfully enduring the trial period could they assume solemn vows and be consecrated as a Bride of Christ. Following this ceremony, it became customary for the nuns to don their habits and, in accordance with their sanctified lives, to be renamed after the holy saints and martyrs. Since the majority of the saints were men, the names of the female saints were quickly used up, forcing nuns to receive such masculine names as Sister Cyprian, Sister Antony, and Sister Aelred. This practice persisted until the middle of the twentieth century, at which time nuns were permitted to assume familiar names which were, for the most part, considerably more feminine.

The nuns were not permitted to leave the monastery for any reason without the permission of the abbess (the name another derivation of the Aramaic *abba)*. The abbess or Mother Superior was chosen by the nuns in a general election and she was obliged to consult with her spiritual sisters in all matters of importance. However, the final decision always came to rest with her, and the nuns were compelled to obey her in a spirit of complete obedience and utter humility.

The nuns of the Benedictine Order (and all subsequent orders) were to speak only when necessary, to refrain from jests and loud laughter, and to walk with their eyes constantly to the ground. They were forbidden to own anything—"not a book, writing tablet, or stylus—in short, not a single item."[29]

The daily schedule was rigorous. They were required to work three to four hours in the morning in the gardens or shops of the monastery, in the kitchen, about the house and chapel, or copying manuscripts. After work, they were to spend two hours in study. In the afternoon, they were granted two hours of rest, followed by a return to work until sunset. They were not to eat until noon, and during the season of Lent not until dusk. From mid-September to Easter, they received one meal a day; in the summer months, two, since the days were longer and the work more arduous. At all times, this schedule of work, study, and sleep was to be regulated by the Divine Office.

18. What is the Divine Office?

The Divine Office was set forth by St. Benedict as a liturgy of prayer, recitations from the Psalms, readings from sacred Scripture, and meditations on the lives of the saints to regulate the daily life of nuns and monks into so-called canonical hours. The nuns and monks were compelled to rise at approximately 2 A.M. (the eighth hour of night) to recite and sing the "nocturns"; at dawn (5 A.M.), they gathered for "lauds" or morning prayer; at six for "prime" (the first hour of daylight); at nine for "terce" (the third hour); at noon for "sext" (the sixth); at three for "none" (the ninth); at sunset for "vespers"; and "compline" at the end of the day. After compline, they were to observe the Grand Silence. Violation of this silence was to be meted out by severe punishment.[30]

St. Benedict based his "canonical hours" on the notion of the "sacred number seven" (septenarius sacratus numerus). Psalm 119, he noted, says that the Lord should be praised seven times a day (164) and once in the middle of the day and once in the middle of the night (62).[31]

The Divine Office continues to regulate monastic life in Catholicism. In recent years, however, since many nuns are involved in such active apostolates as teaching and nursing, a choir is set aside to fulfill the tasks of reciting prime, terce, sext, and none. Moreover, nocturns are commonly observed as private rather than communal devotions.

19. Why are some nuns called "Poor Clares"?

In 1212, a wealthy girl of eighteen named Clara dei Sciffi established a new order for women on the model set forth by St. Francis of Assisi for his followers. His followers, who became known as Franciscans, represented a mendicant order, that is, an order without a monastery or permanent dwelling place. They lived among the poor in the manner of Jesus and his disciples, begged for food, worked at menial tasks, and preached in the market squares. Like the Franciscans, the new order for women—the "poor Clares"—had no fixed income or endowments of any kind. They lived solely on alms. They made clothing and provided shelter for the poor and homeless. They also provided women instruction in letters, hygiene, and the domestic arts. However, unlike their religious brothers—the Franciscans—they were not permitted to leave their convent to engage in active ministry in the streets and marketplaces. They were bound by the decree of papal cloister.

20. *What is the meaning of "cloister"?*

"Cloister" comes from the Latin word *claustrum,* meaning that by which anything is shut up or closed such as a lock, a bar, or a bolt. It was originally used in association with the incarceration of prisoners, but by the seventh century it came to refer to religious convents for women. By this time, such convents were enclosed with thick walls with few entrances, to protect the Brides of Christ from the outside world. This protection was necessary as the barbarian invasions and a state of general lawlessness persisted throughout the Western world. In 692, the Council of Trullo—also known as the Quinisext Council—decreed that nuns were forbidden to leave the enclosures ". . . unless they be induced to do so for the common advantage or other pressing necessity urging on to death, and then only with the blessing of the bishop of that place. . . ."[32] Other church synods, including Ver or Verneuil (755), Fruile (796), and Mainz or Mayence (847), demanded the cloistering of nuns. The Synod of Mainz, for example, insisted that a nun could not leave the monastery for even a spiritual purpose, such as a pilgrimage to Rome.[33] When the first Cluniac monastery was established in 1056, Abbot Hugh specified that once a woman freely entered "this glorious prison" *(gloriosum hunc carcerem)* she would never be free to leave. Inside the convent, nuns were to be dead to the world. Here they were to live, work, die, and be buried. They were held behind the locked doors of the convent and the local bishop controlled the keys.[34] In 1298, Pope Boniface VIII in the bull *Periculoso* decreed universal enclosure or claustration of female religious.

21. *What is the difference between a nun and a religious sister?*

Catholics derive this distinction from the following account of Martha and Mary in the Gospel of Luke: "Now as they went on their way, he [Jesus] entered a village, and a woman named Martha received him into her house. And she had a sister named Mary, who sat at the Lord's feet and listened to his teaching. But Martha was distracted with much serving; and she went to him and said, 'Lord, do you not care that my sister has left me to serve alone? Tell her then to help me.' But the Lord answered, 'Martha, Martha, you are anxious and troubled above many things; one thing is needful. Mary has chosen the good portion, which shall not be taken away from her' " (10:38–42). Mary in Catholic theology represents the contemplative life, the life of prayer and meditation, which characterizes the life of nuns. Martha, on the other hand, represents the active life, the life of service to those in need, which typifies the life of religious sisters. This distinction is generally not acknowledged by the laity and yet it is profound. Nuns profess solemn vows, which render contrary acts illicit and invalid. Religious sisters profess simple vows, which render contrary acts illicit but not invalid. Moreover, by assuming solemn vows, a nun relinquishes all ownership of worldly goods and property. By simple vows, a religious sister gives up the use and administration of her goods but not the ownership.

22. *Whence came religious sisterhood?*

Religious sisterhood is a relatively new development in Catholicism. It traces its roots to 1633, when St. Vincent de Paul and St. Louise de Marillac formed the Sisters of Charity. This order, which was dedicated to corporal acts of charity, became the first Catholic religious society for women that was not bound by the rule of papal cloister. It permitted women to engage in active apostolic work in hospitals, orphanages, asylums, hospices, and battlefields. By 1660, the year that St. Vincent and St. Louise died—there were over forty houses of these sisters.[35] By the nineteenth century, there were thousands of houses of religious sisters throughout the world. By this time, new orders of religious sisters were formed within the old order of nuns. Thus there were Benedictine sisters and Benedictine nuns, Carmelite sisters and Carmelite nuns, Franciscan sisters and Poor Clare nuns, and so on. In 1841, when religious sisterhoods received papal approbation (sanction), the distinction between nuns and sisters was clarified by emerging canon law. Nuns remained in strict papal claustration—dedicated to the perfect life of prayer and reflection. Sisters were held by episcopal or common enclosure, which permitted them to engage in an external ministry.

23. How was the life of religious sisters administered?

Under the sanction of episcopal or common enclosure, religious sisters lived under monastic rules. However, they were permitted to substitute the recitation of the Divine Office with charitable duties. Until the middle of the twentieth century, they lived their lives in an unbroken pattern. They rose around dawn for prayers first, then Mass and Holy Communion. This was followed by breakfast in silence. Following breakfast, they performed their convent chores, cleaning, cooking, baking, gardening, sewing, etcetera. Upon completion of these chores, they were permitted to report to the site of their apostolic mission, for instance, the classrooms of the Catholic schools or the wards of Catholic hospitals. After work, they returned to the convent for more work, prayer, a simple supper, and evening devotions. At all times, the sisters wore the habit of their order (some sisters, like the contemplative nuns, wore hair shirts underneath their habits for mortification). They never entered a rectory or any place where they might be alone with a man. For this reason, they never traveled alone, not even in the company of their parents.

24. Are sisters still bound to this rigid routine?

No. By the 1950s, the first cracks began to appear in the organization of convent life. Under the demands of medical practices and the shortage of trained nurses, sisters in the nursing profession were permitted to adjust their horarium in order to fulfill their professional duties. The sisters who served beyond the convent bedtime were permitted to sleep beyond the five o'clock summons to prayer and were relieved of some of their daily chores. Other fissures also occurred. In

1953, Sr. Mary Emil Penet organized the Sister Formation Conference of the National Catholic Education Association and by forceful argumentation obtained ecclesiastical permission for sisters engaged in the teaching profession (some with only high school diplomas) to depart from the routine revolving around the Divine Office to attend colleges and universities in order to raise the standards of Catholic education.[36] By 1965, when Vatican II came to a close, the hours of religious sisters, by and large, were left to their own discretion and good conscience.

With this new freedom came new and unexpected demands. By the late 1960s, sisters appeared in blouses and bluejeans to join in boycotts, rallies, marches, and sit-ins for a host of social causes. Some, including a group of defectors from the Immaculate Heart of Mary Sisters in Los Angeles, dropped out of their convents to form new religious communities that included married couples and Protestants. Others became involved in the women's liberation movement and shunned any semblance of adherence to the rule of episcopal cloister. This position was upheld by Sr. Margaret Traxler, founder of the National Coalition of American Nuns, who said: "We hope to end domination by priests, no matter what their hierarchical status."[37]

The spirit of rebellion has persisted in the post–Vatican II Church. In 1984, Srs. Barbara Ferraro and Patricia Hussey of the Sisters of Notre Dame di Namur (along with other sisters, including Sr. Margaret Traxler) signed a 1984 advertisement in support of abortion on demand. When the Vatican attempted to pressure the order into expelling the sisters, the order responded by threatening a strike against the Church.[38]

25. What is the present state of religious orders for women in America?

The religious orders for women have displayed the most dramatic decline of any group within the confines of American Catholicism. From 1966 to 1987, the number of sisters and nuns dwindled from 181,000 to 114,000. *Time* projects a more precipitous decline in the next decade, since the average age of a woman in religious life is sixty-two, and the number of new novices extremely low.[39] Because of the shortage of sisters, about one-third of the 19,313 parishes in the

United States have been forced to hire lay women and men to perform tasks previously undertaken by women in religious orders.[40]

26. Are all religious communities in a state of decline?

Yes, but not to the same degree. Those communities which have maintained the essential elements of religious life represented by the *Causortium Perfectae Caritatis* and the members of the Institute on Religious Life have more new postulants than the modernized communities. These two groups in 1988 claimed a membership of thirty-five thousand and were able to maintain their institutional commitments to the Church.

27. What explains the decline in the modernized communities?

Commentators frequently say that secularization is responsible, particularly the tendency in modern culture to stress worldly concerns over the quest for eternal salvation.

Whatever the technical explanation, two definitions of religious life are currently at war with one another, not only within the Church but within the same community. The *historic view* looks upon religious life as a vocation from God to a permanent and approved apostolate of the Church. According to this view, good works and institutional service for the Church are important, but not so fundamental as holiness that comes from a common life and the evangelical counsels. *The modern view* understands religious life not in terms of a community living under a common rule but as a celibate association living and doing something for the Kingdom of God. Apostolates within this view are determined by the individuals, not by the community, which is no longer strictly defined. Moreover, public witness through a recognized habit is deemed unnecessary, along with any supervision by the hierarchy.

28. What are secular institutes?

Secular institutes are societies of men and women living in the world who commit themselves to a life of poverty, chastity, and obedience in order to be Christian witnesses in their everyday working life. They may or may not live together. The major difference between secular institutes and religious communities is the latter's stress on community life and institutional commitment to a Church apostolate. In contrast, members of secular institutes make personal commitments. In recent years, many religious communities have been transformed into secular institutes.

29. When and how did secular institutes come into existence?

They began in the eighteenth century among single men and women of Europe who wished to pursue a holier life in the Church. They received papal approval from Pius XII in 1947. There are approximately thirty-five such institutes in the United States, with a membership running to the thousands. Most of the institutes are small.

NOTES

1. *The Rites of the Catholic Church as Revised by Decree of the Second Vatican Council* (New York: Pueblo Publishing Company, 1980), pp. 140–41.

2. Marina Warner, *Alone of All Her Sex: The Myth and Cult of the Virgin Mary* (New York: Alfred A. Knopf, 1976), p. 128.

3. Robin Lane Fox, *Pagans and Christians* (New York: Alfred A. Knopf, 1987), p. 366.

4. St. Hippolytus, "The Apostolic Tradition," 13, translated by Gregory Dix, in *Readings in Church History,* Vol. I, edited by Colman J. Barry, O.J.B. (New York: Newman Press, 1960), p. 50.

5. Jo Ann McNamara, "The Lives of Consecrated Women in the Fourth Century," in *Distant Echoes,* Vol. 1, *Medieval Religious Women,* edited by John H. Nichols and Lillian Thomas Shank (Kalamazoo, Michigan: Cistercian Publishing Company, 1964), p. 14.

6. Tertullian, "On the Veiling of Virgins," XIV, translated by S. Thelwall, in *Fathers of the Third Century,* Vol. IV in *The Ante Nicene Fathers,* edited by Alexander Roberts and James Donaldson (Grand Rapids: William B. Eerdmans Publishing Company, 1982), pp. 35–36.

7. St. Augustine, cited in Fox, *op. cit.,* p. 367.

8. *Ibid.,* p. 371. See Tertullian, "On the Veiling of Virgins," in *Fathers of the Third Century, op. cit.,* p. 37.

9. *Ibid.* See St. Cyprian, "On the Dress of Virgins," 20, translated by Ernest Wallis, *The Fathers of the Third Century,* Vol. V, *The Ante Nicene Fathers,* edited by Alexander

Roberts and James Donaldson (Grand Rapids: William B. Eerdmans Publishing Company, 1981) p. 435.

10. Barbara J. MacHaffie, *Her Story: Women in the Christian Tradition* (Philadelphia: Fortress Press, 1986), p. 45.

11. Palladius, "The Lausiac History," 8, translated by Robert T. Meyer, Vol. 34, *Ancient Christian Writers,* edited by Johannes Quasten, Walter Burghardt, and Thomas Comerford Lawler (New York: Newman Press, 1964), p. 16.

12. St. Jerome, "Letter 22 (To Eustochium)," translated by F. A. Wright, in *Women and Religion: A Feminist Sourcebook for Christian Thought,* edited by Elizabeth Clark and Herbert Richardson (New York: Harper and Row, 1977), pp. 60–61.

13. St. Teresa of Avila, "The Book of Her Life," 29, 13, translated by Kiernan Kavanaugh, O.C.D. and Otilio Rodriguez, O.C.D., in *The Collected Works of St. Teresa of Avila,* Vol. I (Washington, D.C.: Institute of Carmelite Studies, 1976), pp. 193–94.

14. Tertullian, "On the Veiling of Virgins," 12, in *Fathers of the Third Century, op. cit.,* p. 35.

15. St. Cyprian, "On the Dress of Virgins," 11, in *Fathers of the Third Century, op. cit.,* pp. 434–35.

16. Fox, *op. cit.,* p. 372.

17. St. Augustine, "Letter 212 (To the Consecrated Virgins)," in *Saint Augustine: Letters 204–270,* translated by Sr. Wilfrid Parsons, Vol. 5, *The Fathers of the Church,* edited by Roy Joseph Deferrari, et al. (New York: Fathers of the Church, Inc., 1956), p. 44.

18. Tertullian, "On Exhortation to Chastity," XII, in *Fathers of the Third Century,* translated by S. Thelwall, *op. cit.,* pp. 56–57.

19. St. Cyprian, cited in Fox, *op. cit.,* p. 369.

20. St. Jerome, "Epistle XXII," 14, in *St. Jerome: Letters and Select Works,* translated by W. H. Fremantle, Vol. VI, *The Nicene and Post Nicene Fathers,* Second Series, edited by Philip Schaff and Henry Wace (Grand Rapids: William B. Eerdmans Publishing Company, n.d.), p. 27.

21. Fox, *op. cit.,* p. 369.

22. Jean La Porte, *The Role of Women in Early Christianity* (New York: The Edwin Mellen Press, 1982), p. 80.

23. Jo Ann McNamara, *op. cit.,* p. 19.

24. Will Durant, *The Age of Faith* (New York: Simon and Schuster, 1950), p. 59.

25. *Ibid.*

26. Jo Ann McNamara, *op. cit.,* p. 24.

27. Palladius, *The Lausiac History,* 33, in *Women in the Early Church,* edited by Elizabeth Clark (Wilmington, Delaware: Michael Glazier, 1983), p. 133.

28. St. Augustine, "Letter 212," in *Saint Augustine: Letters 204–270, op. cit.,* pp. 38–51.

29. St. Benedict, *The Rule of St. Benedict,* 33, edited by Timothy Fry, O.S.B., et al. (Collegeville, Minnesota: Liturgical Press, 1980), p. 231.

30. *Ibid.,* 42, p. 243.

31. *Ibid.,* 16, p. 211.

32. "Council of Trullo," Canon XLI, in *The Seven Ecumenical Councils of the Undivided Church,* edited and translated by Henry R. Percival (New York: Edwin S. Gorham, 1901), p. 385.

33. Jane Tibbetts Schulenburg, "Strict Active Enclosure and its Effects on the Female Monastic Movement," in *Distant Echoes,* Vol. I, *Medieval Religious Women,* edited by John A. Nichols and Lillian Thomas Shank (New York: Cistercian Publications, 1984), pp. 56–57.

34. *Ibid.,* pp. 60–61.

35. Lawrence S. Cunningham, *The Catholic Heritage* (New York: Crossroad Publishing, 1983), pp. 38–39.

36. Sara Harris, *The Sisters: The Changing World of the American Nun* (New York: Bobbs-Merrill Company, 1970), p. 7.

37. Sr. Margaret Traxler, quoted in *Religion in America,* edited by Leo Rosten (New York: Simon and Schuster, 1975), p. 402.

38. *Time,* Vol. 130, No. 10 (September 7, 1987), p. 50.

39. *Ibid.*

40. *Ibid.*

ELEVEN

The Third Commandment:

The Mystery of the Mass

. . . the liturgy is the summit toward which the activity of the Church is directed; it is also the fount from which her power flows. For the goal of apostolic endeavor is that all who are made sons of God by faith and baptism should come together to praise God in the midst of his Church, to take part in the Sacrifice and to eat the Lord's Supper. . . .

Vatican II, *Sacrosanctum Concilium,* I, 10

1. *How do Catholics interpret the third commandment: Remember to keep holy the Sabbath Day?*

By the third commandment, Catholics are required to worship God on Sunday by assisting at the Holy Sacrifice of the Mass.

2. *What is the scriptural basis for the Mass?*

The evening before he died (the day before the feast of Passover), Jesus shared his last fellowship meal with his disciples—a meal that would serve as the prototype for the liturgy of the Mass. At this meal, Jesus departed from the usual Passover ritual by washing the feet of his disciples as a sign that they should serve each other with humility (John 13:3–11). Moreover, at the breaking of the bread, before Jesus would have said the traditional Jewish blessing or *berakah,* he gave bread to his disciples telling them that the bread was his body, which they should take and eat. Similarly, he said a blessing over the cup of wine and passed it to them to drink, stating that the cup was the "covenant" of his blood which was "poured out for many for the forgiveness of sins" (Matt. 26:17–29, cf.; Mark 14:17–25; and Luke 22:7–38). Jesus extended the connection between this meal and his sacrificial death by stating: "I tell you, I shall not drink again of this fruit of the vine until that day when I drink it new with you in my Father's kingdom" (Matt. 26:29; Mark 14:25; Luke 22:18). In his first Epistle to the Corinthians, St. Paul told the congregation that they should repeat the ritual of this Last Supper in remembrance of Jesus: "For, as often as you eat the bread and drink the cup, you proclaim the Lord's death until he comes" (11:26).

3. *What were the first worship services like?*

The first services were weekly fellowship or *agape* meals in which the followers of Christ gathered in a spirit of communion with the

Risen Lord. Indeed, the post-Resurrection appearances in the Gospel of Luke were closely related to such gatherings (Luke 24:31, 24:36–43). The services continued to develop within the standard form of the Jewish *berakah*. For this reason, the first liturgical prayers were traditional Jewish prayers with the addition of certain phrases about Jesus, as is evidenced in the following primitive prayers contained in the *Didache* (circa 120):

> We thank you, holy Father, for your sacred name which you have lodged in our hearts, and for the knowledge and faith and immortality which you have revealed through Jesus, your child. To you be glory forever.
>
> Almighty Master, "you have created everything" for the sake of your name, and have given men food and drink to enjoy that they may thank you. But to us have given spiritual food and drink and eternal life through Jesus, your child.
>
> Above all, we thank you that you are mighty. To you be glory forever.[1]

As Christianity spread into the Greek world, converts, unaware of the customs and practices of Judaism, began to take liberties with the Supper by overeating and overdrinking. For such indulgence, they were soundly chastised by St. Paul in 1 Corinthians 11:20–22. "When you meet together, it is not the Lord's Supper that you eat. For in eating, each one goes ahead with his own meal, and one is hungry and another is drunk. What! Do you not have houses to eat and drink in? Or do you despise the church of God and humiliate those who have nothing? What shall I say to you? Shall I commend you in this? No, I will not."

Because of such excesses coupled with the rapid growth of the community, the agape meal became separate from the ritual meal, which became known as the Eucharist (from the Greek "to give thanks"), so named from the prayers of thanksgiving surrounding the *berakah*. This separation, by all evidence, occurred before 110. At this time, Pliny the Younger, upon interrogating Christians to gather information for the Emperor Trajan, reported that Christians met before dawn on a fixed day of the week "to worship Jesus as a God" and gathered later again that day for a common meal.[2]

4. *Describe the first "ritual" meals.*

The first ritual services were structured on the model of the Sabbath liturgy of the synagogue. They began, as St. Justin Martyr affirmed in "First Apology" (circa 150), with the traditional Jewish greeting "The Lord be with you/And with thy spirit," followed by a reading from the "memoirs of the apostles or the writings of the prophets," and an exhortation by the presiding cleric. After the exhortation came a series of prayers followed by the offering of "bread, wine and water." The presiding cleric uttered a prayer of thanksgiving over these gifts to which the people gave their assent with the Jewish declaration "Amen." Communion, then, was distributed to the faithful and sent by means of the deacons to the absent brethren.[3]

5. *Why did the early Christians celebrate the Sabbath on Sunday rather than the prescribed scriptural Sabbath on Saturday?*

Originally, the early Christians celebrated the traditional Jewish Sabbath (Acts 2:42–47), but gathered together on the first day of the week—the day of the Lord's Resurrection—"to break bread" as He had commanded (Acts 20:7) and to "put aside their alms" (1 Cor. 16:2). St. John called it "the Lord's Day," which translated into Latin as *Dominica,* the title still used for Sunday in official Church documents.

St. Ignatius of Antioch in his "Epistle to the Magnesians" (circa 110) referred to the drastic change in keeping the Sabbath that occurred among the early followers of Christ: "Those who lived by ancient practices arrived at a new hope. They ceased to keep the Sabbath and lived by the Lord's Day, on which our life as well as theirs shone forth, thanks to Him and his death. . . ."[4]

Similarly, St. Justin Martyr in his "First Apology" provided the following reasons why Christians celebrated Sunday not Saturday as the day for rest and worship: "We all hold this common gathering on Sunday, since it is the first day, on which God transforming darkness and matter made the universe, and Jesus Christ our Savior rose from the dead on the same day. For they crucified him on the day before Saturday, and on the day after Saturday, he appeared to his apostles and disciples and taught them these things which I have passed on to you. . . ."[5]

6. *Did the early Christians believe in the real presence of Christ in the consecrated elements of bread and wine?*

Yes. In his "Letter to the Corinthians," one of the earliest Christian documents (A.D. 58), St. Paul affirmed that by eating the bread and drinking the cup, Christians were united in an intimate manner, since they truly were partaking of the body and blood of Jesus. "And so," he continued, "whoever eats the bread or drinks the cup of the Lord in an unworthy manner will be guilty of profaning the body and blood of the Lord. Let a man examine himself, and so eat of the bread and drink of the cup. For any one who eats and drinks without discerning the body eats and drinks judgment upon himself." Because of this real presence, the Eucharist was capable of producing not only profound spiritual effects but severe physical effects within the recipient. St. Paul maintained that many in the Church of Corinth were weak and ill—indeed, some had even died—by partaking of the elements without discerning their significance (1 Cor. 11:27–32).

The primitive Christian community's belief in the real presence of Christ in the Eucharist is further affirmed by the following passage from the Gospel of John: "Truly, truly, I say to you, unless you eat the flesh of the Son of Man and drink his blood, you have no life in you; he who eats my flesh and drinks my blood has eternal life, and I will raise him up on the last day. For my flesh is food indeed, and my blood is drink indeed. He who eats my flesh and drinks my blood abides in me, and I in him." (6:52–57).

This scriptural stress of the real presence was greatly intensified by the early Church Fathers in their struggle against Gnosticism. As previously stated, Gnosticism stood as the most formidable threat to primitive Christianity. It represented a syncretism of pagan and Christian thought into a unified system which espoused that Christ was a being sent from the Highest Spirit to bring man true knowledge *(gnosis)* of the spark of divine spirit buried deep within the enslaving matter from which all men had been created by the evil God of this world. Since matter was a product of this evil God, Christ, being pure, did not assume it. For this reason, His mortal appearance was illusionary, and His suffering and death on Calvary an example of divine play-acting to deceive the veil God of this world.

To combat this idea of an illusionary Christ, the Fathers stressed the humanity of Jesus and the reality of his flesh and blood in the Eucharist. St. Ignatius, in his "letter to the Smyrnaeans" (circa 110), warned his readers about the false teachings of Gnosticism by writing: "They hold aloof from the Eucharist and from services of prayer, because they refuse to admit that the Eucharist is the flesh of our Savior Jesus Christ, which suffered for our sins and which, in his goodness, the Father raised [from the dead]. Consequently those who wrangle and dispute God's gift face death."[6] Similarly, St. Justin Martyr in his "First Apology" wrote: "The food we call (the) Eucharist, of which no one is allowed to partake except one who believes that the things we teach are true, and has received the washing of the forgiveness of sins and for rebirth, and who lives as Christ handed down to us. For we do not receive these things as common bread or common drink; but as Jesus Christ our Savior being incarnate by God's word took flesh and blood for our salvation, so also we have been taught that the food consecrated by the word of prayer which comes from him, from which our flesh and blood are nourished by transformation, is the flesh and blood of the incarnate Jesus."[7] And St. Irenaeus in refuting the gnostic claims of Valentinus said, "When the bread from the earth receives the invocation, it is no longer common bread, but the Eucharist consisting of two realities, heavenly and earthly; so also our bodies, when they receive the Eucharist, are no longer corruptible. . . ."[8]

By the end of the third century, the doctrine of the real presence of Christ in the Eucharist was so engrained in Christian belief that it never came into question by Luther and Calvin.

7. *What impact did Constantine's recognition of Christianity as a legitimate religion have on the liturgy?*

After Constantine lifted the legal ban on Christianity with the Edict of Milan (313), Christian worship services were held not in the catacombs around a common table but in great basilicas that had been designed for official state ceremonies. The architecture of the basilica was not conducive to communal participation but for ritual observance. Therefore, the liturgy changed from a spontaneous expression of worship within a prescribed format to a stately ritual of recited prayers and organized activities, centered on the bishop and attendant priests.[9]

Moreover, as congregations grew, the interiors of these churches began to show signs of worldly wealth and prosperity. Walls were richly painted or covered with mosaics, ceilings were gilded, large marble altars took the place of tables, jeweled crosses replaced wooden ones, and gold and silver plates and chalices replaced the former household utensils.[10]

8. Whence come clerical vestments?

Fairly early in his reign, Constantine gave bishops the authority to act as judges in civil suits since they were usually well-educated and respected by the people. For this reason, each bishop was endowed with a sign of his imperial rank, including a special cape, headgear, footwear, and a ring—all of which he was commanded to wear at public functions. Since the liturgy was a public function, bishops wore these vestments while celebrating the Mass. Prior to this, the clergy dressed in the same manner as the laity. Now, however, in addition to the clergy's distinctive dress, they were also accorded many ceremonial honors. They sat on thrones and their presence in processions was accompanied by the sprinkling of incense. Moreover, they were greeted by the people with a genuflection as a sign of respect.

9. Why is the Catholic liturgy called "the Mass"?

In the early Church, participation in the ritual of Communion was limited solely to baptized Christians. Catechumens, while undergoing the years of rigorous spiritual preparation for baptism, were not permitted to witness the consecration of the elements, and so they were dismissed shortly after the sermon by a "ceremony of dismissals" or *missarum solemnia*. Eventually the name for this ceremony was shortened to *missa* or "mass" to designate the entire liturgy, even after the dismissal of the catechumens was dropped from common use after the fifth century.[11]

10. *What does "liturgy" mean?*

Liturgy comes from the Greek word *leitourgia,* which originally referred to any work done for the people or any service accomplished for the common good. Its usage in the late fourth century to describe Christian worship reflects the fact that the agape meal had evolved into a service of ritual sacrifice performed by the bishop and his assistants for the spiritual welfare of the congregation.

11. *Whence comes the cult of the Blessed Sacrament?*

The cult of the Blessed Sacrament developed largely as a reaction to Arianism. Arianism was the most widespread heresy of the first four or five centuries. It arose from the teachings of a presbyter at Alexandria named Arius, who held that Christ was not consubstantial with the Father but represented the *Logos* or the highest being in the created order of things. Arius' teachings were condemned in 325 by the Council of Nicaea, which declared that Christ was "one in being with the Father." Despite this condemnation and the subsequent banishment of Arius, the heresy continued to make inroads into Christian communities. Indeed, many of the barbarian Gallic tribes were converted to the faith not by orthodox clerics but by Arian and semi-Arian bishops.

To check the spread of Arianism, the Nicene Creed was inserted in the Mass after the reading of the Gospel. Moreover, the Mass came to stress not Christ's brotherhood with man but His consubstantiality with God. The Eucharist represented not only the sacrificial offering of Jesus but the awesome presence of God. For this reason, St. Augustine told his readers that the Eucharist was not only to be received but worshipped.[12] And, in the East, St. John Chrysostom spoke of Christ's presence at the holy altar as "a sacrifice at which the very angels tremble."[13]

By the end of the fifth century, the Eucharist was regarded with profound obeisance by the priest. The prayers of the canon of the

Mass were now whispered in solemn reverence to the sacred mystery on the altar. Moreover, immediately after the consecration, the priests were asked to raise the Host above their heads so that the congregation could see it. Later, the chalice was also elevated and a bell was rung so that the people who had been praying would know when to look up to adore the sacrament.

This stress on the ineffable holiness of the Eucharist resulted in a rather precipitous decline in the number of lay communicants. In his "Homily on Ephesians" (circa 390), St. John Chrysostom, after expressing "outrage" at those who "kiss the king of heaven with an unclean soul," ironically continued by stating his concern over the congregation's reluctance to approach the altar: "In vain is the daily Sacrifice, in vain do we stand before the altar, there is no one to partake."[14]

It also gave rise to many superstitions. Some people believed that gazing upon the elevated Host would keep them from sickness and death. Stories spread about hosts that miraculously bled after being broken by sinful priests or chewed by sacrilegious unbelievers. The very word *hocus-pocus* is a bastardization of the Latin words of consecration *Hoc est corpus*.

By the fifteenth century, the cult had resulted in the Catholic devotion of the Benediction of the Blessed Sacrament in which the Host was enshrined in a monstrance and exposed upon the high altar for the people to adore. This devotion was accompanied by the recitation of litanies to the saints and the singing of such hymns as "Tantum Ergo" and "O Salutaris Hostia."

12. *Why is the consecrated bread called the Host?*

Since the laity generally abstained from receiving Communion during the early medieval period, a loaf of bread was no longer needed for the Mass, and a coinlike wafer made of flour and water was substituted in the belief that Christ's last supper had been a Passover meal with unleavened bread. This wafer was commonly called "the Host," from the Latin *hostia,* meaning a "sacrificial victim."

13. *Was the Mass celebrated throughout Christendom in a uniform manner during the Middle Ages?*

No. In the early medieval period, liturgical aberrations abounded, since bishops outside of Rome were permitted to improvise on the episcopal model. Faced with this lack of uniformity, the Emperor Pepin (d. 768) and his son Charlemagne (d. 814) attempted to impose the Roman liturgy on their subjects. The Roman liturgical books were brought across the Alps and distributed to the clergy to copy. The Franco-German clergy not only copied but adapted the Roman liturgy to their particular needs and tastes. They added numerous prayers and enriched the Roman rite with some spectacular and impressive ceremonies, such as the Palm Sunday procession and the Easter Vigil rites.[15] By a strange turn of events, the revised liturgy was brought back to Rome to replace the ancient Roman liturgy. This occurred in 963, when Otto I deposed the corrupt Roman Pontiff John XII on charges of transforming the Lateran Palace into a veritable brothel. After the expulsion of the debauched Pope, Otto took an active part in the reform of the Church. One such reform was the replacement of the old Roman liturgy with the hybrid Franco-Roman liturgy that his clergymen had brought with them. This liturgy was imposed on the whole Church as the official Roman rite by Pope Gregory VII (d. 1085).

14. *Why did Catholics until recent years receive the bread and not the wine?*

The Church, largely in reaction to the heretical teachings of Berenger of Tours (998–1088), maintained that Christ was fully present in every particle of bread and every drop of wine. This teaching led to three liturgical practices: (1) the requirement that the priest keep his "canonical digits" (the thumb and first finger) joined when touching the Host lest a particle drop unnoticed, (2) the dusting of the paten and the rinsing of the chalice after Communion, and (3) the distribution of the ritual meal in the sole element of the wafer. Since Christ was as equally and fully present in the bread as well as the wine, the communicant received the whole Christ by receiving the Host alone.

Moreover, this practice of single distribution prevented the catastrophe of a drop of wine (with Christ fully present in every drop) from spilling onto the floor or an article of clothing.

15. *At what point in the Mass do the elements of bread and wine become the body and blood of Christ?*

From the time of St. Justin Martyr (circa 150), the Church in the West held that the elements became transformed when the words of consecration ("This is my body/This is my blood") were uttered by the priest. St. Ambrose in his work "The Sacraments" (circa 380) wrote:

> . . . bread is bread before the words of the sacraments; when the consecration has been added, from bread it becomes the flesh of Christ. So let us confirm this, how is it possible that what is bread is the body of Christ? By what words, then, is the consecration and by whose expressions? By those of the Lord Jesus. For all the rest that are said in the preceding are said by the priest: praise to God, prayer is offered, there is a petition for the people, for kings and for the rest. When it comes to performing a venerable sacrament, then the priest uses not his own expressions, but he uses the expressions of Christ. Thus the expression of Christ performs this sacrament. What is the expression of Christ? Surely that by which all things are made. The Lord ordered, the heaven was made; the Lord ordered, the earth was made; the Lord ordered, the seas were made; the Lord ordered, every creature was generated. You see then how the creating expression of Christ is. If then there is so great a force in the expression of Lord Christ Jesus, that those things might begin to be which were not, how much more creating that those things be which were, and be changed to something else.[16]

This teaching was rejected by the Church of the East, which held that Christ became present in the Eucharist when the priest invoked the aid of the Holy Spirit to effect the transformation. This teaching was first expressed by St. Cyril of Jerusalem in the following passage from his "Catechetical Lectures": "Then having sanctified ourselves by these spiritual hymns, we beseech merciful God to send forth His Holy Spirit upon the gifts lying before Him; that He may make the bread the Body of Christ and the wine the Blood of Christ; for whatsoever the Holy Ghost has touched is surely sanctified and changed."[17]

16. *What is transubstantiation?*

Transubstantiation is a philosophical term first used by Hildebert of Tours (d. 1133) and other scholastic theologians to describe the transformation of the elements of bread and wine into the body and blood of Jesus. The term reflected the Aristotelian distinction (in an age intoxicated with Aristotle) between substance and accident. Substance is the basic nature of things, while accidents were secondary features, such as size, shape, color, etcetera. This distinction inherent in the term permitted theologians to explain why the elements retained their same appearance after consecration: the substance—the very nature of the bread and wine—was transformed, but the accidents—the size, shape, taste, and smell—remained the same. This metaphysical explanation was upheld by the Fourth Lateran Council in 1215.

17. *When does the sacrifice of the Mass occur?*

The actual sacrifice or immolation of the victim takes place in the consecration of the bread and wine. As St. Thomas Aquinas maintained, this represents the "unbloody" sacrifice of Christ for the sins of the world.[18]

18. *How did the notion of the Mass as an "unbloody sacrifice" become corrupted?*

The medieval theologian John Duns Scotus (1266–1308) held that the Mass was a repetition not a re-presentation of Christ's sacrifice on Calvary. For this reason, Mass was effective in its own right, producing spiritual benefits that could be applied by the priest to the cause of a specific group or individual. The theologian supported this argument by the following analogy:

> When some good has to be distributed among each of the household members according to his need, it is reasonable that the master himself does not do this directly but entrusts it to one or more of his servants. This is general practice in well-ordered families. With equal or even greater

reason, then, this method should prevail in the house of God, the Church, so that not God alone but some minister of the Church distributes the good to be given there in virtue of the sacrifice. Just as it is up to him to determine for whom in particular he intends to offer the sacrifice, so also it pertains to him to dispense or dispose of the good petitioned in virtue of the sacrifice.[19]

Moreover, Scotus argued, it is only fitting that the rewards of this sacrifice be applied to those willing to provide a stipend. "It is reasonable," he wrote, "that in exchange for temporal alms one be obliged to offer the spiritual suffrage of prayers and sacrifice, just as one must return a temporal good for the spiritual benefit of preaching, according to the Apostle" [1 Cor. 9:11].[20] Thus, in accordance with this logic, the holy sacrifice of the Mass came up for sale. A new and lucrative form of ecclesiastical income had been discovered. Private masses, masses without a congregation, began to abound throughout Christendom. By the fifteenth century, thousands of "altar priests" were ordained with the sole function of reciting masses for anyone who paid the price.

19. *What impact did the Council of Trent have on the liturgy?*

The Council of Trent (1545–63) provided the first systematic position on the doctrine of the Eucharist. It affirmed the concept of transubstantiation and upheld the validity of the entire sacrament in the sole element of the Host: "For Christ is whole and entire under the form of bread and under any part of that form . . ."[21] It decreed that children were not required to receive the Eucharist until they reached the age of reason (at age seven). It upheld the adoration of the Blessed Sacrament as a means of worshipping God and set aside a fixed day for the sacrament to be borne reverently in procession through the streets and public places so that the enemies of the Church might be "weakened or broken, or overcome with shame."[22] Moreover, the Council clearly defined the meaning of the Mass. In the Mass, Christ offered Himself in an unbloody manner just as He had offered Himself on Calvary in a bloody manner. Since the Mass represented Christ's own offering of Himself to the Father, it was a pure oblation that could not be contaminated by a wicked or unworthy priest. The sacrifice of the Mass, Trent maintained, did not detract from the importance of Christ's death, but provided the means by which the spiritual benefits of Calvary could be made available to the Church for the remission of the sin.

Trent further addressed such "prevalent abuses" as priests extorting stipends for private Masses, or guaranteeing that a set number of private Masses would free a soul from Purgatory; priests saying Masses many times a day, eliminating prayers and without taking Communion themselves; the selling of "bargain" Masses; and the practice of several Masses being conducted in the same church at the same time, sometimes even while a congregational Mass was being celebrated at the main altar.[23]

In addition, the Council condemned such "less prevalent" abuses as priests elevating the chalice by placing it on their heads; dead bodies being laid on the altar during Mass; hunters coming to the Lord's Supper with hawks and dogs; and processions of the Blessed Sacrament from different churches crossing and breaking into brawls.[24]

To further regulate liturgical abuses, a Roman missal was issued in 1570 under the authority of Pope Pius V. The missal gave detailed instructions on almost every aspect of the Mass from the prayers to be said each day to the tone in which they were to be said, from the number of Masses a priest could celebrate each day to the number of signs of the cross he could make over the consecrated elements. Henceforth, no changes could be made in the Mass without the highest ecclesiastical approval. For this reason, the Catholic Mass in 1960 was almost identical, word for word and gesture for gesture, with the Roman Mass of 1570.[25]

20. *What changes in the Mass were effected by Vatican II?*

The primary aim of Vatican II's "Constitution on the Sacred Liturgy" *(Sancrosanctum Concilium)* was the restoration and promotion of the "full, conscious and active" participation of the faithful in the liturgy (Chapter I, 14). To produce this participation, the Latin rite was replaced by a vernacular liturgy that was, as the Council ordered, "short, clear and free from useless repetitions" (I, 34). Priests were instructed to recite the prayers in an audible manner and the people were expected to respond to the prayers at certain points and to join in the recitation of other prayers, including the Creed and the Our Father.

Since the issuance of this Vatican document in 1964, the papal commission on the liturgy instituted additional changes in the Mass. Members of the laity were recruited as readers and as presenters of the gifts at the offertory procession. Whereas the priest was previously granted little freedom to alter the formula of the service, he was now permitted to improvise greetings and to take various initiatives in order to make the Mass more meaningful to the congregation. Greater emphasis was placed on Scripture by the introduction of a new lectionary with a three-year instead of the former one-year cycle of Sunday readings, and the priest was instructed to preach regularly on the Scriptures.[26]

Other changes permitted the laity to receive Communion in both elements *(Sacramentali Communione, 1970)* and granted deacons and acolytes the right to administer the Eucharist *(Liturgiae Instaurationes, 1970)*.

21. *Are women permitted to distribute the Eucharist?*

No. The Vatican II document "On the Liturgy" *(Liturgiae Instaurationes, 7)* prohibits women (young girls, married, religious) from serving the priest at the altar as acolytes or deaconesses. For this reason, women are prohibited from distributing Holy Communion even in women's chapels, convents, religious schools, and institutes. Women, however, may actively participate in the liturgy in the following manner:

1. by proclaiming the scriptural reading, with the exception of the Gospel
2. by offering the intentions of the Prayer of the Faithful
3. by leading the congregational singing
4. by providing explanatory comments to help the people understand the service
5. by serving as greeters and ushers.

Women may only distribute Communion when called upon to be

extraordinary eucharistic ministers, that is in circumstances when priests or deacons are not available.

22. *Is it a mortal sin for a Catholic deliberately to miss Mass on Sunday?*

Since the intent of the Church is to impose a serious obligation on all Catholics to worship God on Sunday by attending Mass, a deliberate and willful absence from Sunday Mass would of itself be a serious violation of Church law and a serious shirking of one's religious responsibility. Since most church-going Catholics recognize this, an occasional absence for light or insufficient reason might not be mortally sinful; but if the lapse continues beyond two or three occasions, unquestionably a habit or mortal sin was under way.

The Council of Trent passed a series of decrees dealing with the Christian's primary responsibility to attend Mass on all Sundays and holy days of the year. This was upheld by Vatican II's "Constitution on the Sacred Liturgy" *(Sacrosanctum Concilium,* 106), which said:

> By a tradition handed down from the apostles, which took its origin from the very day of Christ's Resurrection, the Church celebrates the paschal mystery every seventh day, which is appropriately called the Lord's Day or Sunday. For on this day, Christ's faithful are bound to come together into one place. They should listen to the Word of God and take part in the Eucharist, thus calling to mind the passion, resurrection and glory of the Lord Jesus and giving thanks to God who "has begotten them again through the resurrection of Christ from the dead" (1 Peter 1:3).

Because of the primacy of this commandment, the authors of *The Teaching of Christ: A Catholic Catechism for Adults* view weekly attendance at Mass as a "good barometer" of the intensity of the Catholic faith in a given society.[27]

23. *According to this barometer, is the Catholic Church in America healthy or ailing?*

It is still reasonably healthy, albeit not nearly as vital as it once was. In 1962, a Gallup poll showed that 82 percent of the Catholics in America attended Mass on a regular basis. Twenty-five years later, a

1987 poll conducted for *Time* by Yankelovich Clancy Shulman showed that 54 percent of the American Catholics attended Mass "weekly or nearly every week." However, the same poll discovered that 38 percent admitted they attended Mass less frequently than they did a decade ago.[28] Considering the population growth, there are ten million less Catholics attending Sunday Mass today than if the old rates of observance were still in force.

24. *Is it permissible for Catholics to fulfill their Sunday obligation by attending Mass on Saturday?*

Yes. The purpose of this concession, according to Vatican II's "Instruction on the Worship of the Eucharistic Mystery" *(Eucharisticum Mysterium)*, II, 28, as issued in 1967, is to permit Catholics to celebrate "more easily" the day of the Resurrection of the Lord. Such Masses, however, are only to be celebrated in the evening, that is, 4 P.M. or later.

NOTES

1. "The Teaching of the Twelve Apostles, Commonly Called the Didache," 9:3–4, translated by Cyril C. Richardson, in *Early Christian Fathers*, edited by Cyril C. Richardson (New York: The Macmillan Company, 1970), p. 175.

2. Henry Chadwick, *The Early Church* (Baltimore: Penguin Books, 1969), p. 28.

3. St. Justin Martyr, "First Apology," 67, translated by Edward Roche Hardy, in *Early Christian Fathers, op. cit.*, p. 287.

4. St. Ignatius, "Epistle to the Magnesians," 9, translated by Cyril C. Richardson, in *Ibid.*, p. 97.

5. St. Justin Martyr, "First Apology," 67–68, in *Ibid.*, pp. 287–88.

6. St. Ignatius, "Epistle to the Smyrnaeans," 7, translated by Cyril C. Richardson, in *Ibid.*, p. 114.

7. St. Justin Martyr, "First Apology," *Ibid.*, p. 286.

8. St. Irenaeus, "Against the Heresies," IV, 8, in *The Apostolic Fathers: Justin Martyr and Irenaeus*, translated by A. Cleveland Coxe, Vol. I, *The Ante Nicene Fathers*, edited by Alexander Roberts and James Donaldson, (Grand Rapids: William B. Eerdmans Publishing Company, 1981), p. 486.

9. Joseph Martos, *Doors to the Sacred* (Garden City, New York: Image Books, 1982), p. 250.

10. *Ibid.*

11. *Ibid.,* p. 252.

12. St. Augustine, "Exposition on Psalm 99," 8, in *St. Augustin: Exposition on the Psalms,* translated by A. Cleveland Coxe, Vol. VIII, *The Nicene and Post Nicene Fathers,* First Series, edited by Philip Schaff (Grand Rapids: William B. Eerdmans Publishing Company, 1956), p. 485.

13. St. John Chrysostom, "Homily II, on Ephesians," translated by Gross Alexander, in *Saint Chrysostom: Homilies on Galatians, Ephesians, Philippians, Colossians, Thessalonians, Timothy, Titus, and Philemon,* Vol. XIII, *The Nicene and Post Nicene Fathers,* First Series, edited by Philip Schaff (Grand Rapids: William B. Eerdmans Publishing Company, 1956), p. 63.

14. *Ibid.,* p. 64.

15. Thomas Bokenkotter, *Essential Catholicism: Dynamics of Faith and Belief* (Garden City, New York: Image Books, 1986), p. 21.

16. St. Ambrose, "The Sacraments," IV:4, in *St. Ambrose: Theological and Dogmatic Works,* edited by Roy J. Deferrari, Vol. 44, *The Fathers of the Church,* edited by Roy Joseph Deferrari et al. (Washington, D.C.: Catholic University Press, 1963), p. 302. Cf., Martos, *op. cit,* p. 256.

17. St. Cyril of Jerusalem, "Catechetical Lecture XXIII," 7, in *The Writings of St. Cyril of Jerusalem and St. Gregory Nazianzen,* translated by Edwin Hamilton Gifford, Vol. VII, *The Nicene and Post Nicene Fathers,* edited by Philip Schaff and Henry Wace (Grand Rapids: William B. Eerdmans Publishing Company, 1958), p. 154. Cf., Martos, *Ibid.*

18. St. Thomas Aquinas, *Summa Theologiae,* Part Three, Question 83, Article 1, Vol. 17, translated by the Fathers of the English Dominican Province (London: Burns, Oates and Washbourne, Ltd., 1923), pp. 433–34.

19. John Duns Scotus, *God and Creature: The Quodlibetal Questions,* 20:32, translated by Felix Alluntis, O.F.M. and Allan B. Walter, O.F.M. (Princeton: Princeton University Press, 1975), p. 454.

20. *Ibid.,* 20:39, p. 456.

21. "Council of Trent," Thirteenth Session, *Canons and Decrees of the Council of Trent,* translated by H. J. Schroeder, O.P. (London: B. Herder Book Company, 1955), p. 75.

22. *Ibid.*

23. *Ibid.* Cf., Martos, *op. cit.,* pp. 287–88.

24. Martos, *loc. cit.*

25. *Ibid.*

26. Bokenkotter, *op. cit.,* p. 218.

27. Ronald Lawler, O.F.M. Cap.; Donald W. Wuerl; Thomas Comerford Lawler, eds., *The Teaching of Christ: A Catholic Catechism for Adults* (Huntington, Indiana: Our Sunday Visitor, 1983), pp. 297–98.

28. *Time,* Vol. 130, No. 10, September 7, 1987, p. 48.

TWELVE

The Fourth Commandment:

The Sociopolitical Teachings

---

of the Church

The Catholic Church has been established by Jesus Christ as MOTHER AND TEACHER of nations, so that all who in the course of centuries come to her loving embrace, may find salvation as well as the fullness of a more excellent life. To this Church, "the pillar and mainstay of the truth," her most holy Founder has entrusted the double task of begetting sons unto herself, and of educating and governing those whom she begets, guiding with maternal providence the life both of individuals and of peoples. The lofty dignity of this life, she has always held in the highest respect and guarded with watchful care.

Pope John XXIII, Mater et Magistra, I

1. *How do Catholics interpret the fourth commandment: Honor your father and your mother?*

By this commandment, Catholics are called upon to esteem, respect, give service to, and when circumstances call for it, to obey their legitimate superiors, beginning with those who sired and bore them. However, the words "father and mother" in the Christian tradition have been understood to include anyone who holds from God legitimate authority over His creatures.[1] These include, besides parents, properly constituted civil officials, pastors, teachers, guardians, and so forth. Conversely, the commandment obliges parents and other individuals in positions of authority to provide for the temporal well-being of their children and subjects. For this reason, the entire corpus of the Church's sociopolitical teachings are rooted in this commandment.

2. *Was the early Church concerned with the affairs of the world?*

No. The early Church, persecuted at first by Jews and later by Romans, had enough to do to survive. It was in no position to reconstruct any social order. What's more, the early Christians believed in the imminent coming of the Kingdom of God and the destruction of "this present evil world" and all its vanity (Gal. 1:4). Since this world was "no continuing city" (Heb. 13:14), Christians were instructed not to be "conformed to the things of the world" (Rom. 12:2) but transformed in expectation of Christ's glorious return to judge the living and the dead (1 Peter 4:5). During this waiting period, social positions were of little concern. Everyone was rather to remain in the station in which they were called: "Were you a slave when called? Never mind. But if you can obtain your freedom, avail yourself of the opportunity. For he who was called in the Lord as a slave is a freedman of the Lord. Likewise he who was free when called is a slave to Christ. You were bought with a price; do not become slaves of men. So, brethren, in whatever state each was called, there let him remain with God" (1 Cor. 7:20–24). Moreover, the apostles said, Christians do not belong to the world but to the Kingdom of God (James 2:5). For this reason, they remain "strangers and exiles" in their fleshly existence, longing for their true home in heaven (Heb. 11:14–16).

Not belonging to the world, Christians sought no changes in the temporal order of social, economic, or political affairs. This order, they believed, had been instituted by God and must be met in a spirit of complete acquiescence. St. Paul wrote: "Let every person be subject to the governing authorities. For there is no authority except from God, and those that exist have been instituted by God. Therefore he who resists the authorities resists what God has appointed, and those who resist will incur judgment" (Rom. 13:1–2).

Following such dictates, the early Christians lived as model citizens. They took no part in the full-scale revolution against Roman rule that erupted in Palestine in 66 and actively sought to disassociate themselves from such zealots.[2] Pliny, in his examination of the Christian community in eastern Bithynia (circa 112), reported that the Christians posed no threat to the prevailing political order and represented nothing more than "an extravagant superstition."[3] Indeed, the early Christians egregiously sought to establish their obedience to Rome. In 155, St. Justin Martyr defended the faith by stating that Christians dutifully pay their taxes and honor all state institutions.[4] Similarly, Tertullian in his "Apology" (197) assured the Roman officials that Christians "are always praying for all emperors, for a safe dynasty, brave armies, a faithful Senate and a quiet world."[5]

This attitude persisted throughout the Patristic period. Writing in 425, forty-five years after Christianity was pronounced the "official religion" of the Roman Empire, St. Augustine wrote: "For, as far as this life of mortals is concerned, which is spent and ended in a few days, what does it matter under whose government a dying man lives?"[6]

3. *How did the early Church view such social evils as slavery?*

Slavery in the early Church was accepted without question as part of the divinely ordained social order. "Slaves," St. Paul wrote to the Ephesians, "be obedient to those who are your earthly masters, with fear and trembling, in singleness of heart, as to Christ" (6:5).

This teaching prevailed throughout the Patristic and medieval periods. St. Augustine, for example, spoke of a slavery as a just condition that had been caused by the sinfulness of man: "The prime cause of slavery is sin, which brings man under the dominion of his fellow— that which does not happen save by the judgment of God, with whom is no unrighteousness, and who knows how to award fit punishments to every variety of offense. . . ."[7]

4. *Did the early Church Fathers have a vision of a just social order?*

Yes. Many Church Fathers, including St. Augustine, upheld the Platonic vision of a society that embodies perfect justice and lasting peace. But this society can only be found in the City of God, which exists in heaven and is the final goal of all believers.[8]

5. *Did the early and/or medieval Church advocate social action?*

If by the phrase "social action" the modern definition is meant, that is, disruption of the social order, the answer is no. Indeed, David J. O'Brien and Thomas Shannon argue that by the Middle Ages an organic social theory emerged in Christianity "which upheld the given social order as ordained by God and made clear the sinfulness of discontent and the futility of efforts at social change."[9] However, social action also means social initiative, and in this sense, the medieval Church gave rise to the widest network of private educational and social agencies in the Western world, including the creation of deacons to take care of the poor, the development of the feudal system with its stress on class cooperation and guilds to protect class interests, the efforts to regulate just wages and just prices through the elimination of usury, and the effect of monks and monasteries on land development and land use.

6. *How did the writings of St. Thomas Aquinas come to serve the feudal order?*

St. Thomas saw the state as properly serving a coercive function by holding sinful man in check by a system of societal regulations.[10] Man has no right to oppose this function, which has been ordained by God as a result of original sin. With the Scriptures in mind, St. Thomas spoke not of social rights but of social duties and the obligations that served to define the proper place of individuals in society. Thus, serfs had responsibilities to their lord, and the feudal lord, in turn, was obligated to manage his feudal manor with justice and charity. Considering the local nature of medieval economics and the lack of national states, there was little social change. Indeed, a feudal mentality was to prevail with Catholicism until the time of Pope Leo XIII and his monumental encyclical *Rerum Novarum* (1891).[11]

7. *What did* Rerum Novarum *have to say that was new?*

Issued in the wake of the industrial revolution, which radically transformed the economy of the Western world and gave rise to secular ideologies such as Marxism that threatened the very existence of the Church, *Rerum Novarum* (On the Condition of Workingmen) represented a bold attempt by the Church to make direct demands for social justice. It spoke of the rights and responsibilities of workers (including their right to protect themselves through trade unions and strikes), the rights and responsibilities of property owners, the problem of child labor, and the "just wage." Concerning the latter, the encyclical said: "While, as a rule, employer and workman may freely agree as to wages, nevertheless, there underlies a dictate of natural justice more impervious and more ancient than any bargain between man and man, viz., that remuneration ought to be sufficient to support the wage earner in reasonable and frugal comfort. If through necessity or fear of a worse evil, a workman accepts harder conditions, because an employer or contractor will afford him no better, he is made a victim of force and injustice."[12]

Rerum Novarum further advocated the sharing of wealth, the role of government in promoting "public well-being and private prosperity," and the right of the Church to pontificate on social issues. Upholding this right, the encyclical said: "No practical solution to the social question will ever be found without the assistance of religion and the Church."

Several future pontiffs took this statement very much to heart.

8. *What did* Rerum Novarum *have to say about the state and the family?*

It said: "The idea that the civil government should, at its own discretion, penetrate and pervade the family and the household is a great and pernicious mistake."[13] Nevertheless, it held that public aid for needy families was in order, as was assistance for those undergoing marital difficulties.

9. *Did this encyclical condone socialism?*

Quite to the contrary, *Rerum Novarum* condemned socialism, stating that the destruction of private property would "rob the lawful possessors, bring the State into a sphere not its own, and cause confusion in the community."[14]

10. *Did the Church officially support the Fascists in the Spanish Civil War?*

Yes, but not because the Church was pro–Fascist. By 1935, the Vatican, in fact, had reached a *modus vivendi* with the Republican government of Spain, based on the following stipulations: (1) that the Republicans would maintain law and order and (2) that they would put an end to the antireligious excesses of the extremists. The Republicans were unable to meet these demands. With the outbreak of national resistance in 1936 under Franco's banner, the Communist extremists destroyed churches and convents, murdering ten bishops, six thousand priests, and sixteen thousand religious and lay leaders. Vatican support understandably turned to the Nationalists.

11. *Did the Church support Mussolini's rise to power?*

Yes. Pope Pius XI felt that Italy needed a "strong man" to establish order and to settle forever the "Roman question"—the question of control and ownership of the Papal States. For this reason, the Vatican withdrew its support from the Catholic Popular Party, causing the resignation of its leader, the priest Don Sturzo. Mussolini rewarded the Church for this action by signing the Lateran Concordat and Treaty. In return for the surrender of papal claims to Italian territory, the treaty granted the Church a munificent amount of money (in excess of ninety million dollars) and complete sovereignty over Vatican City—the forty-acre complex of buildings and gardens around St. Peter's Basilica in Rome—making the complex an independent city-state. In addition, the document accorded Catholicism a privileged status in Italy and imposed Catholic instruction as the norm for religious courses in the state school system.

The Vatican's relationship with the Mussolini government, however, rapidly deteriorated, as evidenced by the issuance of the encyclical *Non Abbiamo Bisogno* (We Have No Need) in 1931, which attacked Fascism for its tyranny and its effort to curb the liberties and activities of the Church. The encyclical made Francis Spellman world famous because Pope Pius XI, fearing Mussolini would suppress its publication, sent the future cardinal to Paris to have it published by the Associated Press.

12. *What was the Church's position toward Hitler?*

Pope Pius XI's encyclical *Mit brennender Sorge* (On the Church and the Third Reich) was, according to C. Falconi, "the first great official public document to confront and criticize Nazism."[15] Smuggled into Germany, the encyclical was read from all Catholic pulpits on Palm Sunday in March of 1937. It denounced the Nazi myth of blood and soil and "neopaganism" of the movement.[16]

13. *How did Pope Pius XII get into so much trouble after his death over the atrocities of the Third Reich?*

The defamation of Pope Pius XII was brought about by the German playwright Rolf Hochhuth who indicted the Pontiff for failing to save the Jews from Hitler. Hochhuth's play *The Deputy* succeeded in slandering the Pope as no research article could do. To this day, those who know nothing about Pope Pius XII accept Hochhuth's assessment, not even aware of the source of their prejudice.

In truth, Pope Pius XII (Eugenio Pacelli) has been cited as one of the great religious leaders of the twentieth century.[17] Outspoken before the rise of Nazism, he collaborated from 1941 onward with Western leaders Franklin D. Roosevelt and Winston Churchill in soothing religious objections to the Western alliance with the Soviet Union so that Catholics would come to understand that Hitler must be seen as a mortal religious and political enemy. The Pope did this despite the fact that he considered Marxism to be the greatest enemy facing the Church and civilization. His revulsion toward Communism can be traced back to his years of service as a nuncio in Munich after World War I.

By 1919, the Socialists had taken control of the Bavarian government and began a purge of all political opponents, a purge which ended only when Archbishop Pacelli condemned it.

From that year until 1925, Archbishop Pacelli followed Marxist activities in Germany very closely. He read the complete works of Marx and Engels, paid several visits to Marx's birthplace at Trier and the University of Bonn where Marx studied from 1835 to 1836, and met with the surviving relatives of Marx and Jenny von Westphalen, Marx's wife.

Gradually, the archbishop came to believe that Communism was not only godless but Satanic. He noticed that Marx's early poems were dedicated to *Oulanem*, a name used in Black Masses and Satanic hymns to denote the devil. He became even more convinced when he discovered that Stalin's pseudonym was *Demonshile* (the Demonic One).[18]

In forty out of his forty-five addresses as papal nuncio, Archbishop Pacelli inveighed against the Antichrist and warned of future struggle between Satan and Jesus (Communism and the Church) for the souls of men.

As stated above, Pope Pius XII did participate in easing Christian objections to the Western alliance with the Soviet Union. Moreover, under his pontificate, the Roman Catholic Church saved more Jewish lives than all other churches, religious institutions, and rescue organizations combined.[19] In Poland alone, the Church provided the ransom money to save over 400,000 Jews from certain death.

Nevertheless, to his dying day in 1958, the Pope remained uneasy about his part in forming the alliance with Stalin. By declaring Hitler to be the greater and more immediate evil, he feared he had acquiesced to a fatal compromise, a compromise that would result in the widespread acceptance of Marxism, even in Catholic circles, and the penetration of this "demonic ideology" into European culture, thought, and politics.

14. *What is the Church's position on Communism?*

The Church has affirmed a vehement opposition to Communism. Pope Leo XIII, in his encyclical *Quod Apostolici Meneris* (On Socialism) issued in 1878, set the tone for the Church's campaign against Marxism by labeling it a "barbaric sect."[20] Pope Pius XI restated this position in his 1931 encyclical *Quadragesimo anno* (Commemorating the Fortieth Anniversary of *Rerum Novarum)* and in a subsequent encyclical *Divini Redemptoris* (On Atheistic Communism), issued in 1937, said: "Communism is intrinsically wrong and no one may collaborate with it in any undertaking whatsoever."[21] In 1949, Pope Pius XII decreed the penalty of excommunication on all Catholics holding formal and willing allegiance to the Communist party.

15. *Why were the teachings of Pope John XXIII so grating to Catholic conservatives?*

In his encyclical *Mater et Magistra* (Mother and Teacher) issued in 1961, Pope John XXIII espoused the "welfare state model," calling for the state to greatly increase its ownership of private property. This led William Buckley to quip, "Mater, yes; Magistra, no." Even more disturbing to conservative thinkers within the Church was the Pope's subsequent encyclical *Pacem in Terris* (Peace on Earth), issued in 1963, in which he attempted to ground the social ethic of the Church on personalism rather than natural law. According to personalism, morality begins and ends with the needs and rights of the human person. The person is the crown and center of reality, absolutely unique as the locus of freedom in the world:

Any human society, if it is to be well-ordered and productive, must lay down as a foundation this principle, namely, that every human being is a person; that is, his nature endowed with intelligence and free will. Indeed, precisely because he is a person he has rights and obligations flowing directly and simultaneously from his very nature. And as these rights and obligations are universal and inviolable, so they cannot in any way be surrendered.[22]

The Pope saw it as the duty of the Church to safeguard and promote this freedom. Therefore, he applauded various movements in the struggle for human rights and dignity, including workers seeking a greater share in the political process, women refusing to tolerate discrimination, and oppressed races emancipating themselves.[23]

The Pope's liberal spirit was captured by Vatican II's "Pastoral Constitution on the Church in the Modern World" *(Gaudium et Spes)*. Promulgated in 1965, it declared the following:

. . . there is a growing awareness of the sublime dignity of the human person, who stands above all things and whose rights and duties are universal and inviolable. He ought, therefore, to have ready access to all that is necessary for living a genuinely human life: for example, food, clothing, housing, the right to freely choose his state of life and set up a family, the right to education, work, to his good name, to respect, to proper knowledge, the right to act according to the dictates of conscience and to safeguard his privacy and rightful freedom even in matters of religion" (26).

16. Did Pope John XXIII soften the Church's position on Communism?

In his encyclical *Pacem in Terris* (159), Pope John allowed for the existence of "elements that are positive and deserving of approval" in movements that originated in "false philosophical teachings regarding the nature, origin and destiny of the universe and of man."[24] Since the issuance of this statement, some Catholics have espoused various forms of socialism. The 1972 "Christians for Socialism" meeting in Santiago, Chile was a dramatic indication of this trend. Moreover, a 1972 commission of French bishops concluded that there are "major elements of

Marxism which have been adapted by Christian workers, which do not seem incompatible with their faith."[25]

17. *Was the social teaching of Pope Paul VI accepted as a religious message?*

Pope Paul VI's major social encyclical *Populorum Progressio* (On the Development of Peoples, 1967) was evaluated by many observers in political terms as a "liberal" platform. In the encyclical (26), he deplored the type of capitalism which "considers profit as the key motive for economic progress, competition as the supreme law of economics, and private ownership of the means of production as an absolute right that has no limits and carries no corresponding social obligation." Noting the expanding distance between the progress of some and the stagnation of others, he called for "bold transformations," "innovations that run deep," and "urgent reforms that must be taken without delay" (32).[26] Moreover, he appeared to imply that the poor have the right to revolution when all else fails: "There are certainly situations whose injustice cries to heaven. When whole populations destitute of necessities live in a state of dependence barring them from all initiative and responsibility, and all opportunity to advance culturally and share in social and political life, recourse to violence as a means to right these wrongs, is a grave temptation" (30).[27]

These radical statements were somewhat tempered by the encyclical's recognition that the Church does not possess the competence to propose concrete solutions to social problems. Such solutions, the Pope concluded, must be instituted by laymen.

18. *How do political pundits read the social leanings of Pope John Paul II?*

They think he upholds a moderate position on social doctrine. In his encyclical *Laborem exercens* (On Human Work, 1981), Pope John Paul II criticized both Marxism and capitalism. Upholding the personalism of his predecessors, he said that "rigid" capitalism must be reformed in order to safeguard the rights of the workers. At the same time, he isolated the numerous personalist problems in the Communist system, including its bureaucratic vision of the individual as a mere cog in a huge machine. The priority of the individual, he maintained, must be placed above the prevailing means of production. For this reason, all systems of government must be judged by their promotion of the basic rights and dignity of the individual person. Upholding the Marxist conception of man as *homo faber,* he said that the most basic right was the right of the worker to gain control over his work. This control should include a greater sense of ownership over "the great work-bench," at which he is working with his fellow man. To achieve this end, the Pope recommended various forms of profit sharing and co-management.[28]

In the same encyclical, Pope John Paul stressed the need for labor unions as "an indispensable element" of modern industrial society in "the struggle for social justice."[29]

In other statements, the Polish Pope emphasized the differing roles of the laity and the clergy in the quest for social justice. Speaking in Brazil, for example, he warned the clergy against participating in partisan struggles for the control of the government. The clergy, he said, must not for the sake of a political cause abandon their true vocation of total consecration to God, testimony to a future life, and a commitment to holiness. While the clergy should project a vision of a just social order, the Pope warned them not to attempt to implement specific social programs, since they lack the expertise. It is incumbent on the laity, he said, to bring about the renewal of the temporal order.[30]

19. *What is liberation theology?*

Liberation theology is a socioreligious reaction to the fideism and intellectualism of traditional Catholicism. The proponents of this "theology" are mostly Latin American Catholics, such as Uruguayan Jesuit Juan Luis Segundo and Brazilian Franciscan Leonardo Boff, who maintain that the traditional categories of the Catholic faith are inade-quate for anyone engaged in the struggle for social justice. They maintain that the Word of God comes neither from the Scriptures nor the tradition of the Church, but from the cries of the poor and ex-ploited. Any interpretation of the Gospel that does not aim at revolutionary action is looked upon as a theological ploy to uphold an unjust socioeconomic order.[31] The concept of liberation from sin leading to eternal salvation, they insist, must be replaced by a new concept of liberation. The Church's "salvation" is tainted by an other-worldly concept of religion, while liberation theology concentrates attention on the process of freeing people from political oppression and economic exploitation in the here and now. Similarly, faith is to be understood not as coming to terms with a transcendent Being but as *praxis,* a term Karl Marx defined as the conscious effort to transform the world for the sake of humanity.

20. *What is Pope John Paul II's view of liberation theology?*

He has severely criticized its tenets and, for a time, silenced radical theologian Leonardo Boff from making political statements. The ban on Boff was lifted in 1986, and the Vatican has decided quietly to tolerate him as long as he steers clear of Marxism and violence. Yet, in the same year, Pope John Paul II journeyed to Bogotá, Colombia, where he reminded the Latin American bishops that they should "firmly maintain the original meaning of Holy Scripture without separating it from the living Church tradition or the authentic interpretation of the Magisterium."[32]

21. *How do the U.S. bishops exercise their teaching role in political matters?*

The U.S. bishops issue policy statements through the United States Catholic Conference (USCC) and the National Council of Catholic Bishops (NCCB). Their judgments are varied and often quite specific. In 1971, for example, they condemned the bombing of Cambodia; called for an immediate end to the Vietnam conflict; and demanded amnesty for all conscientious objectors, including those who had fled to Canada to escape the draft:

. . . we are aware that a number of young men have left the country or have been imprisoned because of their opposition to compulsory military conscription. It is possible that in some cases this was done for unworthy motives, but in general we must presume sincere objections of conscience, especially on the part of those ready to suffer for their convictions. Since we have a pastoral concern for their welfare, we urge civil officials in revising the law to consider granting amnesty to those who have been imprisoned as selective conscientious objectors, and giving those who have emigrated an opportunity to return to the country to show responsibility for their conduct and to be ready to serve in other ways to show that they are sincere objectors.[33]

In 1974, the bishops denounced human rights violations in Chile and Brazil and called for an immediate cutback in federal aid to these countries.[34] Similarly, after the assassination of Archbishop Oscar Romero in 1980, they called for a cutoff in military aid and a monitoring of economic assistance to El Salvador.[35]

22. *Were the U.S. bishops instrumental in pressuring Congress to relinquish U.S. claims to the Panama Canal?*

Yes. In 1976, the National Council of Catholic Bishops passed a resolution intended to pressure Congress into negotiating a new treaty with Panama in order to dissolve "the vestiges of a relationship which more closely resembles the colonial politics of the nineteenth century than the realities of an interdependent world of sovereign and equal states."[36]

23. *Are the U.S. bishops pro-Palestinian?*

Yes. While the bishops recognize the right of Israel to exist as a sovereign nation, they called upon the United Nations to accept the rights of the Palestinians to have a homeland of their own, to participate in all negotiations for a separate state, and to be compensated for their losses by Israel and other members of the "international community."[37] They further advocated the acceptance of all parties of U.N. Resolution 241 (Security Council, 1967) as a basis for negotiations.

24. *Do the U.S. bishops advocate the notion of a welfare state?*

Yes. The bishops have asked for important changes in the U.S. economic system. In 1976, for example, their proposals included full employment for all able-bodied workers, a guaranteed annual income not substantially lower than the median family income for those who cannot work, participation by the poor in welfare policy-making boards, efforts to increase ethnic and racial integration through forced busing and other methods, the replacement of food stamps and other noncash benefits with sizable increases in cash benefits, the continuation and expansion of federal housing for low-to-moderate income families, and an increase in programs for low-income housing rehabilitation and maintenance.[38]

During the same year, the bishops called for folding Medicaid and Medicare into a unified federal health program with no deductibles and no co-insurance (i.e., no portion paid by the recipient).[39]

To finance such domestic social programs, the bishops suggested reliance on general federal revenues as well as direct taxation on employers and the self-employed.

25. By what authority do the U.S. bishops make such social pronouncements?

The bishops invoke this authority on the basis of Vatican II's *Gaudium et Spes* (76) which said: ". . . at all times and in all places the Church should have true freedom to preach the faith, to proclaim its teaching about society, to carry out its task among men without hindrance, and to pass moral judgments even in matters relating to politics, whenever the fundamental rights of man or the salvation of souls requires it. . . ."

Upholding this mandate to assist in the establishment of a just moral order, numerous priests have become political activists, have led marches and demonstrations, have conducted "sit-ins," and have issued statements on a host of political and social issues.

26. What assent of mind do American Catholics owe to the collected statements of the U.S. bishops on social and political issues?

When the bishops are asserting firm and unquestionable Catholic principles, they are owed respect and assent. Such would be statements concerning the inalienable right to life (even in the womb) of all citizens, the right of workers to organize and to obtain a "living wage," and the obligation of the rich to aid the poor.

However, when the bishops propose concrete steps to achieve the proper Christian goal of justice in the world, Catholics have the right to disagree with their pronouncements. Indeed, the bishops themselves maintain that they have no greater insight into national policy matters than anyone else:

"The principles of revelation do not provide specific solutions to many social problems, nor do they constitute a blueprint for organizing society. In proposing concrete policies in the social order, the Church is aware that often the more specific a program or proposal, the more room there may be for persons of sincere faith to disagree."[40]

NOTES

1. John A. Hardon, S. J., *The Catholic Catechism* (Garden City, New York: Doubleday and Company, 1975), p. 319.

2. Henry Chadwick, *The Early Church* (Baltimore: Penguin Books, 1969), p. 22.

3. W.H.C. Frend, *The Rise of Christianity* (Philadelphia: Fortress Press, 1984), p. 50.

4. St. Justin Martyr, "First Apology," 17, translated by Edward Roche Hardy, in *Early Christian Fathers,* edited by Cyril C. Richardson (New York: The Macmillan Company, 1970), p. 253.

5. Tertullian, "Apology," 30, translated by S. Thelwall, in *Latin Christianity: Its Founder Tertullian,* Vol. III, *The Ante Nicene Fathers,* edited by Alexander Roberts and James Donaldson (Grand Rapids: William B. Eerdmans Publishing Company, 1980), p. 42.

6. St. Augustine, "The City of God," V, 13, in *The Political Writings of St. Augustine,* edited by Henry Paolucci (Chicago: Henry Regnery Company, 1962), p. 94.

7. *Ibid.,* XIX, 16, p. 149.

8. *Ibid.,* II, 21, p. 43.

9. David J. O'Brien and Thomas A. Shannon, eds., *Renewing the Earth: Catholic Documents on Peace, Justice and Liberation* (Garden City, New York: Image Books, 1977), p. 18.

10. *Ibid.,* p. 20.

11. Thomas Bokenkotter, *Essential Catholicism: Dynamics of Faith and Belief* (Garden City, New York: Image Books, 1986), p. 358.

12. *Rerum Novarum* in *The Great Encyclicals of Pope Leo XIII* (New York: Benziger Brothers, 1903), p. 236.

13. *Ibid.,* p. 215.

14. *Ibid.,* p. 210.

15. C. Falconi, *The Popes of the Twentieth Century* (Boston: Little, Brown and Company, 1967), p. 230.

16. *Mit brennender Sorge, Encyclical Letter of Pope Pius XI* (Washington, D. C.: National Catholic Welfare Conference, 1937), p. 11. Cf.: Nicholas Cheetham's *Keepers of the Keys* (New York: Charles Scribner's Sons, 1982), p. 284.

17. Malachi Martin, *The Decline and Fall of the Roman Church* (New York: G. P. Putnam's Sons, 1981), p. 269.

18. *Ibid.,* p. 265.

19. Cheetham, *op. cit.,* p. 289.

20. *Quod Apostolici Meneris,* in *The Great Encyclicals of Pope Leo XIII, op. cit.,* p. 22.

21. Pope Pius XI's *Divini Redemptoris,* in *The Papal Encyclicals in Their Historical Context,* edited by Ann Freemantle (New York: G. P. Putnam's Sons, 1956), p. 261.

22. Pope John XXIII, *Pacem in Terris,* 9, in *Renewing the Earth, op. cit.,* p. 126.

23. *Ibid.,* 39–45, pp. 133–35.

24. *Ibid.,* 159, p. 163.

25. Bokenkotter, *op. cit.,* p. 70.

26. Pope Paul VI, *Populorum Progressio,* 32, in *Renewing the Earth, op. cit.,* p. 323.

27. *Ibid.,* 30, p. 323.

28. Bokenkotter, *op. cit.,* pp. 370–71.

29. *Ibid.*

30. *Ibid.,* pp. 371–72.

31. *Ibid.,* p. 37.

32. Pope John Paul II, "Address to the Latin American Bishops," in *Origins,* Vol. 17, No. 35, July 17, 1986, pp. 165–66.

33. "Declaration on Conscientious Objection and Selective Conscientious Objection," in *Pastoral Letters of the United States Catholic Bishops, 1962–1974,* Vol. III, edited by Hugh J. Nolan (Washington, D.C.: United States Catholic Conference, 1984), p. 286.

34. "Statement on Human Rights: Chile and Brazil," *Ibid.,* pp. 453–55.

35. "Resolution on El Salvador," in *Pastoral Letters of the United States Catholic Bishops, 1975–1983,* Vol. IV, edited by Hugh J. Nolan (Washington, D.C.: United States Catholic Conference, 1984), pp. 436–37.

36. "U. S.–Panama Relations," in *Ibid.,* p. 164.

37. "Statement on the Middle East," in *Ibid.,* p. 277.

38. "Political Responsibility: Reflections on an Election Year," in *Ibid.,* pp. 134–35.

39. "Society and the Aged: Toward Reconciliation," in *Ibid.,* p. 145.

40. National Council of Catholic Bishops, "The Bicentennial Consultation: A Response," quoted in J. Brian Benestad's *The Pursuit of a Just Social Order,* (Washington, D.C.: Ethics and Public Policy Center, 1984), p. 4.

THIRTEEN

The Fifth Commandment:

Just and Holy Bloodshed

As he entered Capernaum, a centurion came forward to him, beseeching him and saying, "Lord, my servant is lying paralyzed at home, in terrible distress. And he said to him, "I will come and heal him." But the centurion answered him, "Lord, I am not worthy to have you come under my roof; but only say the word, and my servant will be healed. For I am a man under authority, with soldiers under me; and I say to one, 'Go,' and he goes, and to another, 'Come,' and he comes, and to my slave, 'Do this,' and he does it." When Jesus heard him, he marveled and said to those who followed him, "Truly, I say to you, not even in Israel have I found such faith."

Matthew 8:1–10

In the case of the centurion who said, "I am a man under authority, with soldiers under me, and I say to one, 'Go,' and he goes, and to another, 'Come,' and he comes, and to my slave. 'Do this,' and he does it," Christ gave due praise to his faith. He did not tell him to leave the service.

St. Augustine, *Contra Faustum,* XXII, 74–79

1. *How do Catholics interpret the fifth commandment: You shall not kill?*

By the fifth commandment, Catholics are commanded to take care of their own spiritual and physical well-being and that of others. It forbids murder (including suicide), fighting, anger, hatred, drunkenness, and "bad example."[1]

2. *What is the Church's attitude on war?*

Vatican II's *Gaudium et Spes* (77) says: "The message of the Gospel, which epitomizes the highest ideals and aspirations of mankind, shines anew in our times when it proclaims that the advocates of peace are blessed 'for they shall be called the sons of God.' Accordingly, the Council proposes to outline the true and noble nature of peace, to condemn the savagery of war and earnestly to exhort Christians to cooperate with all in securing a peace based on justice and charity and in promoting the means necessary to attain it."

3. *Was Jesus a pacifist?*

Not really. There are, however, strong elements of pacifism in his teaching, especially the Sermon on the Mount, in which he says, "Blessed are the peacemakers for they shall be called the children of God" (Matt. 5:9), and proceeds to set forth the following: "You have heard that it was said, 'An eye for an eye and a tooth for a tooth.' But I say to you, Do not resist one who is evil. But if any one strikes you on the right cheek, turn to him the left also, and if anyone would sue you and take your coat, let him have your cloak as well; and if any one forces you to go one mile, go with him two miles. . . . You have heard that it was said, 'You love your neighbor and hate your enemy.' But I say to you, Love your enemies and pray for those who persecute you, so that you may be sons of your Father who is in heaven; for he makes the sun rise on the evil and on the good, and sends rain on the just and the unjust" (Matt. 5:38–41, 43–45).

This pacifism is offset by the saying, "I have not come to bring peace but a sword" (Matt. 10:34), and the following enigmatic passage from the Gospel of Luke: "And he said to them, 'When I sent you out with no purse or bag or sandals, did you lack anything?' They said to him, 'Nothing.' He said to them, 'But now, let him who has a purse take it, and likewise a bag. And let him who has no sword sell his mantle and buy one. . . .' And they said to him, 'Lord, Lord, here are two swords.' And he said to them, 'It is enough' " (Luke 22:35–36, 38). If taken literally, this injunction by Jesus in Luke's Gospel is in compliance with the teachings of the Essenes, who forbade the manufacture of arms in their communities but allowed their members to carry arms on their journeys for protection against thieves.[2] In any case, the disciples were certainly armed when Jesus was arrested at the Garden of Gethsemane, for one (purportedly Peter) was said to have drawn his sword and severed the ear of a slave of the high priest (Matt. 26:51). This incident, coupled with the injunction to bear arms, led several rationalist critics, including Hermann Reimarus, to claim that Jesus was a zealot in the tradition of Judas of Galilee who sought to establish his Messiahship by violently overturning Roman rule. Such claims must be dismissed by the fact that Jesus immediately rebuked this violence by saying, "Put your sword back into its place; for all who take the sword shall perish by the sword" (Matt. 26:52).

4. Did the early Church Fathers espouse an antimilitarian position?

No early Christian writer called into question the right of the Empire to have an army. Indeed, it was assumed that the army was necessary for civil life. St. Cyprian praised the good soldiers who defended the camps of their commanders against rebels and enemies and the "glorious generals" of the Roman legions who carry out the commissions entrusted to them.[3] Origen maintained that Christians constantly keep their hands pure in order to pray to God on behalf of the soldiers, who are fighting to ensure the safety of the state.[4] And Lactantius eulogized Constantine for his "military accomplishments" as well as the "probity of his morals."[5]

5. Were some of the early Christians conscientious objectors?

Yes. Tertullian wrote that Christ in disarming Peter disarmed all believers.[6] Elsewhere, he said: "Shall it be held lawful to make an occupation of the sword, when the Lord proclaims that he who uses the sword shall perish by the sword? And shall the son of peace take part in the battle when it does not become him even to sue at law?"[7] Origen wrote that Christians, by Christ's Sermon on the Mount, are forbidden "to bear arms for the commonwealth and to slay men."[8] And St. Clement of Alexandria held that Christian men and women share an equal code of conduct, since Christian men are trained not as soldiers but as peacemakers.[9]

This refusal to accept military service prompted the pagan writer Celsus to say that Christianity was a religion hostile to the well-being of the Empire: "If all men were to do the same as you [the Christians], there would be nothing to prevent the king from being left in utter solitude and desertion and the forces of the empire would fall into the hands of the wildest and most lawless barbarians."[10]

6. Why did the early Christians object to military service?

Their objections to serving in the army were set forth by Tertullian in the following:

1. The Gospel says that no man can serve two masters (Matt. 6:24; Luke 16:13) and Christians are called upon to serve Christ alone.

2. Christians are called upon to avoid all acts of violence and bloodshed (Matt. 5:39).

3. By becoming a Christian, a person is prohibited from participating in pagan culture. He (or she) is prohibited from even appearing in a court of law, let alone serving in the military (Matt. 5:40).

4. Soldiers in the course of their duties might be called upon to do things involving acts of idolatry, such as serving as temple guards or eating meats that were first offered to the gods by pagan priests.[11]

7. Was it permissible for early Christians to accept induction into the military?

Several early Christian writers, including Tertullian and St. Clement of Alexandria, say no. This proscription was vividly dramatized by St. Maximilian of Thebeste who refused induction in 295 by saying: *"Non possum militare, Christianus sum"* (I cannot serve in the military, I am a Christian). However, St. Cyprian in his letters mentions two soldier-martyrs who managed to preserve their integrity as Christians while serving in the military.[12] Indeed, the presence of several believers in the Roman Army at the turn of the fourth century has led some scholars to believe that by this time it must have been permissible for Christians to serve in the military in noncombative roles—as *beneficiarii* (military men assigned to the governors of provinces as administrative aides) and *proctectores* or *proctertores domestici* (soldiers assigned to the custody of prisoners, the care of public transport and the mails, the supervision of ordinances and secretarial duty). Yet, such soldiers persisted in refusing to engage in bloodshed. This is affirmed by the story of St. Maurice, the commander of the Theban legion, who refused to obey Emperor Maximian's order to assault the Gauls near Matigny near Lake Geneva. For this act, the entire legion was reportedly put to death.[13]

8. *What was the attitude of the early Christians to the Roman Empire?*

Despite the periods of terrible persecution, the early Church did not follow the Book of Revelation in identifying the Roman Empire with the Antichrist. Albeit Tertullian and others believed that Rome had been injected with a virus of corruption into its bloodstream,[14] the blessings of the *pax Romana* were much appreciated. St. Irenaeus expressed his appreciation of the fact that the might of the Empire permitted Christians to "walk highways without fear" and to sail seas free from pirates.[15] Tertullian was pleased that his native Carthage under Roman rule enjoyed "piping times of peace and plenty."[16] And Origen saw in the Roman peace the providential means of bringing the Good News of salvation to men of all nations.[17]

9. *What effect did the conversion of Constantine have on the pacifism of the early Church?*

It produced an almost complete reversal in the Church's attitude toward military service. Constantine, as Lactantius pointed out, was viewed as "God's anointed"[18] and his success in routing his imperial rival at the battle of the Milvian Bridge in 312 was attributed to Christ's divine intervention. Before the fateful battle, Constantine reportedly beheld a vision of the cross with the motto: *In hoc signo vinces* (By this sign, you will conquer). He inscribed the cross on the shields of his soldiers and marched against his foes to the glorious victory that reunited the Empire. Strange to say, no spokesman for the Church expressed alarm or outrage that the cross had become a banner for military bloodshed.

The objections of Christians to serving in the imperial forces all but vanished one year after the issuance of the Edict of Milan, when Constantine wrote a letter to the Church Council of Arles (314) in which he presented himself as a "servant of God" *(famulum Dei)* with the "holy bishops of the Savior Christ."[19] The letter stated his aim was to preserve harmony within the Church and suggested that all rebels against the authority of the Roman Church be dispatched to the imperial court for punishment. The state, by the will of the Emperor, was now to serve the Church. It was deemed only fitting that the Church, in turn, should serve the state. For this reason, the Council pronounced a sentence of excommunication on all Christians who persisted in throwing away their weapons even in time of peace (Canon 3).[20]

By the time of Alaric's sack of Rome in 410, pagans, having been polluted by their idolatrous rites, were excluded from the Roman Army: only Christians could serve.[21]

10. *Was the pacifism of the early Church completely eclipsed by the reign of Constantine?*

No. Throughout the fourth century, numerous Christians objected to bearing arms on the basis of conscientious objection. As a new convert, St. Martin of Tours in 336 asked to be released from his military duties when a battle was imminent, on the basis of the Sermon on the Mount. To establish the strength of his pacifistic conviction, he offered to face the barbarian troops with nothing but a crucifix. An eleventh-hour conclusion of peace without battle saved him from this ordeal and he was subsequently allowed to retire from the ranks.[22] A similar example was recorded by Paulinus of Nola, who told of a soldier who refused to fight by stating he had exchanged the weapons of iron for the weapons of Christ. He was dutifully condemned only to be miraculously saved from decapitation when his executioner was stricken blind.[23]

Indeed, the Church retained its aversion to war and bloodshed well into the medieval epoch. In 1076, a council of bishops in Winchester declared that he who killed a man in battle should do penance for a year. He who did not know whether his wounded assailant had died should do penance for forty days. He who did not know how many men he had killed in warfare should do penance one day a week for the remainder of his life.[24]

11. *What was St. Augustine's doctrine of a "just war"?*

St. Augustine, in accordance with the teachings of the Church Fathers, held that war is evil, and yet, he added, it is sometimes necessary, like the work of a jailor or hangman, if "love of violence, revengeful cruelty, fierce and implacable enmity, wild resistance and the lust of power" are not to be permitted to flourish.[25] Indeed, he wrote, it is incorrect to think that the Gospels condemn all acts of warfare: "For if the Christian religion condemned wars of every kind, the command given in the gospel to the soldiers asking counsel as to salvation would rather be to cast away their arms, and withdraw themselves wholly from military service; whereas the word spoken was, 'Do violence to no man, neither accuse any falsely, and be content with your wages' (Luke 3:14), the command to be content with their wages manifestly implying no prohibition to continue in the service."[26] All warfare, however, must have peace as its objective. "Peace should be the object of your desire," he wrote to the Christian governor of a province in Africa, "war should be raised only as a necessity, and waged only that God may by it deliver men from the emergency and preserve them in peace. For peace is not to be sought to kindle war, but war is to be waged in order to obtain peace."[27] A just war, therefore, is one which is undertaken with the intent to achieve or retain peace.

On the basis of this definition, St. Augustine held that a defensive war is almost always a just war. Moreover, he continued, an offensive war may be just if it is waged against a state that either refuses to make reparation for wrongs committed or fails to return the property it has seized. He went so far as to say that offensive wars against power-hungry and evil states may even be viewed as acts of "mercy": "And in mercy, also, if such a thing were possible, even wars might be waged by the good in order that, by bringing under the yoke the unbridled lusts of men, those vices might be abolished which ought, under a just government, to be either extirpated or suppressed."[28]

12. *Whence comes the notion of a "holy war"?*

The idea of a "holy war" is an old one, the Byzantine Emperor Heraclius having preached it to his subjects when the Moslems first conquered the Holy Land in 637. Charlemagne, after crusading against the Moslems in Spain, extended the notion of holy war to his struggle with the pagan Saxons circa 795, shortly before he brought them by force to the faith.[29] However, the idea of a holy war came to full expression in 1095, when Pope Urban II preached the need for a Crusade to save the Holy Land from the hands of the Seljuk Turks. The Turks took Jerusalem from the Fatimids in 1070, and pious pilgrims began to bring to Rome terrifying accounts of the persecution of Christians and the desecration of sacred shrines. Pope Urban II spoke of such atrocities in his masterful sermon to the Christian nobility at the Council of Clermont:

> From the confines of Jerusalem and the city of Constantinople a horrible tale has gone forth and very frequently has been brought to our ears, that a race from the kingdom of the Persians, an accursed race, a race utterly alienated from God, a generation, forsooth, which has neither directed its heart nor entrusted its spirit to God, has invaded the lands of those Christians and has depopulated them by the sword, pillage and fire. . . . They destroy altars, after having defiled them with their uncleanness. They circumcise the Christians, and the blood of the circumcision they either spread upon the altars or pour into the vases of the baptismal font. When they wish to torture people by a base death, they perforate their navels, and, dragging forth the end of the intestines, bind it to a stake: then with flogging they lead the victim around until his viscera have gushed forth, and he falls prostrate upon the ground. Others they bind to a post and

pierce with arrows. Others they compel to extend their necks, and then, attacking them with naked swords, they attempt to cut through the neck with a single blow. What shall I say of the abominable rape of women? To speak of it is worse than to be silent.[30]

The Pope offered complete remission of sin (contingent upon repentance) to all who lost their lives in fighting (and even traveling to fight) the infidels. So forceful was his plea, and so tempting the promise, that the thousands of knights in attendance at Clermont were reported to thunder the response: "Dieu li volt" (God wills it).[31] The knights and nobles sewed red crosses on their tunics and immediately laid plans for the great expedition.

The expedition was to last 250 years and to end in almost complete futility. The First Crusade, however, met with success. Jerusalem fell on June 7, 1099, and, as Raymond of St. Giles, Count of Toulouse, reported to the Pope: ". . . wonderful things were to be seen. Numbers of Saracens were beheaded . . . others were shot with arrows or forced to jump from the towers; others were tortured for several days and then burned in flames. In the streets were seen piles of heads and hands and feet. One rode about everywhere amid the corpses of men and horses."[32]

The Turks eventually retook the Holy Land piece by piece, a development which neither the Second Crusade (1146–48) nor the Third Crusade (1189–92) could arrest. The Fourth Crusade (1199–1204) even failed to reach the Holy Land and ended with the Crusaders sacking Constantinople instead, while the Sixth Crusade (1227–29) was led by the Holy Roman Emperor Frederick II (1194–1250), a man so abominable that the Pope found it necessary to excommunicate him *and his descendents* for all eternity.[33]

13. *What was the primary reason for the Crusades?*

After the collapse of the Carolingian Empire (the Empire established by Charlemagne in 800), Europe fell into a period of "feudal anarchy," in which a condition of almost continuous warfare existed between various territorial principalities. The Church attempted to restrain this bloodletting by proclaiming the "Peace of God," which outlawed war against the clergy, women, and children, and the "Truce of God," which prohibited warfare on holy days, the seasons of Lent and Advent, and special feasts. Those who violated these restraints incurred automatic excommunication. Despite such efforts, the feudal lords and knights persisted in engaging in combat, the one occupation for which they had been bred. Cognizant of this, Pope Urban II saw the Crusade as a means of channeling the cultivated aggression of the knights and nobles in a unified effort to save Europe and Byzantium from Islam. He stated this purpose clearly in his sermon at Clermont:

> Let those who have been accustomed to private war against the faithful carry on to a successful issue a war against the infidels, which ought to have begun ere now. Let those who for a long time have been robbers now become soldiers of Christ. Let those who once fought against brother and relatives now fight against the barbarians, as they ought. . . . Let no obstacle stand in the way of those who are going, but . . . let them zealously undertake the journey under the guidance of the Lord.[34]

To a great extent, the Crusades accomplished the Pope's purpose. The feudal lords united with each other in a righteous cause. Territorial principalities became more sharply defined, ending the state of anarchy and aiding in the rebirth of towns and cities that characterized the twelfth-century Renaissance. Moreover, by becoming transformed into soldiers of Christ, the medieval nobles and knights began to look upon the bearing of arms as a religious experience. Ceremonies surrounding initiation into knighthood assumed the aspects of a sacramental rite, with candidates expected to pray for divine guidance and favor the entire night before their dubbing. Priest bestowed blessings on men and arms alike, sermons were delivered on the nature of knightly virtue, and martial training came to include an emphasis on certain standards of knightly conduct that regularized into precise and highly idealized codes.[35] The Crusades had given rise to the age of chivalry.

14. *Did not the Church also launch a crusade against Christian heretics?*

Yes. In the thirteenth century, the Church inaugurated a massive crusade against the Albigensian or Cathar heresy. Catharism was an eclectic blend of Gnosticism, Manichaeism, and Christianity. Like the Manichaens, the Cathars held that there were two, co-equal universal powers: Jehovah, the Lord of light and ruler of the realm of pure spirit, and Lucifer, the Lord of the material world—"this vale of tears and suffering"—who had imprisoned in the cloying bodies of men the souls of fallen angels. Christ came, the Cathars taught, to redeem these souls and to show them the way back to their home in the realm of pure spirit. But, for the Cathar as for the Gnostic, there was no real incarnation. Christ was a pure spirit who never became enmeshed in the matter of the world.[36]

From these strange beliefs came an extreme form of asceticism. The Cathars, believing in the transmigration of souls, refused to take a life of any kind. Indeed, a certain way for the medieval Church to identify a member of the sect was to ask him to kill a chicken. Moreover, they frowned upon all sexual union, even in marriage, since copulation was the means of manufacturing more matter for use by Lucifer in his entrapment of fleeting souls. This abhorrence of matter further led the Cathars to abstain from eating flesh of any kind, including eggs, milk, butter, and cheese.

This severe religion proved to be highly compelling to disillusioned Crusaders returning from the disasters in the East and the nobles and commoners of Italy and southern France who were at odds with the moral laxity of many members of the orthodox clergy.[37] By 1198, when Pope Innocent III ascended to the See of Peter, the Cathars openly flourished in such Italian cities as Milan, Florence, and Viterbo. In southern France (Provence), their heresy permeated the entire length and breadth of society. The seedbed of the sect, however, appeared to have been the French town of Albi. Hence, Catharism became known as the Albigensian heresy.

When the Cathars, in conjunction with the rich bourgeoisie and the petty nobility, for whom adherence to the heresy provided justification for refusing to pay papal tithes and for plundering ecclesiastical property, openly sought to supplant the Church in southern France, the Church under Innocent III responded in 1209 with a declaration of holy war against the heretics. Northern Frenchmen were enlisted with an offer of plenary indulgences in exchange for forty days of martial service. More importantly, the French nobles were offered the lord-ship of the lands they won from the Cathars as a booty. Hungry for such spiritual and temporal loot, the Crusaders, under Simon de Montfort, ravaged Provence, hanging, beheading, and burning "with unspeakable joy."[38] When Béziers was taken and Arnaud, the papal legate, was asked how to distinguish between the Cathars and the Catholics, he is said to have replied: "Kill them all; God will know his own."[39]

The Albigensian crusade came to an end in 1229. By this time, the heresy was uprooted and much of the southern French countryside devastated. The Church, however, fancied it necessary to take pains to ferret out any remaining heretics for fear that the dread heresy might rise again. In 1227 Pope Gregory IX officially instituted an ecclesiasti-cal vehicle to accomplish this purpose. The Papal Inquisition came into being.

15. What, therefore, is the Inquisition?

The Inquisition was developed by the papacy as a means of inquiry into the existence of heresy within the Church and/or society.

Moderns find it strange, indeed repugnant, that either church or state would inquire into a person's religious beliefs, and worse that either ecclesiastical or civil government would use punitive measures to enforce orthodoxy or social conformity to a church's religious standards. This attitude, of course, is the outgrowth of contemporary popular opinion, which considers religion a matter of personal taste, not of truth or right, not a matter or concern to government and, if one accepts private judgment as a fundamental religious norm, not even anything which church authority can or should circumscribe. However, such a world view was not the popular opinion of the Middle Ages when the Catholic Church was the source of Christian truth and where society, though often corrupt, was culturally Catho-lic, with the state itself committed to maintain that culture intact.

Long before the Church decreed any particular punishment for heretics, public opinion throughout Europe had shown itself savagely hostile to heretics, many of whom met their death by lynching. Public opinion in those lands not long removed from invasions by barbarians demanded harsh penalties for civil and religious crimes. The same inquisitions and legal punishments too, including vigilante activities, violence by activists, and police brutality, go on in modern society whenever the threats are other than religious, to public health; to national security; to ethnic, class, or racial self-interest; to restrictive laws of one kind or another, and so forth.

Church historian Philip Hughes called the Inquisition a "tribunal set up by the papacy and responsible to the popes whose business it was to discover and punish Catholics who adopted heresy."[40]

The Inquisition was begun in part under pressure from Catholic princes, who considered heretics threats to their royal rule, and marked a departure from Catholic tradition for the Church to go beyond its usual punishment for heresy, which was excommunication. The so-called Roman Inquisition was a much more judicious tribunal than those which eventually fell under the control of princely authority, as in Spain. Several popes developed a ferocious distaste for Spanish procedures and the Spanish themselves, notably the reforming Pope Paul IV of Tridentine (Council of Trent) fame. (Early Protestant reforms used similar inquisitorial methods to rout out social or moral deviants, not infrequently Catholics.)

16. *Who was Torquemada?*

Tomás De Torquemada, Dominican priest, is the name most frequently associated with the worst excesses of the Spanish Inquisition, and defamed the name "inquisition" itself.

Born in 1420 of Jewish descent, he became confessor to Queen Isabella I and her husband, King Ferdinand V. Although appointed as an Inquisitor in 1482 to trim the sails of early Inquisitors, who meted out unjust punishments, he rose to a position of dominance, using his powers to investigate and punish on an unprecedented scale crypto-Jews who had been insincerely or forcibly converted to Christianity, apostates, witches, and other spiritual offenders. Since Isabella and Ferdinand supported Torquemada, complaints to the Pope were ineffective. Pope Alexander VI, who excommunicated Savonarola in Italy for preaching excesses, appointed four extra Inquisitors to restrain Torquemada but without much effect on his conduct. The police system Torquemada established survived his death in 1498 for several generations.

Exceptionally intolerant even for times that were harsh, he is responsible for the bad repute of the Spanish Inquisition and the delight of anti-Catholics ever since.

17. How did the Inquisition work?

The Inquisition was conducted by mendicant friars, Dominicans and the Franciscans, under the direct authority of the Pope. The Dominicans proved themselves to be especially talented in heresy hunting and, in time, became known as *Domini canes* or "the dogs of the Lord."[41] After an Inquisitor arrived in a particular area, an inquisitorial court was established, consisting of twelve men chosen by the local secular ruler from a list presented to him by the local bishop and the Inquisitor. The heretics were given a week to come forward of their own accord in exchange for a mild punishment. Upon coming forward, they were required to relate the names of fellow heretics and their friends and acquaintances. The named suspects were summoned before the tribunal, interrogated repeatedly, and kept in prison between hearings. Most of the accused did not know the precise nature of the offense for which they were accused but, nevertheless, were compelled to provide answers to a host of questions ranging from their Christian beliefs to their daily diet. From this interrogation came the names of more and more suspects. Accused persons could be tried in their absence and even after their deaths. Two condemnatory witnesses were required. Confessed heretics, seeking clemency, were allowed to serve as witnesses against others; wives and children were allowed to testify against, but not for, husbands and fathers.

The punishment system was comprehensive and permitted the Inquisitor to distinguish between different types of penalty. Those who had heretical leanings and simple believers were required to perform extraordinary penances, including the wearing of yellow repentance crosses on their chest and back for long periods of time, flagellations within their native town or district, and pilgrimages to holy shrines. A relatively large number of those accused were condemned to imprisonment for limited periods or life.[42] The Inquisitors, however, were far harsher in their treatment of resolute heretics who either refused to recant or neglected to perform their prescribed penance. Such heretics were handed over to the civil authorities, who were responsible for ensuring that the death penalty was carried out. It was the state not the Church that bore the responsibility for the executions. The Church, on the basis of Christ's teachings and the pacifism of the Church Fathers, righteously refused to pronounce a sentence of death on its subjects. It upheld as a motto, *Ecclesia abhorret a sanguine* (The Church shrinks from blood), and cautioned the secular authorities to avoid all bloodshed in its infliction of due punishment *(animadversio debita)* on condemned prisoners. For this reason, the heretics were burned at the stake.[43]

Since mere contact with a Cathar was a punishable offense, large sections of the population came under suspicion. At times, the general population enthusiastically joined in the hunt for heretics—at times lynching alleged Cathars long before the Church began to persecute.[44] At other times, the arrival of an Inquisitor in a town or village produced an atmosphere of unmitigated terror. In 1235, Bishop Raymond of Falga and his fellow Inquisitors were attacked and driven from the county of Toulouse by the local count. Seven years later, ten Inquisitors were murdered in Avignonet. And, in 1239, the Dominican monastery in Orvieto was besieged by an angry mob.[45]

Nonetheless, the systematic search for heretics persisted. In 1245, 5,471 people from the area of Lavaur were called before the inquisitorial court.[46] The searches were equally meticulous in other regions of southern France. In one day in 1239, Robert the Dominican sent 180 prisoners to the stake, including the local bishop, who, in his opinion, had given too much freedom to heretics.[47]

18. Did the Church condone the use of torture?

Yes. The use of torture was sanctioned by Pope Innocent IV in the bull *Ad extripanda* (1251). The Pope, however, advised that torture should only be used once, and should be kept "this side of loss of limb and danger of death."[48] The Inquisitors interpreted "only once" as meaning only once for each examination.

19. *Why were the medieval popes involved in so many wars?*

The direct involvement of papal forces in warfare was largely a result of the so-called Babylonian captivity of the Church. In 1296, Pope Boniface VIII and Philip IV, King of France, surnamed "the Fair," were enmeshed in a struggle over papal versus civil authority. The controversy arose when Philip imposed a levy of taxation on clerical income in France without the consent of the Pope. The Pope responded by issuing a defiant bull, *Clericis laicos,* which prohibited the clergy from paying any kind of tax to lay rulers. Philip, then, called a council to judge the Pope on trumped-up charges of heresy, blasphemy, murder, sodomy, and sorcery. The Pope, in turn, drew up another bull to excommunicate the French King. This prompted Philip to dispatch armed forces to the papal palace at Anagni, near Rome. The forces brutally seized the eighty-six-year-old Pontiff with the intent of bringing him to trial before Philip's makeshift council in France. After three days of turmoil, Pope Boniface was freed from his captors by the outraged citizens of Anagni. The shock of the assault, however, proved to be mortal, and, within a month, the Pope was dead.

Following Pope Boniface's death, a French pope—Clement V— was elected under the influence of Philip the Fair. The newly elected Pope did not return to Rome, mainly because he feared Italian reprisals for the French treatment of Boniface and the French influence in securing his election. A secondary reason, perhaps, was his devotion to his French mistress, the beautiful Countess of Perigord.[49] In 1309, Pope Clement V settled in Avignon, a city in southern France near the mouth of the Rhone. Thereafter, under six French popes in succession, Avignon became the center of Christianity, while Rome fell into decay and ruin.

An offshoot of this "Babylonian captivity" (so named by Petrarch) was that the popes in Avignon could no longer retain control of the Papal States, which had been seized by local nobles including the Visconti, who threatened in 1360 to become the dominant power in Italy. To drive these forces from its holdings, the papacy recruited mercenary armies and initiated a series of ferocious wars that were to persist with greater and lesser intensity for over 150 years. During this time, 64 percent of the papal income was spent on warfare.[50]

20. *Didn't many of the medieval popes lead armies and directly engage in bloodshed?*

Yes. One of the first warrior popes was the great reformer Leo IX (1048–1054). In 1052, the German Emperor Henry III donated the duchy of Benevento to the papacy. However, the resident Duke of Benevento, Pandulf by name, refused to recognize this gift. Pope Leo, in turn, asked the Emperor to provide him with a German army in order to oust Pandulf and his Norman forces from the duchy. The Pope received from Henry a force of only seven hundred men; to these he added some untrained Italians and set out on a campaign against Pandulf and the Normans. The campaign was a miserable failure. Pope Leo's forces were quickly routed by the Normans, who captured the Pope only to fall to their knees to beg his pardon for killing his men.[51]

The most famous or infamous of the warrior popes was Julius II, the patron of Raphael and Michelangelo. When he ascended to the See of Peter, Pope Julius found that the Papal States, despite the bloody efforts of his predecessor Pope Alexander VI and Alexander's son Caesar Borgia, had not been reconquered from the local dictators. Summoning forces from France, Germany, and Spain, Pope Julius rode at the head of a formidable army. After regaining Perusia, the papal forces launched an attack on Bologna, an attack which Pope Julius fortified with a bull of excommunication against anyone who resisted his army and an offer of a plenary indulgence to any man who killed any of his opponents.[52] This was a new brand of warfare and his enemies quickly raised the white flag. The same tactics worked in Venice, which surrendered to the Pope in 1510.

Pope Julius II spent the three remaining years of his pontificate battling the French, who refused to abandon the Italian territories they had conquered under the papal flag.

The conquests of this last warrior pope proved to be long-lasting, and the Papal States remained loyal to the Church until the national revolution of 1870, which ended the temporal power of the papacy.

21. *Does the Church still uphold the doctrine of a "just war"?*

In accordance with the teachings of St. Augustine, Vatican II's *Gaudium et Spes* (79) maintained that a war can be just under the following conditions: (1) when a state is morally certain that its rights are being violated and that it is faced with certain and imminent danger; (2) when the cause of war is in proportion to the evils that are part of every war; (3) when every peaceful method of settlement has been ineffective; and (4) when there is a well-grounded hope of bettering the human condition by the conflict.

22. *What is the Church's position toward nuclear warfare?*

The development of nuclear arms forced the Church to reappraise its position toward war at the Second Vatican Council and to proclaim the following: "Every act of war directed to the indiscriminate destruction of whole cities or vast areas with their inhabitants is a crime against God and man, which merits firm and unequivocal condemnation" *(Gaudium et Spes,* 80).

The U.S. bishops in their 1983 pastoral "The Challenge of Peace" stated their concern this way: ". . . nuclear war threatens the existence of our planet; this is a more menacing threat than any the world has known. It is neither tolerable nor necessary that human beings live under this threat."[53] The document upheld the following beliefs:

1. Catholic teaching begins with a presumption against war and for peaceful settlement of disputes. In exceptional cases, determined by the moral principles of the just-war tradition, some uses of force are permitted.

2. Every nation has a right and duty to defend itself against unjust aggression.

3. It is not permissible to direct nuclear or conventional weapons to the indiscriminate destruction of whole cities or vast areas with their populations. The intentional killing of innocent civilians and noncombatants is always wrong.

4. Under current world conditions, deterrence based on weapons between super-powers, not as an end in itself but as a step toward progressive nuclear disarmament, must be judged to be morally acceptable.[54]

NOTES

1. *Baltimore Catechism,* No. 2 (New York: W. H. Sadlier, 1945), p. 99.
2. Roland H. Bainton, *Christian Attitudes Toward War and Peace* (New York: Abingdon Press, 1960), p. 57.
3. St. Cyprian, "Epistle 73," 10, in *Saint Cyprian: Letters (1–81),* translated by Sr. Rose Bernard Donna, C.S.J., Vol. 5, *The Fathers of the Church,* edited by Roy Joseph Deferrari et al. (Washington, D.C.: Catholic University of America Press, 1964), p. 272.
4. Origen, "Against Celsus," VIII, 73, translated by A. Cleveland Coxe, in *Fathers of the Third Century,* Vol. 5, *The Ante Nicene Fathers,* edited by Alexander Roberts and James Donaldson (Grand Rapids: William B. Eerdmans Publishing Company, 1982), p. 668.
5. Lactantius, "The Death of the Persecutors," 18, in *Lactantius: The Minor Works,* translated by Sr. Mary Francis McDonald, Vol. 54, *The Fathers of the Church,* edited by Roy Joseph Deferrari et al. (Washington, D.C.: The Catholic University Press of America, 1965), p. 160.
6. Tertullian, "On Idolatry," 19, in *Early Latin Theology,* translated by S. L. Greenslade, Vol. V, *The Library of Christian Classics,* edited by John Baillie, John T. McNeill, and Henry P. Van Deusen (Philadelphia: Westminster Press, 1956), p. 105.
7. Tertullian, *De Corona,* XI, translated by Dr. Holmes, in *Latin Christianity: Its Founder, Tertullian,* Vol. III, *The Ante Nicene Fathers,* edited by Alexander Roberts and James Donaldson (Grand Rapids: William B. Eerdmans Publishing Company, 1980), p. 99.
8. Origen, *loc. cit.*
9. St. Clement of Alexandria, *Stromata* (The Miscellanies), IV, 8, in *Fathers of the Third Century, op. cit.,* p. 435.
10. Celsus, quoted in Origen's "Against Celsus," VII, 68, in *Fathers of the Third Century, op. cit.,* p. 665.
11. Tertullian, *De Corona,* in *Early Latin Theology, op. cit.,* pp. 99–100. Cf., Lawrence Cunningham, *The Catholic Heritage* (New York: Crossroad Publishing, 1983), p. 67.
12. St. Cyprian, "Letter 83," quoted in Bainton, *op. cit.,* p. 68.
13. Cunningham, *loc. cit.*
14. Tertullian, "Ad Nationes," translated by S. Thelwall, IX in *Fathers of the Third Century, op. cit.,* pp. 117–21.
15. St. Irenaeus, "Against Heresies," 34, 4, in *The Apostolic Fathers: Justin Martyr and Irenaeus,* translated by A. Cleveland Coxe, Vol. I, *The Ante Nicene Fathers,* edited

by Alexander Roberts and James Donaldson (Grand Rapids: William B. Eerdmans Publishing Company, 1981), p. 512.

16. Tertullian, "Ad Nationes," I, 1, in *Fathers of the Third Century, op. cit.*, p. 5.

17. Origen, "Against Celsus," in *Fathers of the Third Century, op. cit.*, pp. 443–44.

18. Lactantius, *loc. cit.*

19. W. H. C. Frend, *The Rise of Christianity* (Philadelphia: Fortress Press, 1984), p. 486.

20. *Ibid.*

21. Bainton, *op. cit.*, p. 88.

22. Sulpitius Severus, "Life of St. Martin," IV, translated by Alexander Roberts, Vol. XI, *Nicene and Post Nicene Fathers,* Second Series, edited by Philip Schaff and Henry Wace, (Grand Rapids: William B. Eerdmans Publishing Company, 1955), p. 6.

23. Bainton, *op. cit.*, p. 89.

24. *Ibid.*, p. 109.

25. St. Augustine, "Contra Faustum," XII, 74, in *The Political Writings of St. Augustine,* edited by Henry Paolucci (Chicago: Henry Regnery Company, 1962), p. 164.

26. St. Augustine, "Letter 189," 4, in *Ibid.*, p. 180.

27. *Ibid.*, p. 182.

28. St. Augustine, "Letter 188," 15, in *Ibid.*, pp. 179–80.

29. Jeffrey Burton Russell, *A History of Medieval Christianity: Prophecy and Order* (New York: Thomas Y. Crowell Company, 1968), pp. 157–58.

30. Pope Urban II's Sermon at Clermont, in Charles T. Wood's *The Quest for Eternity: Medieval Manners and Morals* (Garden City, New York: Doubleday and Company, 1971), pp. 128–29.

31. Maurice Keen, *A History of Medieval Europe* (New York: Frederick A. Praeger, 1967), p. 97.

32. Raymond of St. Giles, quoted in Will Durant's *The Age of Faith* (New York: Simon and Schuster, 1950), p. 592.

33. Wood, *op. cit.*, p. 120.

34. *Ibid.*, p. 129.

35. *Ibid.*, p. 134.

36. Keen, *op. cit.*, p. 116.

37. Bainton, *op. cit.*, p. 115.

38. *Ibid.*

39. *Ibid.*

40. Philip J. Hughes, *A Popular History of the Catholic Church* (New York: The Macmillan Company, 1962), p. 129.

41. Durant, *op. cit.*, p. 783.

42. Martin Erbstossen, *Heretics in the Middle Ages,* translated by Janet Fraser (Leipzig, Germany: Edition Leipzig, 1984), p. 137.

43. Durant, *op. cit.*, p. 783.

44. *Ibid.,* pp. 777–78.

45. Erbstossen, *op. cit.,* p. 138.

46. *Ibid.,* p. 140.

47. Durant, *op. cit.,* p. 780.

48. Thomas Bokenkotter, *A Concise History of the Catholic Church* (Garden City, New York: Image Books, 1979), p. 141. Cf., *Ibid.,* p. 783.

49. Barbara Tuchman, *A Distant Mirror* (New York: Alfred A. Knopf, 1978), pp. 25–26.

50. Bainton, *op. cit.,* p. 117.

51. Durant, *op. cit.,* p. 543.

52. Will Durant, *The Renaissance* (New York: Simon and Schuster, 1953), p. 443.

53. "The Challenge of Peace," 3, in *Pastoral Letters of the United States Catholic Bishops, 1975–1983,* Vol. IV edited by Hugh J. Nolan, (Washington, D.C.: United States Catholic Conference, 1984), p. 494.

54. *Ibid.,* pp. 494–95.

FOURTEEN

Unholy Murder:

The Crime of Abortion

The first right of the human person is the right to life. He has other goods of which none are more precious. Hence it must be protected above all others. It does not belong to society, nor does it belong to public authority in any form to recognize this right for some and not for others; all discrimination is evil, whether it is founded on race, sex, color or religion. It is not recognition by another that constitutes this right. This right is antecedent to its recognition; it demands recognition and it is strictly unjust to refuse it.

The Congregation for the Doctrine of Faith,
Quaestio de abortu, 1974, 7

1. *What is the Church's position on abortion?*

The "Declaration on Procured Abortion" published by the Sacred Congregation of the Doctrine of the Faith on November 18, 1974, summarized Catholic teaching as it has existed from the beginning of the Church. At various times, Church authority has called it "murder," a "grave fault," an "abominable crime." But however it has been described, abortion, when it involves the direct killing of human life, is gravely immoral. Not even civil law can be its sanction. Said the Congregation: "Man can never obey a law which is in itself immoral, and such is the case of a law which would admit in principle the license of abortion." Furthermore, "it is inadmissible that doctors or nurses should find themselves obliged to cooperate closely in abortions and have to choose between the Law of God and their professional situation."[1]

The word *abortion* is sometimes misused or used loosely to cover the indirect killing of a fetus, as in the removal of a cancerous uterus or following surgery on a Fallopian tube during an ectopic pregnancy. Such surgery is permissible because it is directed at the cure of a mother's disease, not the killing of a fetus, which is an unintended but unfortunate effect. This distinction between direct and indirect killing is important, because it keeps final authority over innocent life and death in the hands of the Creator of life and precludes any human being from claiming the right to kill another innocent human being directly. The immorality of abortion is absolute.

In the nineteenth century, it was not uncommon for doctors to resort to "craniotomy" (cutting up a baby in the womb beginning with the head; hence the name) when a pregnant woman was in difficulty. Opposition to this procedure (a direct killing) by the Church led to the development of the Caesarian section, so called because Julius Caesar was supposedly born in this manner. Today there are many speculative questions that remain unanswered, but by the time a woman discovers she is pregnant, there is no question that which she carries is a human being. In complicated surgical matters, the counsel of a competent moral theologian may be necessary. But the general principle is clear and the penalty for Catholic abortionists specified in the 1983 Code of Canon Law (No. 1398): "A person who procures a complete abortion incurs an automatic excommunication." Pope Paul VI addressed this subject many times. In 1972, he declared that this teaching of the Church "has not changed and is unchangeable."

2. *Is this teaching scriptural?*

The Book of Exodus contains the following injunction concerning an abortion caused by a third party: "When men have a fight and hurt a pregnant woman, so that she suffers a miscarriage, but no further injury, the guilty one shall be fined as much as the woman's husband demands of him, and he shall pay in the presence of judges. But if an injury ensues, you shall give life for a life, an eye for an eye, a tooth for a tooth, a hand for a hand, a foot for a foot, a burn for a burn, a wound for a wound" (20:22–25). This passage offers weak scriptural justification for an unqualified condemnation of abortion, since it is more concerned with the rights of the husband and wife than the right to life of the unborn child. There is no other passage relating to abortion in the Old Testament and the subject is not explicitly mentioned in the New Testament.

Catholics employ other scriptural passages to uphold their stance. The 1974 "Declaration on Procured Abortion" (22), for example, states the following:

. . . the Lord proclaims in the Gospel: "God is God, not of the dead, but of the living" (Mt. 22:32) And death like sin will be definitely defeated by resurrection in Christ (cf. 1 Cor. 15:20–227). Thus we understand that human life, even on this earth, is precious. Infused by the Creator, life is again taken back by him (cf. Gen. 2:7; Wis. 15:11). It remains under his protection: man's blood cries out to him (cf. Gen. 4:10) and he will demand an account of it, "for in the image of God man was made" (Gen.

9:5–6). The commandment of God is formal: "You shall not kill" (Ex. 20:13). Life is at the same time a gift and a responsibility. It is received as a "talent" (cf. Mt. 25:14–30); it must be put to proper use. In order that life may bring forth fruit, many tasks are offered to man in this world and he must not shirk them. More important still, the Christian knows that eternal life depends on what, with the grace of God, he does with his life on earth.

The tradition of the Church has always held that human life must be protected and favored from the beginning, just as at the various stages of its development.[2]

3. Did the early Church condemn abortion?

Yes. The *Didache* or "The Teachings of the Apostles," one of the oldest Christian documents (circa 120), contains in its lessons for *catechumens* (individuals undergoing religious instruction) the following injunctions against abortion and infanticide (both of which were common practice in pagan Rome): "You shall not kill an unborn child or murder a newborn infant."[3] This equation of abortion with homicide was upheld by Tertullian. In his treatise, "On the Veiling of Virgins" (206), he sharply criticized overly zealous parents who forced their young daughters to accept the veil by making a vow of perpetual virginity. Such force, he noted, often resulted in women rebelling against the veil by "sinful audacities." To make matters worse, some, he said, had been known to "cover up their failures," i.e., to conceal their pregnancies, by committing homicide by means of procured abortion.[4] In 250, St. Cyprian in an attack on the presbyter Novatian, whom he accused of kicking his pregnant wife in the stomach to cause a miscarriage, spoke of abortion as "parricide," a crime far worse than simple homicide in the code of Roman law.[5]

4. What was the penance for abortion?

By the time of the Council of Elvira in Spain (305), abortion was judged to be so heinous a sin that a woman who purposefully destroyed the child in her womb, when the child was conceived by an act of premarital fornication or adultery, was held to be guilty of a sin that merited double damnation. For this reason, she could not be restored to Communion for the rest of her life. Since this severe sentence smacked of Novatianism, that is, the belief that some sins committed after baptism cannot be forgiven, this harsh canon was modified by the Council of Ancyra in 314, which prescribed a penance of ten years for anyone who destroyed a fetus in the womb.[6]

5. *But didn't the early Church believe that abortion was murder only after the child was fully formed as a human being in the womb of the mother?*

Yes. This belief originally came from a faulty translation of the Book of Exodus in the Septuagint, the Greek version of the Hebrew Scriptures, which was produced approximately 250 years before the birth of Christ. This version of the Old Testament was accepted by the Church Fathers, who, for the most part, knew Greek and not Hebrew. The crucial text—Exodus 20:22–25—reads as follows in the Septuagint: "If two men strive and smite a woman, and her child is imperfectly formed, he shall be forced to pay a penalty; as the woman's husband shall lay upon him, he shall pay with a valuation. But if the child be formed, he shall pay with his life." Therefore, the *lex talonis* ("an eye for an eye," etcetera) only applied when a child was formed. This raised the crucial question: when is a child formed—at what stage in the process of gestation does the fetus become a human being with an immortal soul?

Following Aristotle's study of aborted fetuses, Lactantius early in the fourth century argued that a fetus became formed and infused with a soul forty days after conception.[7] One hundred years later, St. Augustine attempted to provide a more theological answer to this pressing dilemma. Commenting on John 2:18–22, in which Jesus says that he will rebuild the temple in three days if anyone destroys it, St. Augustine maintained that Jesus by these words provided insight into the formation of infants:

> In the first six days [the fetus] is similar to a kind of milk, in the following nine days it is changed to blood, then in the following twelve days it becomes solid, in the remaining ten and eight days the features of all its members achieve complete formation, and in the remaining time until

birth it grows in size. Therefore to forty-five days add 1, which signifies the sum (because 6, 9, 12, 10 and 8 brought together into one sum make 45); add 1, as was said, and the result is 46. When this number is multiplied by 6, which stands at the head of the series, 276 results, i.e., nine months and six days. This is the time between March 25th (the day on which the Lord is believed to have been conceived, since he also suffered and died on that day) to December 25th (the day on which he was born). Therefore, it is not absurd to say that the temple, which signifies his body, was built in forty-six years, so that there were as many years in the construction of the temple as there were days in the completing of the Lord's body.[8]

Although Churchmen vacillated between Aristotle's forty days and St. Augustine's forty-six days in the formation of fetuses, with most opting for Aristotle's scientific explanation, the distinction between formed and unformed fetuses remained unchallenged. Thus different penances were issued for different stages of abortion. The seventh-century Penitentials, for example, prescribed a penance of one year for a woman who consented to an abortion before the fetus was formed and the penance of homicide (three to ten years) for one who consented to or performed such an act forty days after insemination *(accepti semines)*.

Shortly after the turn of the thirteenth century, this distinction in punishment for the crime of abortion received the highest ecclesiatical approval. Pope Innocent III became faced with the problem of a Carthusian prior regarding a monk in the prior's charge. The monk, while indulging in some act of levity with a woman whom he had made pregnant, caused an abortion. This raised the question whether the monk would have to give up his ministry. According to canon law, he would have to do so if found guilty of homicide. Innocent III's response in his *Sicut ex litteram* stated that if the *conceptus* was not yet *vivifactus,* the monk could continue his ministry; otherwise, he could not.[9] This was an implicit recognition by the Church of the distinction between formed and unformed (animated and unanimated) fetuses, and the classification of only the abortion of the former as homicide.

6. How did the medieval Church view the abortion of an unformed fetus?

Such an abortion was viewed as grievous sin *(maleficium)* since it represented a heinous attempt at birth control. Still and all, the Church Fathers persisted to speak of what emitted from the womb before the forty-day formation period for male fetuses as *effluxions* or corrupt semen. They further believed, in accordance with Aristotle, that female fetuses required a formation period of ninety days.

7. Why did they believe it required a longer time for the formation of female fetuses?

Medieval theologians, following the twelfth-century rediscovery of Aristotle, held that a female is conceived when there is some defect either in the form of the fetus (the semen) or the matter (the *menstra* and menstral blood). St. Thomas, however, allowed for the possibility that such a defect may be caused by an extrinsic force: "For the active power in the seed of the male tends to produce something like itself, perfect in masculinity; but the procreation of a female is the result either of the debility of the active power, or some insuitability of the material, or some change effected by external influences, like the south wind, for example, which is damp. . . ."[10]

8. But didn't Pope Sixtus V impose a penalty of immediate excommunication on women who consented to or performed an abortion of any kind, i.e., before or after the formation of the fetus?

Yes. During the Renaissance, the practice of abortion became so widespread in Italy that Pope Sixtus V in his apostolic constitution *Effraenatam,* issued in 1588, attached the penalty of immediate excommunication to the crime of abortion. This penalty was pronounced not only on pregnant women but on anyone who gave advice, assistance, a potion, or another kind of medicine for the commission of the crime. Moreover, absolution from this penalty was reserved to the Supreme Pontiff, except in cases when the one who incurred the punishment was in danger of death.[11] This legislation did not make the traditional distinction between formed and unformed fetuses. For this reason, it was modified shortly after the death of Pope Sixtus V by Pope Gregory XIV, who in a new apostolic constitution, *Sedes apostolica,* issued in 1591, limited the penalty of immediate excommunication to the abortion of "animated" fetuses. Moreover, by this document, the Pope no longer reserved the sole right to pronounce an absolution from this penalty, but granted this right to local bishops and the clerics delegated to them.[12] Pope Gregory's constitution remained in effect for almost three hundred years, being revised by Pope Pius IX in 1869.

9. *Why was this position revised?*

The theory of delayed animation was severely undermined by medical findings of the nineteenth century. By this time, embryologists discovered the role of sperm (which some moral theologians in their microscopic studies labeled *insecta* or *vermiculi)* and the female egg or *ovum* in the formation of a zygote. For this reason, the Church no longer could speak of the distinction between formed and unformed, animate and inanimate, fetuses. Indeed, this distinction already had been dissolved in the ethical discourses of Cardinal Thomas Marie Gousset (1792–1866).

In 1869, Pope Pius IX issued new legislation regarding abortion— legislation that abolished the former distinction in penalties regarding the abortion of formed and unformed fetuses. Henceforth, anyone causing an abortion, whatever the stage of fetal development, incurred immediate excommunication, provided that the attempt actually succeeded. This legislation passed through several pontificates and was incorporated in the Code of Canon Law published in 1917.[13] It remained unaltered when the Code was revised in 1983 and remains in full force in the Church today.

10. *Does the Church acknowledge that its firm position regarding abortion often comes into conflict with other important human values?*

Yes. The 1974 "Declaration on Abortion" (14) states that the Church by denying abortion

. . . endangers important values which men normally hold in great esteem and which may sometimes even seem to have priority. We do not deny these very grave difficulties. It may be a serious question of health, sometimes of life or death for the mother; it may be the burden represented by an additional child, especially if there are good reasons to fear that the child will be abnormal or retarded; it may be an importance attributed in different classes of society to considerations of honor or dishonor, of loss of social standing, and so forth. We proclaim only that none of these can ever objectively confer the right to dispose another's life, even when that life is only just beginning. . . .[14]

11. *Is it permissible for a young girl who is a victim of rape to undergo an abortion?*

No. As stated in Question 1, the deliberate killing of a fetus is a morally heinous act in any but a life-threatening situation. However, a common medical practice in today's hospitals and clinics is not to perform a surgical abortion on a rape victim but to administer a dose of a diethystilbestrol hormone known as DES. This synthetic female hormone (estrogen) affects the wall of the uterus so that new life (the zygote) cannot attach itself and develop further. It, therefore, passes from the mother and is lost. Such a procedure, in the eyes of the Church, constitutes an unlawful abortion, meriting the penalty of automatic excommunication.[15]

12. *Is it permissible for a Catholic nurse to assist a doctor in performing an abortion?*

No. Anyone who assists in an abortion in any way is guilty of homicide. This stands true even for the receptionist in an abortion clinic.

13. *Is the Church's teaching on abortion widely accepted by the faithful?*

No. According to a poll conducted by Yankelovich Clancy Shulman for *Time* magazine in 1987, the opinions of American Catholics on abortion do not differ greatly from those of Protestants. Only 14 percent of the Catholics polled agreed with the Church's teaching that abortion should be illegal in all but life-threatening circumstances, as did 12 percent of the Protestants. Fifty-seven percent of the Catholic respondents and 52 percent of the Protestants said they approved of abortion for pregnancies resulting from rape. And 27 percent of the Catholics along with 34 percent of the Protestants maintained that a woman should be permitted to obtain an abortion upon demand until the fetus is "viable," as U.S. law allows, no matter what the reason.[16]

NOTES

1. "Declaration on Procured Abortion," No. 22, in *Vatican Council II*, Vol. 2, "More Postconciliar Documents," edited by Austin Flannery, O.P. (Northport, New York: Costello Publishing Company, 1982), p. 449.

2. *Ibid.*, 5 and 6, pp. 442–43.

3. "Didache or The Teaching of the Twelve Apostles," 2, translated by Francis X. Glimm; Joseph M. F. Marique, S. J.; and Gerald G. Walsh, S. J., Vol. I, *The Apostolic Fathers*, edited by Ludwig Schopp et al. (New York: Cima Publishing Company, 1947), p. 172.

4. Tertullian, "On the Veiling of Virgins," XIV, translated by S. Thelwall, *Fathers of the Third Century*, Vol. IV, *The Ante Nicene Fathers*, edited by Alexander Roberts and James Donaldson (Grand Rapids: William B. Eerdmans Publishing Company, 1982), p. 36.

5. St. Cyprian, "Epistle 52," 2, in *St. Cyprian: Letters, (1–81);* translated by Sr. Rose Bernard Donna, C.S.J., Vol. 5, in *The Fathers of the Church*, edited by Roy Joseph Deferrari et al. (Washington, D.C.: Catholic University of America Press, 1964), p. 129.

6. "The Canons of the Council of Ancyra," Canon XXI, in *Seven Ecumenical Councils of the Undivided Church*, edited by Henry R. Percival (New York: Edwin S. Gorham, 1901), p. 73.

7. Lactantius, "The Workmanship of God," 12, in *Lactantius: The Minor Works*, translated by Sr. Mary Francis McDonald, C.S.J., Vol. 54, *The Fathers of the Church*, edited by Roy Joseph Deferrari et al. (Washington, D. C.: Catholic University of America Press, 1965), p. 39.

8. St. Augustine, "Eighty-three Different Questions," Question 56, translated by David L. Masher, Vol. 70, *The Fathers of the Church*, edited by Hermigild Dressler et al. (Washington, D.C.: Catholic University of America Press, 1977), p. 98.

9. John Connery, S. J., *Abortion: The Development of the Roman Catholic Perspective* (New York: Loyola University Press, 1977), pp. 96–97.

10. St. Thomas Aquinas, *Summa Theologiae*, I, Question 92, Article 1, Addenda 1, translated by the Blackfriars, Vol. XIII (New York: McGraw-Hill Book Company, 1964), p. 37.

11. Connery, *op. cit.*, p. 148.

12. *Ibid.*

13. *Ibid.,* p. 167.
14. "Declaration on Procured Abortion," 14, *op. cit.,* p. 446.
15. John J. Dietzen, *The New Question Box* (Peoria: Guildhall, 1986), pp. 390–91.
16. *Time,* Vol. 130, No. 10, September 7, 1987, p. 48.

FIFTEEN

The Sixth

and Ninth Commandments:

The Church and Sex

Married love is uniquely expressed and perfected by the acts proper to marriage by which intimate and chaste union of the spouses takes place are noble and honorable; the truly human performance of these acts fosters the self-giving they signify and enriches the spouses in joy and gratitude. Endorsed by mutual fidelity and, above all, consecrated by Christ's sacrament, this love abides faithfully in mind and body in prosperity and adversity and hence excludes both adultery and divorce.

Vatican II, Gaudium et Spes, 49

1. *How do Catholics interpret the sixth and ninth commandments: You shall not commit adultery and You shall not covet your neighbor's wife?*

By these commandments, Catholic catechists insist that people approach their sexual life with full consciousness of its sacred value and in a moral manner. Among the virtues necessary for its proper use is temperance or moderation, usually spoken of as chastity.[1]

2. *Why are these commandments always joined as one in Catholic moral thought?*

In the Scriptures, the sixth and ninth commandments are made one by Jesus. In the Gospel of Matthew, he revises the law of Moses by saying: "You have learned how it was said: You shall not commit adultery. But I say to you: if a man looks at a woman lustfully, he has already committed adultery in his heart" (5:27–28). Similarly, in the Gospel of Mark, he says: "whoever divorces his wife and marries another has already committed adultery with her." The Church Fathers from St. Augustine to St. Thomas Aquinas maintained this union of commandments in their discussions of premarital sex and adultery.

3. *What were the apostolic teachings on marriage and sexuality?*

The teachings of primitive Christianity on marriage and sexuality may be summarized as follows:

a. God from the beginning intended man and woman to use their sexual powers within marriage (Matt. 19:4–6; cf. Mark 10:7–9).

b. Marriage is an exclusive and indissoluble union between one man and one woman (1. Cor. 7:10–11).

c. The married state calls for fidelity, fruitfulness, and love (Eph. 5:28).

d. Children have special value in the Kingdom of God (Mark 9:36–37).

4. *How did these teachings differ from those of the pagan world?*

They represented a radical departure from the norms of the Greek and Roman world into which Christianity was born. In classic Greek civilization, mutual fidelity and chastity were unknown; the murder of newborn children by exposure was taken for granted; the status of mother and faithful wife was that of ignorant drudge; homosexuality was extremely common (albeit it was decried as a serious offense against nature in Plato's *Laws*) and, at least in Sparta, idealized. In Rome the father held the power of life and death over his wife and children, concubinage was commonplace among the upper classes, abortion and infanticide were acceptable practices, husbands alone had the prerogative of divorce, and so forth.

5. *What was the social impact of the Christian world view on the Roman Empire?*

With the passage of time, the chief contributions of Christianity to pagan culture became as follows: respect for life, rejection of the male-female double standards of morality, and the exaltation of monogamy, fidelity, and chastity as positive virtues.

6. *Were the early Church Fathers stricter than their Jewish predecessors in matters of sexual morality?*

Yes. However, the central part of the Church's teaching on sexual conduct is derived from Jewish tradition. Like the Jews, the early Christians identified adultery with murder (Lev. 20:10) and fornication with apostasy (2 Chron. 2:11; Isa. 23:17; Ezek. 16:29, etcetera). As for homosexuality, the early Epistles reflect the Jewish view that it is an "utter abomination unto the Lord" (Lev. 18:22). Yet Christians and Jews were sharply divided on the question of sexual continence.[2] Traditional Judaism encouraged marriage and upheld an affirmative attitude toward marital sex as part of the goodness of God's creation. This attitude is most clearly evidenced in the injunction which serves as a persistent refrain in the Book of Genesis: "Be fruitful and multiply, bring forth abundantly in the earth and multiply in it" (1:22, 8:17, 9:7, 35:11). Christianity, however, came to uphold the ideal of virginity and viewed sexual renunciation as a means of obtaining a place of prominence in the Kingdom of God.

7. Whence came this ideal of virginity?

The primary source of this ideal, as Robin Lane Fox points out in *Pagans and Christians,* is Jesus himself.[3] In the Gospel of Matthew, Jesus commends those who are "eunuchs for the sake of the kingdom of heaven" (19:10–12). Similarly, in the Gospel of Luke, he says: "The children of this age marry and are given in marriage but those judged worthy of a place in the world to come and of a place in the age to come do not" (20:35–36). This notion of living in the spiritual manner of eunuchs and angels vis-à-vis the carnality of mortal man was fortified not only by the words but the example of Jesus. Jesus never married, and Jewish bachelors in their thirties were a rarity in Palestine, since they lived in opposition to the law of Moses.[4] Moreover, Jesus commanded his apostles to relinquish their wives and children in order to dedicate themselves completely to the cause of the Kingdom of God (Matt. 19:29; Mark 10:29; Luke 18:29). Such strong sayings have led many scholars to see a relationship between Jesus and the Dead Sea sect of Essenes. Among the Essenes, there was an inner group of "Covenantors," who awaited the imminent coming of the Kingdom of God in a state of fasting and sexual abstinence.[5]

The New Testament emphasis on chastity is further stressed by the accounts of Mary and the virgin birth of Jesus. By the second century, these accounts were greatly embellished by apocalyptic works such as "The Gospel of the Nativity" and "The Protoevangelium of James." In the latter work, Salome, after hearing a report of the miraculous birth of Jesus from a midwife who had attended the delivery, set out to verify Mary's alleged "intactness" for herself. As Mary was sleeping, Salome stole into the cave and "put forward her finger to test her condition," only to have her finger severely singed for her sinful curiosity.[6]

8. *Was this ideal unique in the Roman world?*

Yes. Rome had its vestal virgins who watched over the city's sacred fire, virgin priestesses and *galli* served deities of the mystery religions such as Cybele, and chaste female slaves or *hierodules* who attended the rites of the goddess Diana. Such chastity in the pagan world, however, was a ritual requirement (since virginity was often viewed as a source of magical power) and not an ascetic statement about morality and the corruption of the flesh as it was in Christianity. Moreover, Christianity upheld this virtue for men as well as women. Male virgins were most uncommon in ancient Rome, since Roman society neither required nor expected men to remain chaste before marriage. Unmarried men were rather encouraged to expend their passion on slaves and prostitutes, the only objection to the latter being their expense. With the dawn of the Christian era, epitaphs began to appear with the word *virginus* as a statement of a deceased man's virtue and dedication to Christ. This word's scarce usage in classical antiquity testifies to the uniqueness of this Christian virtue.

Being unique, this ideal was, at times, extremely difficult to uphold, and nowhere are the difficulties more clearly stated than in the third-century treatise "On Virginity," which has been traditionally and most likely spuriously attributed to St. Clement. In this work, the writer provides a fellow Christian with fatherly advice on how to avoid temptation while engaged in missionary ventures. When the young missionary arrives in a new location, he immediately should seek out lodgings with fellow male celibates, or, in the case of an emergency, with a holy married couple. If, by adverse fortune, he should arrive at a community where the only Christians are women, he should seek shelter in the home of the oldest of the Christian cronies, preferably in a room that is farthest away from the place where she is sleeping. If, by the worst possible circumstance, he should arrive in a place where the only Christian is an attractive woman, he should not stop nor pray but "run away from her as from the face of a serpent."[7]

9. *Is not virginity in Christianity a negative virtue that represents a denial of the goodness of creation?*

Strange to say, the early Church viewed virginity as a positive virtue, a means by which the faithful could aspire to the state of angels and reverse the tragic effects of the Fall of Adam and Eve. Indeed, sexual abstinence was seen as the sole means by which a believer could regain a true simplicity of heart in his or her Christian journey through this "no abiding city." St. Cyprian argued that, whereas sex takes a man's mind from God, chastity permits him to concentrate on God alone and thereby obtain increased freedom from the fetters of the material world.[8]

But the price of this freedom was high. By the fourth century, spiritual counselors encouraged the virgins in their charge to enhance the holiness of their lives through acts of mortification of the flesh (such as self-flagellation) and prolonged periods of fasting from food and wine. Such measures, they came to realize, often result in amenorrhea, the cessation of menstruation. Amenorrhea represented tangible proof of the virgin's ability to reverse the Fall and to achieve a pristine wholeness of being. However, the discipline bolstered the belief that the so-called *via negativa* (the way to God by rejecting the demands of the flesh) produced positive results; the transformation of mature women—sexual women—into innocent children of God. This spiritual advice, best expressed in St. Jerome's letter to the virgin Eustochium, was repeated down the centuries in convents throughout Christianity, where religious sisters attempted to attain sanctity by the hair shirt, the scourge, and the stone, which they used to beat against their breasts in the manner exemplified by St. Jerome in painting after painting, including Leonardo's unfinished masterpiece in the Vatican.[9] Although the Church in modern times came to frown upon self-flagellation in religious communities, the other ascetic practices were still employed with moderation. In the 1950s, for example, the novices at Woodstock, the former Jesuit seminary in Maryland, were still given a spiked band to wear on their thighs as a penance.[10]

10. *Did the early Church encourage castration?*

No, albeit some Church Fathers on the scriptural basis of Matthew 19:12 approved of it. St. Justin Martyr, for example, wrote of a young Christian who asked a physician in Alexandria to castrate him. However, since castration was banned by Roman law, the physician instructed him to apply for permission to undergo such surgery from the provincial governor. The youth complied and was filled with chagrin when the governor denied his request. The incident is significant primarily because St. Justin speaks of the young man's efforts to sever the source of his libidinal urgings as something admirable.[11] Other Church Fathers went further. Origen, it is said, castrated himself on the basis of an all-too-literal interpretation of Matthew 18:7-9: "For it is necessary that temptations come, but woe to the man by whom the temptation comes! And if your hand or your foot causes you to sin, cut it off and throw it from you; for it is better for you to enter life maimed or lame than with two hands or two feet to be thrown into the eternal fire. And if your eye causes you to sin, pluck it out and throw it from you; it is better for you to enter life with one eye than with two eyes to be thrown into the hell of fire."

While such acts of self-mutilation were uncommon in the early Church, there were enough occurrences of such radical acts that the Council of Nicaea addressed them in its first canon, calling for all clergymen who have castrated themselves to terminate their ministry.[12] In 496, the Synod of Trullo condemned such clergymen as "self-murderers" and "enemies to the workmanship of God."[13]

11. *Does the Church consider virginity a higher state than marriage?*

Yes. This teaching finds its scriptural basis in St. Paul's first Epistle to the Corinthians:

"It is well for a man not to touch a woman. But because of the temptation to immorality, each man should have his own wife and each wife her husband. The husband should give to his wife her conjugal rights and likewise the wife to her husband. For the wife does not rule over her body, but her husband does; likewise the husband does not rule over his body, but his wife does. Do not refuse one another except perhaps for a season, that you may devote yourself to prayer; but then come back together again, lest Satan tempt you through lack of self-control. I say this by way of concession, not of command. I wish that all were as I myself am. But each has his own special gift from God, one of one kind and one of another. To the unmarried and the widows, I say that it's well for them to remain single as I do. But if they cannot exercise self-control, they should marry. For it is better to marry than to burn" (7:1–9).

From this teaching and the example of Christ, the Church Fathers, almost to the point of monotony, spoke of celibacy as a higher state. Though sanctified by God as a means of procreation, marriage, St. Jerome argued, could only count as thirty-fold in spiritual value compared to the sixty-fold of widowhood and the one hundred-fold of virginity.[14]

St. Gregory of Nyssa referred to the marriage of one of his students as a "sad tragedy,"[15] and St. Ambrose labeled it a "galling burden" and urged those of his disciples who were contemplating marriage to think of the state of domestic servitude to which wedded bliss soon deteriorated.[16] The most sincere praise of marriage during the Patristic age came from St. Jerome, who said: "I praise wedlock, I praise marriage, but it is because they produce virgins for me. I gather the rose from the thorn, the gold from the earth, the pearl from the oyster. Shall the ploughman plough all day? Shall he not enjoy the fruit of his labor? Wedlock is the more honored when the fruit of wedlock is the more loved."[17]

Even more telling is "The Testament of our Lord," which presented the proper order for the reception of Holy Communion in the post-Nicene Church: first bishops, presbyters, and deacons; then widows, virgins, and deaconesses; and finally married adults and children.[18]

This teaching of the superiority of virginity was echoed by theologians throughout the medieval period and became defined as a solemn dogma by the Council of Trent in 1552, which decreed: "If anyone says that the married state excels the state of virginity or celibacy, and that it is better or happier to be united in matrimony than to remain in virginity or celibacy, let him be anathema."[19]

In 1981, Pope John Paul II reinforced this dogma in his apostolic exhortation "The Christian Family in the Modern World" *(Familiaris Consortio)* by stating:

"Virginity or celibacy, by liberating the human heart in a unique way, 'so as to make it burn with greater love for God and for all humanity,' bears witness that the Kingdom of God and his justice is that pearl of great price which is preferred to every other value no matter how great, and hence must be sought as the only definitive value. It is for this reason that the Church, throughout her history, has always defended the superiority of this charism to that of marriage, by reason of the wholly singular link which it has with the Kingdom of God"[20].

12. *Does the Church teach that sexual intercourse within the confines of marriage can be sinful?*

The Church traditionally has taught that there are times when it might be sinful, such as when its exercise injures the dignity of the spouse. St. Augustine argued that married couples turn intercourse into a sinful act when they use it exclusively for the gratification of lust (concupiscence) to the exclusion of the desire for offspring.[21] Such an act is sinful, he said, even if no attempt is made to prevent propagation "either by wrong desire or evil appliance."[22] Throughout the Middle Ages, the Church advised couples to restrain the likelihood of concupiscence through periods of sexual abstinence. Priests sometimes advised couples to abstain from intercourse on Thursdays in memory of Christ's arrest, on Fridays in memory of His death, on Saturdays in honor of the Virgin Mary, on Sundays in honor of His Resurrection, or on Mondays in honor of the faithful departed.[23]

The question concerning the sinfulness of sexual congress within the confines of matrimony was still debated by the scholastic theologians in the twelfth and thirteenth centuries. St. Thomas Aquinas believed that marital sex on occasion may be either venial or mortal sin, depending on the degree of lust. He wrote: ". . . if pleasure be sought in such a way as to exclude the honesty of marriage; so that, to wit, it is not as a wife but as a woman that a man treats his wife, and that he is ready to use her in the same way if she were not his wife, it is mortal sin; wherefore if such a man is said to be too ardent a lover of his wife, because his ardor carries him away from the goods of marriage, so that it would not be sought in another than his wife, it is venial sin."[24]

This view of the importance of the virtue of chastity in marriage continues to prevail in the Church of the twentieth century. In 1951, Pope Pius XII in an "Address to Midwives" condemned the unbridled pursuit of sexual pleasure in marriage as "hedonism" by saying: "If nature aimed exclusively or even primarily at a mutual gift and a mutual possession of couples for pleasure, if it had ordained that act solely to make their personal experience happy in the highest degree and not stimulate them in the service of life, then the Creator would have adopted another plan in the formation and constitution of the natural act."[25] In 1981, Pope John Paul II in "The Christian Family in the Modern World" continued to exhort Catholic couples to be chaste in marriage by control of their sexual desire and moderate in their sexual activity (36).

13. What is the Church's stance on homosexuality?

The Church condemns homosexual acts as particularly heinous sins. This teaching is based on several passages in the Old and New Testaments. Leviticus stated the moral law, "You shall not lie with a man as with a woman" (18:22) and prescribed a death penalty for those who engaged in such acts (20:13). In the New Testament, St. Paul spoke of idolatrous pagans who were completely consumed with "vile affections:" ". . . for their women exchanged natural relations for the unnatural, and the men likewise gave up natural relations with women and were consumed with passion for one another, men committing shameless acts with men and receiving in their own persons the due penalty for their error" (Rom. 1:26–27). In an even more explicit passage, St. Paul said: "Know yet not that the unrighteous shall not inherit the Kingdom of God? Be not deceived, for neither fornicators, nor idolators, nor adulterers, nor effeminate, nor abusers of themselves with mankind, nor thieves, nor covetous, nor drunkard, nor revilers, nor extortioners, shall inherit the Kingdom of God" (1 Cor. 6:9–10). The terms "effeminate" and "abusers of themselves" are translations of the Greek words *malakoi* and *arsenokoitoi* (in the Latin

Vulgate: *molles* and *masculorum concubitores),* the former denoting males passively engaging in homosexual acts, the latter referring to those who actively engage in such actions.

The Church Fathers remained deeply concerned about the mere possibility of the sin among the body of believers. St. John Chrysostom, for example, cautioned parents not to let their male children's hair grow long for fear they might appear effete. Indeed, he regarded any attempt by a male to enhance his appearance as dangerously effeminate and unnatural, and cautioned parents to have their young sons in the constant protection of attendants for fear of "lurking" pederasts in public squares and open alleyways.[26] St. Basil said that men who have committed "shameful acts" with other men should be excluded from the sacraments for a period of fifteen years, a severe punishment with which St. Gregory of Nyssa soundly affirmed.[27]

In the seventh century, the *Cummean Penitential,* which was used by priests as a guide for prescribing acts of penance, mandated that homosexual acts must be be punished by a period of four to seven years of fasting and prayer. By the fourteenth century, sins of this nature were considered so grave that they could only be absolved by the pronouncement of a bishop.[28]

The gravity of such sins was upheld by the Church in its 1975 "Declaration on Certain Problems of Sexual Ethics" *(Personae humanae).* The Vatican document, however, advised pastors to be "considerate and kind" in their care of homosexuals in their congregations by instilling within them the hope of one day overcoming their difficulties. "However," the document continued, "it is not permissible to employ any pastoral method or theory to provide moral justification for their actions, on the grounds that they are in keeping with their condition. Sexual relations between persons of the same sex are necessarily and essentially disordered according to the objective moral order. Sacred scripture condemns them as gravely depraved and even portrays them as the tragic consequence of rejecting God."[29]

14. *What do Catholics mean by natural law?*

When the Second Vatican Council wished "to recall first of all the permanent binding force of natural law and its all-embracing principles," the Council Fathers employed the term "natural law" as a special term with a definite meaning (*Gaudium et Spes,* 79). The Council was not speaking of the "laws of nature" in the same way physicists or biologists speak of the laws which control the planets or the structure of the human body. Nor was "natural law" to be confused with anything Christ said about the Church or the sacraments or about those canonical requirements that the Church establishes for Catholics. By natural law, the Council Fathers meant those norms of human behavior which have been implanted in human nature by God and which an individual by the use of reason can discern and apply to his/ her conduct. Thus, the Church teaches, thoughtful people can know right from wrong, even without the light of revelation. The reason why the Ten Commandments enjoy lasting endurance, according to this argument, is because they express the fundamental content of God's natural law: You shall not kill the innocent, steal another man's wife or property, etc. Indeed, for Catholics, the only Mosaic commandment that is not a "natural law" is the one prescribing a holy Sabbath.

15. What is the traditional Catholic interpretation of the natural law of sexual morality?

The traditional Catholic interpretation of the natural law which governs sexual morality has its basis in St. Paul's Letter to the Romans (quoted above) in which he speaks of women changing the "natural use" of sex into that which is "against nature," and of men giving up "natural relations" with women by being "consumed with passion" for other men (1:26–27). This reference to nature as a criteria for right action was a concept advanced by Stoic and Neo-Platonic philosophers who had a great impact on St. Paul and his contemporaries.

The Stoic philosophers from Chrysippus to Cicero upheld nature as a guide for conduct and believed that a person should be rationally self-sufficient and not a slave to the demands of his/her irrational body. Such freedom could only be achieved by a spirit of disinterestedness to base passions and instincts. Moreover, according to the stoics, reason decrees that sexual activity must be guided by the finality inscribed within it by nature. Imbued with such ideals, St. Justin

Martyr wrote that Christians live in the manner of true philosophers since they marry only to have children. Otherwise, he said, they remain completely continent.[30] Similarly, St. Clement of Alexandria held that Christians who intend to beget children should approach their wives with a chaste and controlled will, for to engage in intercourse for purposes other than procreation is to do injury to nature.[31]

Of particular moral repugnance to the Church Fathers was any attempt at birth control. St. John Chrysostom held the use of contraceptives to be worse than homicide.[32] And St. Augustine spoke of married couples who practice birth control as fornicators engaged in "criminal conduct."[33]

St. Thomas Aquinas made a distinction between sins against nature and sins of lust (fornication, adultery, seduction, rape) in seriousness because they represented perversions of the God-given purpose of human sexuality. Aquinas divided sins against nature into the following four categories: (1) procuring ejaculation without coitus, i.e., masturbation; (2) copulation with nonhuman creatures, i.e., bestiality; venereal acts between members of the same sex; and (4) deviation between married partners from the proper manner of sexual intercourse *(naturalis modus concumbandi)*, i.e., face-to-face contact with the woman on her back. Of those, he concluded, the most grievous sins were bestiality and homosexuality.[34]

16. *Does the Church continue to uphold this belief in the natural law of sexuality?*

Yes. Pope Paul VI in his encyclical "On the Regulation of Births" *(Humanae vitae)*, issued in 1968, said that married couples must respect "the laws of the generative process" as ministers of the design established by the Church"[35] In 1975, the Sacred Congregation for the Doctrine of Faith in "The Declaration on Sexual Ethics" said that the Church ". . . continues to preserve without ceasing and to transmit without error . . . the principles of the moral order which spring from human nature itself. . . ."

17. *Does the Church continue to condemn masturbation as an immoral act?*

Yes. Masturbation freely and deliberately committed is a mortal sin *(mortale peccatum)*, which, if unrepented, incurs God's displeasure. In its latest statement on sexual ethics, the Church denied that it is, as some psychologists claim, a "normal concomitant of growth toward sexual maturity." Masturbation, in the eyes of the Church, is rather "an intrinsically and gravely disoriented action." "The principal argument of this truth," the Vatican said in its "Declaration on Certain Problems of Sexual Ethics," "is that the deliberate use of the sexual faculty, for whatever reason, outside of marriage is essentially contrary to its purpose." (9).

18. *What is the Church's present position on birth control?*

The Church has never wavered from the teachings of the Fathers on birth control. This was evidenced by Pope Paul VI's encyclical *Humanae vitae* (1968) which insisted that Catholics must always keep their love relationship open to God's intervention of new life. For this reason, they condemned all artificial means of birth control (including condoms, pills, withdrawals, and post-coital dousing procedures) as immoral and unnatural: "Every act that intends to impede procreation must be repudiated, whether the act is intended as an end to be attained or as a means to be used, and whether it is done in anticipation of marital intercourse or during it, or while having its natural consequence"(14). This position was upheld by Pope John Paul II in his Apostolic Constitution *Familiaris consortio* (32), as issued in 1981.

19. *Are Catholics prohibited from taking any measures to limit the size of their families?*

No. Catholics may adopt methods of Natural Family Planning which, unlike the rhythm methods of old, pinpoints with remarkable accuracy the fertility period of the woman in a given month, thus enabling a couple to seek or to avoid pregnancy, depending on their good reasons. The Church does not recommend any particular Natural Family Planning method, except to declare that family planning of this kind is permissible for a couple's good reason. This natural method of family planning has established itself to be reliable. Indeed, Pope John Paul II commended recent successes in this field.

20. *What specifically comes under the heading of Natural Family Planning?*

Natural Family Planning enables couples to project the likelihood of pregnancy through the instrumental knowledge of the woman's basal temperature and the time of her mucous secretions.

21. *How have Catholics in their moral principles been affected by the sexual revolution?*

Catholics have not remained unaffected. A 1981 Knights of Columbus–sponsored study of eighteen to thirty-year-old Catholics in the United States showed that 90 percent disagreed with the Church's position on birth control and almost as many disagreed with Catholic norms on divorce and premarital sex. From 1973 to 1983, the rate of divorce among Catholics grew from one out of seven to one out of four. More than seven million Catholics have been through a divorce or legal separation. A 1985 Gallup poll reports the general Catholic population is now more tolerant of premarital sex than Protestants—only 33 percent of Catholics disapproving, compared to the Protestants' 46 percent. Only fifteen years earlier, 70 percent of both communities considered such conduct absolutely immoral.[36]

NOTES

1. John A. Hardon, S. J., *The Catholic Catechism* (Garden City, New York: Doubleday and Company, 1975), p. 353.

2. Robin Lane Fox, *Pagans and Christians* (New York: Alfred A. Knopf, 1987), p. 351.

3. *Ibid.*, p. 362.

4. *Ibid.*, p. 363.

5. *Ibid.*, p. 365.

6. "The Protoevangelium of James," quoted in *Women and Religion: A Feminist*

Sourcebook for Christian Thought, edited by Elizabeth Clark and Herbert Richardson (New York: Harper and Row, 1977), p. 35.

7. "The Second Epistle of Saint Clement Concerning Virginity," I–IV, in *The Clementine Homilies,* translated by A. Cleveland Coxe, Vol. VII, *The Ante Nicene Fathers,* edited by Alexander Roberts and James Donaldson (Grand Rapids: William B. Eerdmans Publishing Company, 1951), pp. 61–62; Fox, *op. cit.,* p. 360.

8. St. Cyprian, "On the Dress of Virgins," 20–22, translated by Ernest Wallis in *Fathers of the Third Century,* Vol. V, *The Ante Nicene Fathers,* edited by Alexander Roberts and James Donaldson (Grand Rapids: William B. Eerdmans Publishing Company, 1981), pp. 435–36.

9. Marina Warner, *Alone of All Her Sex: The Myth and Cult of The Virgin Mary* (New York: Alfred A. Knopf, 1976), pp. 74–75.

10. *Ibid.*

11. St. Justin Martyr, "First Apology," 29, in *The Apostolic Fathers: Justin Martyr and Irenaeus,* translated by A. Cleveland Coxe, Vol. I, *The Ante Nicene Fathers,* edited by Alexander Roberts and James Donaldson (Grand Rapids: William B. Eerdmans Publishing Company, 1981), p. 172.

12. "The Canons of the Council of Nicea," Canon 1, in *The Seven Ecumenical Councils of the Undivided Church,* edited and translated by Henry R. Percival (New York: Edwin S. Gorham, 1901), p. 8.

13. "The Synod of Trullo," Canon XXIII, in *Ibid.,* p. 595.

14. St. Jerome, "Against Jovinian," in *Women and Religion, op. cit.,* p. 61.

15. St. Gregory of Nyssa, "On Virginity," III, in *Select Writings and Letters of Gregory, Bishop of Nyssa,* translated by William Moore and Henry Austin Wilson, Vol. V, *The Nicene and Post Nicene Fathers,* Second Series, edited by Philip Schaff and Henry Wace (Grand Rapids: William B. Eerdmans Publishing Company, 1955), p. 345.

16. St. Ambrose, "Concerning Virgins," I, 6, in *The Principal Works of St. Ambrose,* translated by H. DeRomestin, Vol. X, *The Nicene and Post Nicene Fathers,* Second Series, edited by Philip Schaff and Henry Wace (Grand Rapids: William B. Eerdmans Publishing Company, 1955), pp. 367–68. See also Vern L. Bullough, "The Christian Inheritance," in *Sexual Practices and the Medieval Church,* edited by Vern L. Bullough and James Brundage (Buffalo: Prometheus Books, 1982), p. 8.

17. St. Jerome, "Letter 22 (To Eustochium: the Virgin's Profession)," translated by F. A. Wright, in *Women and Religion, op. cit.,* p. 60. See also Vern L. Bullough, *loc. cit.*

18. Charles R. Meyer, *Man of God: A Study of the Priesthood* (Garden City, New York: Doubleday and Company, 1974), pp. 68–69.

19. *Canons and Decrees of the Council of Trent,* Canon 10, translated by H. J. Schroeder (London: B. Herder Book Company, 1955), p. 182.

20. Pope John Paul II, "The Christian Family in the Modern World," *(Familiares Consortio)* No. 22, in *Vatican Council II,* Vol. II, *More Postconciliar Documents,* edited

by Austin Flannery, O.P., (Northport, N.Y.: Costello Publishing Company, 1982), p. 827.

21. St. Augustine, "On Marriage and Concupiscence," 1, 5, 4, in *Women and Religion, op. cit.,* p. 72.

22. *Ibid.,* 1, 17, 15, p. 75.

23. Warner, *op. cit.,* p. 77.

24. St. Thomas Aquinas, *Summa Theologiae,* III Supplement, Question 49, Article 6, in *Women and Religion, op. cit.,* p. 85.

25. Pope Pius XII, "Moral Questions Affecting Married Life," 60 (Washington, D.C.: National Catholic Welfare Conference, 1951), p. 21.

26. St. John Chrysostom, Homily LXXIII, 3, cited in Vern L. Bullough, "Formation of Ideals: Christian Theory and Christian Practice," in *Sexual Practices and the Medieval Church, op. cit.,* p. 18.

27. St. Basil, "Letter 217," 62, and St. Gregory of Nyssa, *Epistula Canonica,* 4, cited in *Ibid.,* p. 18.

28. Reay Tannahill, *Sex in History* (New York: Stein and Day, 1981), pp. 158–59.

29. The Sacred Congregation of the Doctrine of the Faith, "Declaration on Certain Problems of Sexual Ethics," *(Personae Humanae),* No. 8, in *Vatican Council II,* Vol. II, *op. cit.,* p. 491.

30. St. Justin Martyr, "First Apology," 29, *loc. cit.*

31. St. Clement of Alexandria, "On Marriage," *Stromateis,* 3, in *Women and Religion, op. cit.,* p. 47.

32. St. John Chrysostom, "On Account of Fornication," cited in Vern L. Bullough, "Formation of Ideals: Christian Theory and Christian Practice," *Sexual Practices and the Medieval Church, op. cit.,* p. 15.

33. St. Augustine, "On Marriage and Concupiscence," 1, 17, 15, in *Women and Religion, op. cit.,* p. 75.

34. St. Thomas Aquinas, *Summa Theologiae,* II, II, Question 154, Articles 11 and 12, cited in Vern L. Bullough, "The Sin Against Nature and Homosexuality," in *Sexual Practices and the Medieval Church, op. cit.,* p. 85.

35. Pope Paul VI, "Encyclical Letter on the Regulation of Births," *(Humanae Vitae),* No. 11, in *Vatican Council II,* Vol. II, *op. cit.,* p. 403.

36. George A. Kelly, "Schooling and the Values of People," Columbia, Vol. 29, No. 6, June 1986, pp. 22–29.

SIXTEEN

The Seventh

and Tenth Commandments:

The Church and Its Temporality

And all who believed were together and had all things in common; and they sold their possessions and goods and distributed them to all, as any had need.

Acts 2:44–45

The Catholic Church has an innate right to acquire, retain, administer and alienate temporal goods in pursuit of its proper ends independent of civil power. The following ends are especially proper to the Church: to order divine worship; to provide decent support for the clergy and other ministers; to perform the works of the sacred apostolate and of charity, especially towards the needy.

Canon 1254 of the New Code of Canon Law

1. *How do Catholics interpret the seventh commandment, You shall not steal, and the tenth, You shall not covet your neighbor's goods?*

These commandments forbid stealing, cheating, dishonesty, keeping what belongs to others, unjust damage to other people's property, accepting bribes as public officials, failing to live up to business agreements, etc. The commandments further reach into the human psyche, expecting illicit urges in these directions to be kept in check.[1] They apply also to the temporality of the Church.

2. *What is meant by "temporality?"*

Temporality in Catholic terminology, means the Church's worldly possessions—the manpower, the buildings, the monies, the investments, the artifacts which are used to conduct its mission on earth. Sometimes, they are used wisely, sometimes badly.

The scholar James Gollin, in a study on the wealth of the Church, made the following observation: "Every act of religion, ancient or modern, ceremonies or spontaneous, makes use of the things of this world; and regrettable though the fact may be, the things of this world cost money. Because a pilgrim church, like a church militant, marches on its stomach, someone will always have to worry about the state of the exchequer."[2]

3. *Cannot the Church's involvement with worldly goods be a dangerous enterprise?*

Yes, since the New Testament describes the love of money as "the root of all evil" (1 Tim. 6:10). The dangers of greed, avarice, and miserliness cannot be gainsayed, and throughout its long history the Church has been known as much for its scoundrels as its monastic popes and poor Franciscans.

James Gollin, initially scandalized to learn that the Vatican owned 18 percent of a zinc mine in the Belgian Congo (Zaire), toward the end of his five hundred pages of text concluded: "I think we should wish the Church well in its struggle for spiritual renewal and economic survival. Catholic or not, Christian or not, we gain by the work it does in education, in charity, in mercy. We owe a debt to the Church as the curator of so much of our cultural heritage, and as the exemplar of the remarkable idea—remarkable at least in our time and our land—that money isn't everything."[3]

4. *Where did the Church obtain the reputation for having vast wealth?*

Although vast sums of money pass through the Church and although the Church more often than not is money poor, it is the "holdings" down the ages that comprise the enormous wealth of the Church. During the first centuries, the Church of the Catacombs was poverty stricken, but beginning in 324 the Roman Emperor Constantine, now a convert, gave the Church the Lateran Palace, Vatican Hill, and what is now the Pope's summer residence, Gandolfo. At the same time, when rich and aristocratic Roman families abandoned paganism for Christianity, the Church of Rome became the object of their benefaction. In almost no time at all the Church of Christ went from rags to riches.

By the end of the sixth century, the material holdings of the Church around Rome and in Naples, Calabria and Sicily had become vast. The annual revenues from Calabria, and Sicily alone amounted to more that thirty five thousand gold florins. by 764, Pope Paul I assumed the worldly title of *dux plebis* (leader of the people) and began to speak to his followers of *pars nostra Romanorum* (our Roman ecclesiastical state).

The civil jurisdiction was further enlarged by the famous donation of Pepin the Short in 756. In exchange for the exalted title of *Patricius Romanus,* the Frankish King Pepin bequeathed to the papacy all of the Italian cities he had conquered from the Lombards along with their territories. Pope Stephen II thus received two large northeastern areas of Italy. One, comprising 4,542 square miles, centered around Ravenna. It was later called the Romagna. The other, which comprised 3,692 square miles, lay below Ravenna and stretched down into central Italy. It was called the March of Ancona.[4]

Twenty-one years later, the citizens of Rome gathered in a parliament and conferred upon the Pope supreme authority over them.

5. *What were the Papal States?*

They were sixteen thousand square miles of territory in what is now modern Italy, divided in the Middle Ages into various *patrimonia* (estates)—the patrimony of Tuscany, the patrimony of Perugia, the patrimony of the March of Ancona, the patrimony of Romagna, the patrimony of Bologna, and so on.[5]

In addition to these jurisdictions, which were governed directly by the popes, at the close of the eighth century the Pontiff also acquired feudal power over most of Portugal, the Navarre and Aragon provinces of Spain, England, Ireland, Bulgaria, Corsica, Sardinia, and the Kingdom of Sicily, all of which provided yearly taxes to the See of Peter. It was an advantage then to become a feudal vassal of the Pope. The Pope's hegemony was by now richly endowed and the Pope a political person to be reckoned with by the princes of this world. As a result, a large bureaucracy of clerics, bishops, priests, deacons, and laymen were called upon to administer papal towns, papal fleets, papal treasuries. Abuses took root almost immediately, not the least of which was simony.

6. *What is simony?*

Simony is the sale of church offices and services. Throughout the medieval period, church offices were often bestowed on generous patrons. More scandalous to a later day was the occasional use of bribery by a powerful family to acquire the papacy for a relative. At the lowest point, perhaps, Benedict IX, a layman whose personal life was violent and dissolute, with the aid of the counts in Tusculum, was appointed Pope in 1032. For twelve years he was a competent pontiff, but in due time the laity drove him from the Lateran Palace, only to have the Tusculan counts restore him to office, not once, but twice.[6]

This was an unusual procedure but also a fact of history. Although officially condemned by the Council of Rheims in 1049 and by reforming pontiffs such as Pope Gregory VII (d. 1085) and Pope Urban VI (d. 1389), the problem of simony returned like the recurrent plague throughout the Middle Ages.

7. *Did the Church ever impose a system of taxation on the faithful?*

Yes. The most common tax was on benefices and dignities. Every parish, diocese, priory, monastery and cathedral was considered to be a benefice. Ecclesiastical dignities ran from simple parish priest to bishop, archbishop, abbot, prior, and cardinal. The theory was that all benefices and dignities belonged to the Pope and were his to award as he wished. Those who wished to possess a benefice or acquire an ecclesiastical dignity often paid for it, usually the sum of one-third to one-half of the annual income of the benefice. Later, the tax became standard. Those who refused to pay taxes were sometimes excommunicated. After the death of a dignity, his benefice along with his personal possessions were handed over to the papacy and promptly resold.[7]

Other means of taxation were not excluded. In 1199, Pope Innocent II directed all bishops to send a fortieth of their revenue to Rome, which they, in turn, recovered from mandatory tithes on secular holdings.[8] A *cens* or tax was levied also on all monasteries, convents and churches that came directly under papal protection.

Additional sources of revenue were found in fees for the granting of dispensations from canonical impediments (such as the permission of a consanguineous marriage) and the sale of indulgences.

8. *What are indulgences?*

The concept of an indulgence was developed primarily from the teachings of St. Anselm of Canterbury (1033–1109), who held that Christ by His passion and death had paid back to God more than was required for man's debt of sin. For this reason, Christ had earned a surfeit of merit.[9] Additional merits were earned by the holy martyrs and saints in their dedication to God. These merits, it was believed, were kept in a heavenly treasure chest which was placed in the hands of the Vicar of Christ on earth, the Bishop of Rome. By the fourteenth century, this notion of a treasure chest of merits was related to the sacrament of penance. Through their divine power to forgive sin, priests possessed the ability to shrive man of the guilt of sin (the *culpa*) and thereby save him from eternal damnation. But the scales of God's justice at all times had to be balanced. And although man might be absolved of the guilt of sin, he still had to bear the punishment (or *poena*) for his transgression of God's law. This punishment was meted out by confessors in the form of a penance. Moreover, since almost all men die before they can fully perform their penance, the balance, it was believed, had to be paid by a period of suffering in Purgatory.

In 1343, Pope Clement VI sanctioned the belief that the Pope could draw on the treasure chest of merits to cancel out all or part of an individual's unperformed penances as payment for a supererogatory act of faith and charity, an act over and above what is required for salvation. Thus a penitent after performing the prescribed penance for his or her transgressions, could earn a share from the treasure chest of merits by performing such additional good works as making a pilgrimage, joining a Crusade against the Turks, draining a swamp on ecclesiastical property, or assisting in the construction of a hospital or church. The substitution of blood money *(wergeld)* for punishment was a long-established practice in secular courts. For this reason, no real furor occurred when it became employed as an acceptable means of performing a supererogatory act of penance. Therefore, a shriven penitent, by making a monetary payment to Rome, could receive enough merits to obtain a partial or plenary (full) "favor of remission" or indulgence from any or all unperformed penances at the time of his death.

At this same time, the Church began teaching that favors of remission could be applied to souls in Purgatory. This teaching served to minimize the aspect of personal penance that was integral to the original concept of an indulgence and it opened the door to abuses.

The first abuse took place during the pontificate of Pope Boniface IX (1389–1404), who declared 1400 to be a Jubilee Year. On the occasion of such Jubilees, the Church held that a penitent could obtain a plenary indulgence by making a pilgrimage to Rome and praying at the sacred shrines. Pope Boniface, however, said that such a pilgrimage was not necessary for this Jubilee. Full remission of any unpaid penance could be obtained simply by saying prayers in a local church and paying a fixed amount of money for an officially sealed letter of indulgence to a duly appointed "pardoner" of the Church.[10]

9. How widespread were the abuses?

Throughout the fifteenth and early sixteenth centuries, pardoners sold indulgences throughout Christendom on a percentage basis without requiring repentance, confession or prayer. In 1517, one such pardoner—a Dominican named Tetzel—appeared in Wittenberg, Germany ostensibly to raise funds for the refurbishing of St. Peter's Basilica. Reportedly, he sold plenary indulgences for dearly departed souls by reciting the jingle, "As soon as the money in the coffer rings, the soul from purgatory's fire springs."[11]

Hearing reports of Tetzel's sales techniques, Martin Luther, an Augustinian friar, who by this time had lost faith in the sacramental function of the Church, used the pardoner as his excuse to launch what came to be known as the Protestant Reformation.

10. Did the Church correct such abuses?

Yes. The wholesale sale of indulgences was condemned as follows by the Council of Trent (1545–63):

> In granting indulgences the Council decrees that all criminal gain therewith connected be entirely done away with as a source of grievous abuse among the Christian people; and, as to other disorders arising from superstition, ignorance, irreverence, or any course whatsoever—since these, on account of the widespread corruption, cannot be removed by special prohibitions—the Council lays upon each bishop the duty of finding out such abuses as exist in his own diocese, of bringing them before the next provincial synod, and of reporting them, with the assent of the other bishops, to the Roman Pontiff.[12]

11. *How did the Church come to lose the Papal States and many of its worldly possessions?*

After the Reformation, revenues from benefices, legacies and gifts, especially from Northern Europe, were lost. Moreover, during the colonial expansion of the seventeenth and eighteenth centuries, the papacy did not invest in the foreign colonized markets which provided both capital and raw material to the burgeoning industrialist class, nor did it take advantage of new inventions, such as the steam engine, the flying shuttle, and the water frame, which were revolutionizing means of production. The Papal States remained an economy in stagnation.

At the beginning of Pope Clement XI's reign in 1700, the papal debt stood at fifteen million scudi (roughly comparable in value to one dollar). By 1730, the debt was sixty million scudi. Thirty years later, the debt hovered around eighty million scudi.[13] The total population of the *patrimonia* from Tuscany to Perugia was now beyond two million, with starvation and beggary the order of the day. Papal revenues from Portugal, Spain, Naples, and Sicily were seized by National Governments, while the papal estates in France and Italy were similarly lost.

Greater hardships for the papacy still lay ahead. On November 2, 1789, the moment of the French Revolution, all Church property in France was declared "at the disposal of the Nation." The new National Assembly decreed that henceforth French bishops were forbidden to contribute local monies to papal support. With the arrival of Napoleon (1796), a tribute of twenty-one million scudi was laid on the Papal States. The Vatican was forced to compel everyone from cardinals to sharecroppers to send their personal values to the Vatican, an amount insufficient to meet the budgetary demands on the Pope. In retaliation, Napoleon's troops stripped the Roman palaces, churches, and convents of gold, silver, and precious stones, removed art works —paintings, sculptures, tapestries, manuscripts, and ceramic treasures —from Rome to Paris. The Church in Rome was left bare.[14]

After the collapse of the Napoleonic Empire, the Congress of Vienna (1815) restored some of the priceless treasury and offered Rome inadequate indemnities. Although eighteen provinces of the papal territories were intact, the days of the temporal glory of Roman Catholicism were over.

The last Pope-King *(il Papa Re)* was Pius IX (1846–1878). By 1860, papal rule had been disbanded by the Piedmontese government in fifteen of the eighteen papal provinces, leaving rebellion in its wake. On August 19, 1870, national troops of the united Italy took possession of the patrimony of St. Peter, the Roman province itself. Pope Pius IX was left governor of only 480,000 square meters on and around Vatican Hill, whereupon he declared himself a prisoner within the Vatican and refused to leave even for a short absence. Until 1922, his successors followed suit, none ever appearing on the front balcony of St. Peter's even to give the papal blessing of a new pontiff.

12. *How did the Church recover its economic base?*

The Italian government signed a concordat with Mussolini in 1929 that granted the Church the freedom to conduct its own affairs in a new state called Vatican City (Stato della Città del Vaticano), independent of the Italian government. There was little friendship on either side. In addition, the concordat provided reparation (approximately ninety million dollars) for the losses the Church suffered during the merger in 1870 of the Papal States into a united Italy, and all ecclesiastical corporations were granted tax-exempt status.[15]

13. *Did the new Vatican City stabilize the Pope's financial difficulties?*

Yes. Pope Pius XI created a financial agency, *The Special Administration of the Holy See,* under the direction of Bernardino Nogara, a genius in monetary investments, who immediately invested the ninety million dollars (mostly in Italian government bonds) in an incredible variety of Italian concerns. Governmental-supported financial companies, insurance companies, public utilities, public and private construction firms, furnishings, hotels, mining and metallurgical products, farming products, munitions, pharmaceuticals, cement, paper, timber, ceramics, pasta, engineering firms, railways, passenger shipping, telephone and telecommunications, real estate, and banking became elements of a widely diversified portfolio.[16]

During this pre–World War II period, Pope Pius XI assembled a circle of professionals and prelates (including Patrick Cardinal Hayes of New York) to manage the financial and legal affairs of the Vatican, with Nogara remaining the central figure. Other laymen began to emerge as powerful figures, especially Enrico Galeazzi, whose importance grew by virtue of his personal relationship with the future Archbishop of New York (Francis Spellman) and a future pope (Eugenio Pacelli, who became Pius XII).

14. *What financial measures did Pope Pius XII initiate?*

In 1942, Pope Pius XII in accordance with the designs of Nogara formed *The Institute for Religious Works* (IOR). Commonly called "the Vatican Bank," this agency was established to administer the Church's capital as a separate corporate entity with complete independence from the other offices and agencies of the Holy See. Answerable only to the Pope, it is not a bank in the customary sense; its services are not available to the public, only to the heads of religious orders, to Catholic educational and social agencies, to diplomats accredited to the Holy See, to the Pope and members of his Curia.

Through this agency, the Vatican established links with an array of other banks (Rothchild's, Crédit Suisse, Hambros, Morgan Guaranty, Bankers Trust, Chase Manhattan, and Continental Illinois) and greatly expanded its investments in Italian securities.[17]

15. *What complications and/or controversies did this amassment of capital create for the Church?*

In 1968 the Vatican became associated by the press with Michele Sindona, an alleged mob figure. At this time the Italian government under Giovanni Leone threatened to remove the Vatican Bank's tax-exempt status, a move that would have cost the Church millions in lost revenue. Faced with this threat and the embarrassing revelation that the Vatican had invested in Italian pharmaceutical firms that were manufacturing birth control pills, Pope Paul VI decided to transfer vast Vatican holdings out of Italy and into the tax-free Eurodollar market.[18] To accomplish this, he created the *Prefecture of Economic Affairs,* chaired by Cardinal Egidio Vagnozzi who proceeded to engage the services of Sindona, a rising star in the world of international finance. Sindona's task was to broker the sale of Societa Generale Immobiliare, a Vatican holding which was one of Italy's largest real estate companies. Instead of selling the firm, he bought it himself. This transfer of holdings, according to *Time* magazine's longtime Vatican correspondent Wilton Wynn, represented the extent of Sindona's dealings with the Vatican in an official capacity, but was enough to provide the press with the opportunity to describe him as "the Vatican's top financial adviser."[19]

By 1970, Sindona had established his own financial empire. In 1972, he purchased the Franklin National Bank of New York. Two years later, the Franklin National collapsed. That same year Sindona's European banks were declared insolvent. An investigative committee, appointed by the Bank of Italy, reported that in one of the financier's banks the net losses through Sindona's unrecorded foreign exchange contracts and irregular fiduciary contracts were in excess of $500 million. The Italian press reported the Vatican's loss to be as high as $80 million, although Vatican sources maintained that its true loss was a tenth of that figure.[20] In any case, all this prompted the media to speak of Sindona as a "Vatican financial partner." Sindona, however, persistently stated that he had never gone into financial ventures with the Vatican.[21]

16. *What happened to Sindona?*

On March 27, 1980, Sindona was convicted of sixty-eight counts of misappropriation of funds, perjury, and fraud involving the Franklin National Bank. He was fined $207,000 and sentenced to twenty-five years in prison. In January 1982, he was indicted in Palermo with seventy-five others for operating $600 million plus in heroin trade between the United States and Sicily.[22]

Sindona was extradicted in 1984 to Milan, where he was tried and found guilty of bank fraud and murder in connection with the failure of Banca Privata Italiana. In March 1986, he died of arsenic poisoning in his cell in Voghera prison near Milan.

17. *What was the Ambrosiano affair?*

Throughout the 1970s the Vatican Bank had relations on a bank-to-bank basis with the Banco Ambrosiano in Milan, considered a Catholic bank with a good reputation whose chief executive officer was Roberto Calvi. Archbishop Paul Marcinkus, the head of the Vatican Bank, sat on the board of one of Ambrosiano's subsidiary branches in the Bahamas. In 1975, an elaborate plot was hatched by Calvi that came to involve the Vatican Bank in a notorious international scandal.

The affair began when Calvi started to "loan" huge sums of Ambrosiano's money to eight "dummy" corporations in Panama. These corporations, in turn, used the borrowed money to purchase shares of Ambrosiano stock. When asked for collateral, the Panamanian companies simply posted the Ambrosiano stock they had purchased. Calvi then began to declare huge stock dividends and rights offerings that doubled and redoubled the shares outstanding. Calvi publicly supported the inflated stock values with optimistic announcements and market-rigging stock purchases. The Panamanian companies used their increased stock holdings to borrow more money with which they purchased more stock. The companies never paid interest on their borrowings. They simply added the accrued interest to their loan balances and backed their new obligation for collateral with more Ambrosiano stock.[23]

Italian authorities claim that Calvi used the Vatican Bank as a conduit to set up the dummy corporations, giving Ambrosiano lenders the impression that the Vatican Bank was a direct party to the transactions. In addition, they maintain that most of the loan money was unnecessarily transferred to the dummy corporations through the Vatican Bank, enabling the Vatican to earn huge fees for currency conversions. Finally the authorities contend that the Vatican Bank may have profited directly from the scheme by selling its shares of Ambrosiano stock at the artificially high prices engineered by Calvi.[24]

Vatican officials have persistently refuted these allegations as part of an election-year campaign to smear the Vatican and maintain that the Vatican Bank was but one of seventy banks involved in dealings with Ambrosiano during this period.

In 1979, Calvi's maneuverings began to go awry. The Ambrosiano bank was obliged to pay interest on the increasing deposits to make the loans. As the interest rates soared in banks throughout the world, Calvi found himself in an expensive bind. In 1981, he was asked by Ambrosiano officials for definite proof that the Vatican Bank maintained some measure of control over the shares of Ambrosiano stock that were accumulating in the Panamanian corporations. Calvi, at this time, approached Archbishop Marcinkus for documentation that could be used to attest to the Vatican's control of these firms. Marcinkus complied by issuing "letters of patronage" in which he assured lenders that the Panamanian firms were responsible companies whose purposes were known and approved by the Vatican Bank. Wilton Wynn explains that these letters, which served to perpetuate the monumental fraud, were issued by the archbishop in a naive manner as a gesture of goodwill to Calvi. He writes: "The letters were not guarantees; they were nothing that would back up a loan, only kind words for Calvi's companies. Also they had been issued on September 1, 1981, which was after all Calvi's indebtedness had been incurred. Not a single loan was secured, or even influenced on the basis of those letters. Furthermore, Marcinkus had a note from Calvi cancelling the letters and promising that they would never be used in any way to cause 'any damage, present or future' to the Vatican Bank. Marcinkus had issued the letters under pressure from friends of Calvi and to give the banker time to set his house in order. The letters expired in June 1982, and after that Marcinkus flatly refused to give Calvi any further help."[25]

Despite the issuance of Vatican documentation, Calvi's attempts to shore up the hidden losses of Ambrosiano failed. He was convicted in July 1981 of exporting $27 million illegally from Italy and was sentenced to four years in jail and a $13.7 million fine. He was released on bail only to be confronted by the Bank of Italy for an explanation of the $1.3 billion in loans to the Panamanian companies.

Calvi could offer no explanation and on June 10, 1982, fled from Italy. Several days later his secretary committed suicide by leaping from the fourth floor of the Banco Ambrosiano. On June 18, 1982, Calvi's body was found hanging from Blackfriars Bridge in London.[26]

18. *What was the outcome of the Ambrosiano affair?*

Calvi was dead. But most of the $1.3 billion remained missing. Ambrosiano creditor banks, in search of repayment, claimed that the Vatican was a principal participant in the failure, citing the "letters of patronage." In response to such charges, Pope John Paul II's Secretary of State Agostino Casaroli proposed to the Italian government the appointment of six-man commission to make a thorough investigation of the affair: three were to be named by the Vatican and three by the Italian Ministry of the Treasury. The government complied. The commission's report, however, proved to be inconclusive. It failed to demonstrate that the Vatican officials were guilty of wrongdoing and further failed to remove the suspicion of a Vatican conspiracy with Calvi. The Holy See's public relations problem persisted.

Dissatisfied with these findings, Ambrosiano's creditors continued to threaten lawsuits against the Vatican. Archbishop Marcinkus looked upon such threats as little more than efforts at blackmail brought about by the banking community's awareness of the Vatican's vulnerability to malfeasance. He expressed outrage at the proposal advanced by Cardinal Casaroli of resolving the matter quietly, even at a heavy cost. "If we keep sweeping things under the carpet," Marcinkus complained, "after a while it will pile so high we'll stumble on it."[27]

But the matter demanded an immediate settlement. The Italian government initiated a criminal investigation into the affair, while the press persisted in its search for a Vatican connection to the Panamanian companies. Indeed, to the Church's embarrassment, someone had listed the companies in the records of the Banca del Gottarda in Switzerland and attributed their ownership to the Vatican.[28] The radical Rome daily *La Repubblica* began to carry a two-page cartoon on the head of the Vatican Bank entitled "The Adventures of Paul Marcinkus." Marcinkus was not intimidated. Wilton Wynn writes, "Marcinkus saw the threat of lawsuits and the press campaigns as a kind of blackmail to force the Vatican to pay up. He argued that articles were being planted in the press and lawsuits threatened because other banks had gotten burned and they knew the Vatican was an easy target. He insisted that these banks would have fought to the bitter end if they had been in the Vatican's situation. But they knew the Holy See preferred to settled things quietly, even at a heavy cost."[29]

Finally, Pope John Paul II decided to place the affair behind him once and for all. With the approval of his fifteen-man financial advisory commission of cardinals, he offered a "goodwill renumeration" of $250 million to Ambrosiano creditors. On May 25, 1984, the creditors formally accepted this offer in writing at the headquarters of the European Trade Association in Geneva.

The Geneva settlement averted the possibility of a long and damaging court trial for the Vatican, but it did not close the case. The criminal investigation continued on a quiet but persistent course. On February 26, 1987, the investigating magistrates concluded that the Vatican Bank had acted as an umbrella for Calvi's illicit dealings abroad; that it owned a substantial share of Banco Ambrosiano; and that it shared responsibility for the bank's failure.[30] Arrest warrants were issued for the three top Vatican bankers: Archbishop Marcinkus, Luigi Mennini, and Pellegrino del Strobel.

The arrests, however, were not made. To protect its officials, the Vatican pointed to Article Eleven of the Lateran Treaty of 1929, which served to regulate matters between the Holy See and Italy. The article stipulated that there can be no interference by the Italian government in "the central institutions of the Catholic Church."[31] Italy's highest court upheld this article and ruled that Marcinkus and his two colleagues could not be arrested and brought to trial in Italy. As of this writing, the three Vatican bankers remain safe from extradition within the sanctuary of the sovereign state of Vatican City.

19. *What is the present state of Vatican finances?*

On March 9, 1989, the Vatican predicted a record deficit of slightly more than $78 million for the Holy See's operating budget in 1989. Official details of the budget showed that the shortfall will be the largest since the Vatican began releasing selective figures about its finances in the wake of the Ambrosiano affair (1984). The 1988 deficit was $63.8 million. The causes for the 1989 deficit, according to Vatican sources, are threefold: an increase over the past twenty years in the number of offices, committees, and nunciatures to various governments from about 35 to approximately 116; a sharp rise in the salaries of lay workers at the Vatican and their pensions; and a severe drop in the value of the dollar on which the Vatican income depends. A special commission of cardinals appointed by Pope John Paul II to oversee finances and prevent further scandal said that the deficit is expected to increase in 1990 and 1991, and warned that the reserve funds of the Vatican are now depleted. They called for reduction of Vatican spending, undertook steps to increase Peter's Pence, (which in 1988 came to just short of $53 million, most of it contributed by the rich churches of the United States and West Germany), initiated fundraising projects for the Holy See, and advised that the Holy See should regularly publish its balance sheet of incomes and expenditures. The commission further unveiled plans for the reorganization of the Vatican Bank.

The income of the Vatican Bank, which is viewed by the Church as a separate corporate entity, is not included in the financial report.

NOTES

1. John A. Hardon, S. J., *The Catholic Catechism* (Garden City, New York: Doubleday and Company, 1975), p. 383.

2. James Gollin, *Worldly Goods* (New York: Random House, 1971), p. 33.

3. *Ibid.,* p. 497.

4. Malachi Martin, *Rich Church, Poor Church* (New York: G. P. Putnam's Sons, 1984), p. 113.

5. *Ibid.,* p. 114.

6. Will Durant, *The Age of Faith* (New York: Simon and Schuster, 1950), p. 540. See also E. R. Chamberlin, *The Bad Popes* (New York: Dorset Books, 1969), pp. 67–74.

7. Martin, *op. cit.,* p. 124.

8. Durant, *op. cit.,* p. 767.

9. St. Anselm of Canterbury, "Why God Became Man," II, XIX, translated by Eugene R. Fairweather, in *A Scholastic Miscellany*, Vol. X, *The Library of Christian Classics,* edited by John Baillie, John T. McNeill, and Henry P. Van Deusen (Philadelphia: Westminster Press, 1956), pp. 180–81.

10. Martin, *op. cit.,* p. 126.

11. *Ibid.*

12. "Decree of the Council of Trent," Twenty-First Session, Chapter IX, in *Canons and Decrees of the Council of Trent,* translated by H. J. Schroeder, (St. Louis: B. Herder and Company, 1955), p. 142.

13. Martin, *op. cit.,* p. 155.

14. *Ibid.,* p. 159.

15. *Ibid.,* pp. 27–31.

16. *Ibid.,* pp. 40–41.

17. David A. Yallop, *In God's Name* (New York: Bantam Books, 1984), p. 97.

18. Martin, *op. cit.,* pp. 61–62.

19. Wilton Wynn, *Keepers of the Keys: John XXIII, Paul VI and John Paul II— Three Who Changed the Church* (New York: Random House, 1988), p. 158.

20. Wynn, *loc. cit.*

21. *Ibid.*

22. Martin, *op. cit.,* p. 68.

23. *Newsweek,* September 13, 1982, p. 66.

24. *Ibid.,* p. 67.

25. Wynn, *op. cit.,* pp. 167–68.

26. *Time,* September 13, 1982, p. 28.

27. Marcinkus quoted in Wynn's *Keepers of the Keys, op. cit.,* p. 172.

28. *Ibid.,* p. 166.

29. Wynn, *op. cit.,* p. 172.

30. *Ibid.*

31. *Ibid.,* p. 174.

SEVENTEEN

The Eighth Commandment:

Forbidden Books and Films

. . . It is necessary to apply to the cinema a supreme rule which must direct and regulate the highest art in order that it may not find itself in continual conflict with Christian morality, or even simply with human morality based upon natural law. The essential purpose of art, its *raison d'être,* is to assist in the perfecting of the moral personality, which is man. For this reason, it must be moral. . . .

Pope Pius XI, "On Motion Pictures" *(Vigilanti Cura),* 1936

1. *What does the eighth commandment, You shall not bear false witness against your neighbor, oblige Christians to do?*

Positively, that they speak the truth; negatively, that they foreswear lying, lying under oath, revealing in public other people's private faults (detraction), worse, telling public lies about them (calumny), and so forth. With the invention first of the printing press, then daily newspapers, and in our times electronic media and computer devices of all kinds, the harm done by false witness can be irreparable, especially when committed outside of the courtroom.[1]

2. *Is there any way to protect the community from public detractors, pornographers, and other serious abuses of free speech?*

Normally, public authority limits expressions that are a threat to the stability of the body politic or to public morals. When citizens agree on what those threats are, legislators have an easier time protecting the common good than when people are generally opposed to limitations on freedom at all. Nonetheless, most people recognize the right of government to protect itself from potential seditionists, traitors, criminals, child abusers, and so forth. Civil courts judge cases and determine penalties for those who misuse speech or publish material that exceeds bounds of freedom defined in law. The state often censors published material, certainly during wartime or plague or rioting, which endangers the freedom of other citizens to live in peace. Usually, private citizens can only censor their own works out of deference to public opinion. Practically, they have no authority to exercise strict censorship.

3. *What, therefore, is censorship?*

It is an action by which public authority controls, limits, or suppresses expressions or public displays that threaten the common good.

4. Are picket lines or boycotts forms of censorship?

No, they are in reality means of persuasion because pickets and boycotters cannot enforce the restrictions they propose. In principle, these actions are forms of public enlightenment, although devotees of absolute freedom wrongly call them censorship. Criticism, even if highly organized, is not censorship.

5. What is the attitude of the Catholic Church to such things as censorship and boycotts?

As long ago as 1957 the U.S. bishops granted the right of civil authority to safeguard public morals but suggested that it hold for freedom more than for restraint, and restraint only as a last resort. The Church is also a long-time defender of the legitimacy of strikes and boycotts, correctly used.

6. Does the Church practice censorship?

Yes, for reasons not dissimilar to those of the state, except that the motive in the Church's case is the salvation of souls and the protection of the faithful from false teachers or from those who would corrupt Christian morals. Ecclesiastical censorship began with St. Paul at Ephesus, when books on magic were burned (Acts 19:19). In the fifth century, St. Augustine submitted his works to others for prior censorship. Universities enacted censorship laws in the thirteenth century.

7. How does the Church apply censorship in practice?

Almost every major diocese has a censor appointed by the bishop to examine writings before their publication to make sure that they contain nothing contrary to Catholic doctrine. The censor conveys his approval of the given work by giving a *Nihil Obstat* (Nothing Stands in the Way), which permits the bishop to grant his *Imprimatur* (Let it Be Printed). In normal times, both authors and publishers are pleased to have *Imprimaturs* on their books as a seal of official Catholic approval. During times of ecclesiastical upheaval, there is a tendency to publish books that distort or deny the faith, usually without an *Imprimatur* or with one carelessly given.

8. *Does the Church censor all books?*

No. Censorship is only required for the following books: (1) books of holy Scripture as well as commentaries or annotations on any part of Scripture; (2) books that deal with Scripture, theology, Church history, canon law, natural theology, and ethics; (3) books of prayer and all works of a devotional, ascetic, catechetical, or mystical nature; and (4) all books that contain sacred images or pictures.[2]

9. *What was the* Index Librorum Prohibitorum?

In the sixteenth century, with the advent of the mass production of manuscripts, the Church initiated the *Index Librorum Prohibitorum* (The List of Forbidden Books) to safeguard the flock from works that might corrupt faith and morals. By 1966, the list had become unwieldy. Moreover, with more and more books being produced through advance technology in the printing industry, it had become impossible for the Congregation of the Doctrine of Faith to keep an up-to-date list of all the works that stood in opposition to Catholic doctrine. Therefore, the publication of the *Index* came to an end in 1966 with a reminder that Catholics should still be alert to doctrinal error.

10. *What books had been condemned by the* Index?

The *Index* condemned the works of the Reformers, anti-Catholic tracts, and non-Catholic versions of the Scriptures. In addition, it prohibited the reading of many works of philosophy and fiction. Most of these works were by French writers, including Victor Hugo's *Les Miserables;* Pascal's *Pensées;* and the complete works of Jean-Jacques Rousseau, Voltaire, Ernst Renan, and Stendhal. The most prominent modern writers on the list were André Gide, Jean-Paul Sartre, and Alberto Moravia.

The *Index* was never systematic, an unlikely expectation in a worldwide Church. Georges Sand, for instance, was condemned for indecency but not D. H. Lawrence, Émile Zola's *Nana* but not James Joyce's *Ulysses.*[3]

11. *How does the Church protect the faithful today from erroneous or harmful publications?*

The New Code of Canon Law (Canons 822–32) places responsibility on pastors to be vigilant about harmful books and to denounce them, as necessary. Their special concern must be directed to the following books: (1) books of sacred Scriptures and their vernacular translations; (2) liturgical books and their translations; (3) prayer books; (4) text books on religious matters; (5) decrees of ecclesiastical authority; (6) publications that attack the Catholic religion or good morals. In most cases, these books require approval by ecclesiastical authority: bishops are to supervise the writings of clerics and their appearance on television or radio.

12. *What was the Legion of Decency?*

In April 1934, the American bishops established the Legion of Decency for the purpose of establishing norms for judging the moral contents of films. When the suggested Code was pressed upon the Hollywood producers, they, at first, refused to accept it. In response, the United States bishops gathered written pledges from eleven million Americans, all swearing they would boycott the films of any studio that failed to adopt the Code as its standard policy for production. Hollywood set up its own machinery, with Judge Will Hays as "movie czar," declaring films objectionable or unobjectionable.

Movies avoided all scenes of gross brutality and sexual promiscuity. Illegal or immoral lifestyles were not to be treated favorably. Marriage was depicted as a sacred institution. Certain words, such as *sex,* were forbidden.[4]

In 1936, Pope Pius XI issued an encyclical "On Motion Pictures" *(Vigilanti Cura)* in which he praised the Legion of Decency for its salubrious effect on the film industry: "Because of your vigilance and because of the pressure which has been brought to bear by public opinion, the motion picture has shown improvement from the moral standpoint: crime and vice are portrayed less frequently; sin no longer is so openly approved or acclaimed; false ideals of life no longer are presented in so flagrant a manner to the impressionable minds of youth."[5]

Minor infractions of the Code resulted in a film being classified as morally objectionable, while major infractions—such as the use of the word *virgin* in Otto Preminger's 1953 film *The Moon Is Blue*—resulted in the film being condemned. Such condemnation had severe effects at the box office, since Catholics were directed not to see such works under the threat of mortal sin.

In the wake of Vatican II, the Code began to break down. This was first evidenced by the Legion's acceptance of *Who's Afraid of Virginia Woolf* in 1966 as permissible viewing for discerning adults. Gradually, the Legion in the name of art became more and more lenient. By 1969, it approved as "morally acceptable for adults" a film entitled *Medium Cool* that had received an "X" rating from the Motion Picture Association of America. Several years later, it condemned *Dirty Harry* for its excessive violence, while granting an "A-4" (acceptable for adults) rating for *The Exorcist*. Perplexed critics, such as Colin L. Westerbeck, could not understand how the Legion could condemn a film in which the protagonist triumphs over evil, while it accepted another in which evil overcomes the power of the cross.[6]

In 1973, the Legion was disbanded and replaced by the United States Catholic Conference (USCC) Department of Film and Broadcasting, later to become the Department of Communications.

13. *Does the Church still condemn movies?*

No. The USCC Department of Communications, however, rates some films as being "morally offensive." Recent films to merit this rating include *Bull Durham, Rambo III, Die Hard,* and *The Last Temptation of Christ.*

NOTES

1. John A. Hardon, S. J., *The Catholic Catechism* (Garden City, New York: Doubleday and Company, 1975), p. 41.

2. Richard C. Broderick, *The Catholic Encyclopedia* (New York: Thomas Nelson, Inc., 1975), p. 102.

3. Bernard Wall, "The Index Librorum," in *Versions of Censorship,* edited by John McCormick and Marie MacInnes (Garden City, New York: Anchor Books, 1962), pp. 47–51.

4. Gerald Mast, *A Short History of the Movies,* 3rd edition (Indianapolis: Bobbs-Merrill Educational Publishing, 1981), p. 219.

5. Pope Pius XI, "On Motion Pictures *(Vigilanti Cura)"* (Washington, D.C.: National Catholic Welfare Conference, 1936), p. 5.

6. Colin L. Westerbeck, quoted in Gail Linda Robinson's "Censorship and the Contemporary Cinema," in *An Intellectual Freedom Primer,* edited by Charles H. Busha (Littleton, Colorado: Libraries Unlimited, 1977), p. 181.

EIGHTEEN

The Forgiveness

of Sins

All the faithful of both sexes shall after they have reached the age of discretion faithfully confess all their sins at least once a year to their own priest and perform to the best of their ability the penance imposed, receiving reverently at least at Easter the sacrament of the Eucharist, unless perchance at the advice of their own priest they may for a good reason abstain; otherwise they shall be cut off from the Church during life and deprived of a Christian burial in death.

The Fourth Lateran Council, 1215, Canon XXI

1. *What is the sacrament of penance?*

It is a holy rite (sacrament) of the Church instituted by Christ for the purpose of reconciling sinners to God for sins they committed after baptism. Reconciling sinners with God is the function of all revealed religion, Jewish or Christian. It is Catholic teaching that members of the Church in serious sin normally restore their relationship to God through this sacrament by the will of Christ, who, on the first Easter night, told the apostles: "Receive the Holy Spirit. If you forgive the sins of any, they are forgiven; if you retain the sins of any, they are retained." (John 20:23). From the beginning of the Church, penance and the forgiveness of sins were essential facts of Christian belief based on Christ forgiving sin Himself. (Matt. 9:8) and then conferring on his apostles the power of binding and loosing. What they bind or loose, God binds or looses (Matt. 18:18).

2. *What is involved in the sacrament of penance?*

For the forgiveness of sin by means of this rite, the Catholic must be sorry for his (or her) sins, confess them to a priest, receive his absolution, and promise to do the penance imposed on him, as reparation for his sins.

3. *Is "forgiveness of sins" through ritual a Christian invention?*

The Catholic practice of "auricular confession," private confession of sin directed to the ear of a priest, is actually rooted in Jewish tradition. According to the law of Moses, the Torah, a transgression against the Commandments constituted a break in the covenant between God and the people of Israel that had to be amended by an act of restitution. Such acts consisted of sacrifices and sin offerings, prayers and lamentations, fastings and fines, property restitutions and corporal

punishments.[1] Moreover, in order to keep the people pure and undefiled, the high priest each year on the Day of Attonement confessed
the corporate sins of the nation to God. Afterward, he placed his hand
on the head of a live goat, signifying the transference of these iniqui-
ties into the body of the beast. The goat was then driven far into the
wilderness (Lev. 16:21). Jewish law further required the confession of
individual sins, such as the touching of anything unclean or the utter-
ing of a rash oath (Lev. 5:16). By the time of Jesus, rabbinical books
suggested that the confession of such sins to a rabbi constituted a
sincere act of repentance. The rabbi, upon hearing the confession, was
to prescribe a suitable means of atonement, such as sleeping on the
ground, wearing sackcloth and ashes, almsgiving, prayer, and fasting.[2]
This practice persisted in the early Church. James, in his Epistle, advised Christians to confess their sins to one another that they might be
healed (5:16). By 230, Origen advised his fellow believers to confess
their sins to their spiritual leaders, who possessed the fruits of the Holy
Spirit.[3] And St. Cyprian, a decade later, spoke of such confession as
salutary medicine for the sickness of sin.[4]

4. What do we know about the practice of penance in the early Church?

Not as much as we would like. It was one thing for Christ to tell
the apostles to forgive sins, quite another for the apostles and their
successors to know what this would mean in practice. Furthermore,
the extant documents from two thousand years ago are few in number. We do know that St. Paul excommunicated an incestuous Christian (1 Cor. 5:5) and pardoned another "in the person of Christ" (2
Cor. 2:11). These are considered sacramental acts of binding and loosing. Pope Clement I (92–101) the third successor of Peter, makes clear
that penance for the forgiveness of sin was a common Christian belief,
but does not specify how this was being accomplished in the Rome of
his time. During the second and third centuries, controversy broke out
whether sins committed after baptism could be forgiven more than
once, and whether grave sins such as adultery, homicide, idolatry, or
apostasy could be forgiven at all. The Greek Orthodox, the earliest
part of the Eastern Church, recognize penance as a sacrament, as do
many Anglo-Catholics and Lutherans. What records of the early

Church we do have indicate a process of development in the discipline.

5. *Was the penance private, as it is today?*

Not so far as we can judge from the records. The penitential discipline then was public for the most part. The first step involved was confession to the bishop or in the large churches to a priest-penitentiary. After confession, the sinner was enrolled in the order of penitents. Whether or not the sinner was exhorted or obliged to confess to the community, his or her secret sins is not known.

6. *What was the ritual of forgiveness in those centuries?*

Ordinary or routine sin (so-called *quotidiana* by Tertullian and others) could be forgiven through the process of confession, Holy Communion, and good works. But not so mortal sin—*crimena mortalis*—such as adultery, fraud, manslaughter, and apostasy.[5] The early Church stressed one ritual for the forgiveness of such transgressions: baptism. And since there could only be one baptism, there could be no forgiveness of mortal sin after baptism. This explains why bishops were called upon to officiate at all rituals of baptism in primitive Christianity. Only the bishops possessed the sacerdotal power to forgive sins through their "vicarious ordination" as apostles.[6]

Throughout the first three Christian centuries, the words of Jesus to his disciples in John 20:22–23 ("Receive the Holy Spirit. If you forgive the sins of any; they are forgiven; if you retain the sins of any, they are retained") were interpreted in relationship to baptism. St. Cyprian testified to this by writing: "It is in baptism that we all of us receive the remission of sins. Now the Lord proves this in his Gospel that sins can be remitted only through those who possess the Holy Spirit. For when he sent his disciples out after the Resurrection, he said this, 'As the Father hath sent me, even so I send you.' And when he said this, he breathed on them and saith unto them, 'Receive ye the Holy Ghost; whose soever sins ye remit, they shall be remitted unto him; whose soever sins ye retain, they shall be retained.' This passage shows that only he who possesses the Holy Spirit can baptize."[7]

7. What happened to those who committed scandalous sins after baptism?

In accordance with the teachings of St. Paul, they were driven from the Church and handed over to Satan: "I wrote to you not to associate with anyone who bears the name of brother if he is guilty of immorality or greed, or is an idolater, reviler, drunkard, or robber—not even to eat with such a one. For what have I to do with judging outsiders? Is it not those inside the Church whom you are to judge? God judges those outside. Drive the wicked person from among you" (1 Cor. 5:11–13). The Christian community as the "body of Christ" was to be kept "holy, blameless and undefiled" (Heb. 7:26)

During the first Christian centuries, those accused—even self-suspected—of committing a mortal sin were brought to bishops who were held on the authority of Jesus to possess the rabbinical power of binding and loosing sin (Matt. 16:19; John 20:23). Those judged guilty of such sin were bound to their transgressions and excommunicated from the Church. Those who were judged innocent were loosed from their transgressions and received back into the fellowship. However, there was no way back through works of mercy or tears of remorse for those who were bound.

8. When and why did the Church soften this strict teaching?

The first sign of softening in the belief of no forgiveness of mortal sin after baptism appeared between 100 and 130 in a document called "The Shepherd of Hermas." In this document, Hermas relates the following mandate which was conveyed to him by a vision:

"Sir," I said (to the vision), "I have been told by some teachers that there is no other repentance except the one (that was vouchsafed us) when we went into the water and received remission of our former sins." He said to me: "You have been correctly told; such is the case. For, the person who has received remission of sins must no longer sin, but live in purity. However, since you are enquiring accurately into everything, I shall clarify the matter for you, without giving an excuse either to those who now believe or are destined to believe on the Lord. For, those who now believe or are destined to believe do not have repentance for sins, but they do have remission of their former sins. The Lord, then, has prescribed repentance for those who were called before these days. For, the Lord has knowledge of hearts and knows all things in advance, the weakness of human beings and cunning craft of the Devil, the evil he will do to the servants of God and his wickedness against them. Therefore, the Lord in His exceeding mercy took pity on His creatures and prescribed the occasion for repentance. Authority over this repentance He has given to me. But this I say to you," he said. "After that solemn and holy call, if a man sins after severe temptation by the Devil, he has one chance of repentance. But if he sins and repents offhandedly, it is unprofitable for such a man. Only with difficulty will he live."[8]

This teaching of a second repentance caught hold in many Christian communities in the wake of periods of widespread persecution. Faced with torture or death, many Christians renounced the faith and made sacrifices to the pagan gods. Others managed to purchase certificates that attested to their offering of such sacrifices. When the persecutions subsided, many of these lapsed Christians sought reentry into the Church. Some bishops refused such requests on the basis of 1 Corinthians 5:11–13. Others took a more lenient view and said that such grievous sinners could be received back into fellowship after a period of severe purgation for their idolatry but only once, since repeated forgiveness would make a mockery of God's mercy. They, including St. Clement of Alexandria, justified this on the basis of 2 Corinthians 2:5–11, in which St. Paul urged forgiveness for a person who had caused pain to the congregation since he displayed signs of true repentance. Tertullian spoke of this one chance of forgiveness as a single spar adrift in a tempestuous sea to which sinners must cling for salvation. Elsewhere, he described it as the sole antidote to the poisons of Satan that could be administered but once.[9]

This antidote to *crimena mortalia* was painful. Such penitents stood outside the primitive Church in sackcloth and ashes begging the brethren to pray for them. Those who sought a bath or a change of clothing or meat or drink were not deemed worthy of forgiveness. They were expected to spend their days and nights in fasting and prayer, mortifying their flesh and making "outcries of loud lamentation." Only by this severe discipline of repentance, called "exomologesis," could heinous sin be forgiven. Tertullian wrote: ". . . while it exomologesis abases a man, it raises him; while it covers him with squalor, it renders him clean; while it accuses, it excuses; while it condemns, it absolves."[10] Absolution, therefore, was brought about by the process of this discipline, not by a pronouncement.

The process could last for months, even years. When at last the congregation was convinced that the conversion of the sinner was complete, the bishop imposed hands on him as a sign of his reacceptance into the community.[11]

9. *What was the influence of the Council of Nicaea?*

Early heresies (such as Montanism) denied the bishop's right to forgive those guilty of serious sins. The Church's first General Council (325) responded with a condemnation and a demand that reconciliation be conducted according to Catholic norms.

10. *How did the penitential system change once the Church emerged from the catacombs?*

After the Council of Nicaea in 325, the penitential system became standardized throughout Christianity, and several classes of penitents could be easily distinguished within and without the Church. Outside the gates of the Church stood the "weepers," who were covered with sackcloth and ashes, prostrate at the feet of the faithful, begging for their prayers as they entered the churchyard. Inside the gates stood the catechumens (those preparing for baptism) and the "hearers," who were allowed to hear the Scriptures and the sermon but were dismissed before the celebration of the Eucharist. In the back of the Church were the "kneelers," who were allowed to remain in the nave and to join in the recitation of certain prayers. Before being dismissed with the catechumens and hearers, they prostrated themselves before the bishop and begged for God's mercy. The Church, an historian of the time said, echoed with their wailing and lamenting.[12] The bishop imposed his hands upon them and recited a prayer of exorcism. The last group of penitents were the "co-standers" or *consistentes* who were allowed to remain after the other penitents were dismissed but were not allowed to partake of Holy Communion.[13]

This organization of penitents into various classes or grades was promulgated by the practice of canonical penance and persisted for the next four hundred years.

11. *What was canonical penance?*

During the fourth century, bishops were appointed to serve as judges in civil disputes and their decisions were enforced by Roman law. They conformed to their juridical position in dress, manner, means of address, and thought. As they pronounced sentences on wrongdoers in the name of the Emperor, so they pronounced penances on sinners in the name of God. These penances became regulated by directives and codified into "canons" or "rules" (in the same manner in which Roman law was codified). The list of mortal sins, at this time, was greatly increased and became distinguished by form and degree of gravity. Repentance, which was originally understood as the process by which a sinner reestablished his proper relationship with God, became regarded as a penalty imposed for a violation of a canon of the Church. Long and severe penances were deemed necessary to meet the demands of divine justice, in the same manner that long prison sentences were meted out to meet the letter of Roman law.[14]

Outside of this canonical system—with the bishop pronouncing sentence—there was no means of forgiveness of mortal sin. Private repentance to God or a priest was not enough. St. Augustine voiced this by writing: ". . . those who govern the Church have rightly appointed times of penitence, that the Church in which the sins are remitted may be satisfied, and outside the Church sins are not remitted. . . ."[15]

12. *Describe these "canons" for mortal sin.*

A list of the standard canons is found in a letter by St. Basil the Great. Those who denied Christ were deemed the most serious sinners and were assigned to serve as "weepers" for the rest of their lives. Such sinners could only receive the sacrament of Holy Communion in the hour of death. Those guilty of homicide, sorcery, or incest were to be excommunicated for twenty years: four years as "weepers," five as "hearers," seven as "kneelers," and four as "co-standers" without communion. Adulterers and homosexuals were to be excommunicated for fifteen years: four as "weepers," five as "hearers," four as "kneelers," and two as "co-standers." Perjurers and tomb-breakers were to be excommunicated for ten years: two as "weepers," three as "hearers," four as "kneelers," and one as "co-standers."[16]

13. What happened to the practice of canonical penance?

Few Christians were willing to undergo the rigors and humiliation of public penance. For this reason, they either deferred confessing their mortal sins until they were on their death beds and were assured of receiving forgiveness in accordance with the teachings of the Council of Nicaea, or they postponed baptism until they were late in life. The latter was the most common practice, since one could recover from an illness after receiving the second repentance, only later to lapse without any hope for forgiveness. Constantine refused to be baptized until the day of his death. St. Monica was unwilling to submit St. Augustine to baptism, even when he became seriously ill. And St. Ambrose only consented to baptism upon being consecrated as Bishop of Milan at the age of thirty-four.[17]

14. How did private confession come into common practice in Catholicism?

Private confession throughout this time persisted in the Church for sins that were not deemed "deadly" to the soul. By the fourth century, a canon of the Church specified that those in religious life (monks, nuns, priests, etcetera) should not be subjected to public penance because of the disgrace this might cause the Church. Therefore, the religious (especially monks within the confines of communal life) developed their own penitential system of private confession for mortal and less serious *(leviora)* sins.

In 440, the monks who became the first missionaries to Ireland brought this penitential system with them. As itinerant ministers in an uncivilized land, they found it impossible to impose the system of canonical penance on the Celtic converts, who repeatedly turned back to their barbaric ways. Moreover, since the monks had to cover great distances, they could not always be on hand to grant the final forgiveness of sins to those who were dying. And so, they imposed the same means of forgiving serious and "routine" sins on their flock that they employed with their fellow clerics in the monastery. On one trip, they would hear the confessions of the tribesfolk and assign suitable penances. On a second trip, they would ensure that the penances were preformed and then would pray with the penitents to ask the favor of God's forgiveness. Not being bishops, they did not impose hands on the penitents: they merely imparted a blessing through the sign of the cross.[18]

By the sixth century, the monks of Ireland began to employ penitential books to bring a measure of uniformity to the penances prescribed for certain sins. On one side of such books was the sin, and, on the opposite side, the correct penalty or "tariff" to be paid. For example, concerning the sin of gluttony, one book held the following: "He who suffers excessive distention of the stomach and the pain of sateity shall do penance (of total fasting) for one day. If he suffers to the point of vomiting, though he is not in a state of infirmity, he shall do penance for seven days."[19]

At this same time, Ireland and England had been thoroughly Christianized, and the Celtic monks embarked on the mission of spreading the Gospel to barbarian tribes throughout continental Europe. Within a few years, they traveled prodigious distances, founding monasteries, building churches, and establishing schools in France, Switzerland, northern Italy, and Spain. And wherever they went, they brought their penitential system with them.[20]

The Church, at first, looked with grave displeasure upon this practice of private penance as a means of cheapening forgiveness by violating the dogma (since it had been canonically defined by the Council of Nicaea) of one repentance after baptism. The regional Synod of Toledo, for example, in 589 condemned the practice by stating: "We have heard that in some churches in Spain the faithful are doing penance not in accordance with the canonical rule but in another detestable way, that is, they ask a priest to grant them pardon as many times as it pleases them to sin. We wish to put an end to this abominable presumption, and, accordingly this sacred council decrees that penances should be given in the manner prescribed by the ancient canons."[21] As late as 813, the bishops of France at councils in Reims,

Tours, and Chalon-sur-Saône called for the restoration of the ancient penitential discipline and condemned the penitential books as filled with errors and written by misguided authors.[22]

But it proved to be impossible to uproot the Irish system. The penitential books continued to proliferate, and the new discipline to spread. "Out of this conflict, Ladislas Orys writes, "a new balance emerged of an enduring yet precarious compromise . . . public penance should be done for public and notorious wrongdoing; private penance was allowed for individual sins. . . ."[23]

By 1215, private penance was so widely accepted that the Fourth Lateran Council decreed that the faithful should confess their sins at least once a year to their own priest.[24]

15. *Are priests held to possess the power to forgive all sins?*

The power of priests to forgive sins is imparted to them by their bishops, who, in turn, inherit the power of binding and loosing sins from the apostles through the process of apostolic succession. For this reason, extraordinary sins (then as now) are often referred to the direct jurisdiction of a bishop or the Pope.

16. *Can Catholic clergy absolve all sins?*

Yes, unless canon law says that absolution is reserved to a higher authority, to the bishop or the Pope for example, as in cases of excommunication. The substantial meaning of excommunication is that the person is deprived of the sacraments. In former days, excommunication also involved separation from other Christians. When King Robert of France was excommunicated in 998 for marrying his first cousin, he was abandoned by all his courtiers and nearly all his servants.[25]

17. *But didn't the practice of private penance constitute a relaxation of Church discipline and give rise to numerous abuses?*

Not at first. The punishments meted out by clerics during the so-called Dark Ages were most severe and served as a deterrent to sin and crime in an age when civil law was almost nonexistent. Typical penances were as follows: for theft, restoration of the stolen property plus compensation; for adultery, payment of damages to the injured party plus total abstinence from sex for the remainder of one's life; for fighting and bloodshed, scourging and a prohibition to carry arms; for murder and other crimes that might arouse vengeance, compulsory pilgrimage, that is, exile.[26]

Since these penances were so severe and could vary in length from a few days for a simple lie to a lifetime for a false oath, by the tenth century priests began to commute penances, substituting shorter but more intense punishments for longer and milder ones, especially in cases when the penitent was ill or of advanced age. Therefore, a year of mild fasting could be commuted to three days of complete abstinence from food and drink coupled with continuous readings from the psalms and self-flagellation.[27]

Abuses soon arose. According to feudal law, it was permissible for one man to accept the punishment of another. For this reason, several penitential books allowed a person to perform a penance for someone else. Feudal lords employed their subjects to fast and pray for them. Moreover, through the use of commutation, it became possible for a nobleman to accomplish a seven-year fast in three days with the aid of a small army by adhering to the following formula:

> The penitent will pay twelve men to fast three days for him on bread, water and vegetables. Then he will get 7×120 men to fast three days. The total of $(12 \times 3) + (120 \times 7 \times 3) = 2,556$ days $= 7$ years.[28]

18. *How did the Church correct such abuses?*

During the twelfth century, the Church began teaching that the forgiveness of sins was contingent not upon the performance of a satisfactory penalty for sin but upon the sinner's state of true contrition, that is, a sorrow for sin based upon a love of God's goodness, and not attrition, that is, a sorrow for sin based upon a fear of God's justice. This teaching was first advanced by Peter Abelard (d. 1142) and later by his disciple Peter Lombard (d. 1160). It was accepted by the fathers of scholasticism, St. Albertus Magnus (d. 1280) and St. Thomas Aquinas (d. 1274), and proclaimed as dogma by the Council of Florence (1438–45).[29]

19. *If contrition is the essential element in forgiveness, why does the Church insist on the need of confessing sins to a priest?*

St. Thomas Aquinas explained the need of auricular confession in terms of the Aristotelian distinction between matter and form. The matter of the sacrament of penance consists of the priest's words, "I absolve you from your sins in the name of the Father, the Son and the Holy Spirit." For St. Thomas, these words possessed true spiritual power and were capable of transforming the sinner's sincere contrition into perfect contrition, thereby removing the guilt of sin.

This teaching was modified by John Duns Scotus (d. 1308), who said that it was not necessary for a man to reach a state of sincere contrition in order for the sacrament to be efficacious (grace-infusing). After all, it is impossible to know when one truly reaches a state of repentance based on an unadulterated love of God. Christ, Scotus argued, instituted the sacrament as a sure means of obtaining forgiveness. All that is required from the sinner is a sense of sorrow for his offenses, even if this sorrow is caused by imperfect contrition or attrition. When the words of absolution are spoken, he continued, grace is infused *ex opere operato* into the soul of the sinner, purifying it of foulness of sin.[30] This teaching, which was set forth as dogma by the Council of Trent (1545–63), firmly established the role of the priest and the sacramental effects of absolution in bold and precise language.

20. *If sin is held to be absolved by the priest* ex opere operato, *what is the purpose of performing acts of penance?*

Scotus drew a critical distinction between the guilt or *culpa* and the penalty or *poena* of sin. Through the sacrament of penance, God in his mercy removes the guilt or *culpa* of sin and thereby saves the penitent (in the case of mortal sin) from eternal damnation. But each sin must be punished in order to meet the demands of God's justice. Therefore, it is necessary for a priest to prescribe a fitting punishment or *poena* for each offense. This punishment could be either voluntarily endured in this life or involuntarily endured in the fires of Purgatory.

21. *Why did Luther reject the Catholic teaching on penance?*

Luther was really ambivalent in his views on penance. In his early writings, he spoke of it as a sacrament. In his later writings, he did not. Throughout his career, he resisted all attempts to do away with the practice of private confession. He wrote: "Yes, I would rather have the Pope's tyranny of fasting, ceremony, vestments, serving trays, capes and whatever else I could stand without doing violence to my faith, than have confession taken away from Christians."[31]

However, he rejected the belief that true contrition or any other "work" by man could merit God's forgiveness. Christ, he said, had earned forgiveness once and for all by His death on the cross. This forgiveness could be appropriated to man by faith alone. Since confession merely permitted Christians to realize that the blood of Christ covered their sins and that they should rejoice in their salvation. Therefore, the effect of confession was not a metaphysical cleansing of sin but an experience of peace that came from faith in Christ's work.

22. *Did the Council of Trent alter the teachings of the medieval Church on penance?*

No. Trent reaffirmed that the sacrament of penance consisted of the components of contrition, confession, absolution, and satisfaction. Regarding contrition, the Council held that perfect contrition "reconciles man with God before the sacrament is actually received." However, such contrition must include the ardent desire to receive the sacrament. Moreover, imperfect contrition is sufficient for a valid reception of penance, since fear "is a gift of God and an impulse of the Holy Ghost."[32]

Regarding confession, the Council said that penitents must enumerate their sins so that the priest as a judge will be permitted to weigh the gravity of the offenses in order to impose a proper penalty.

Regarding absolution, the Council maintained that the words of the priest *(Ego te absolvo)* were not merely an announcement of God's forgiveness but a pronouncement by the priest acting in God's name through the power imparted to the Church by Christ.

Regarding satisfaction, the Council decreed: "We should not have our sins forgiven without any satisfaction, for otherwise we would be tempted to regard sins lightly and offend the Holy spirit by falling into more serious sin." It ordered priests not "to wink at sins and deal too indulgently with penitents" by imposing "very light works for serious sins."[33] Such works were to be viewed as deterrents to crime and a means of making just restitution to the honor of God.

23. What is the "seal of confession"?

By canon law, priests are prohibited from disclosing anything that is related to them in sacramental confession. This "seal" of absolute secrecy applies whether the confession was finished or not, whether it was worthy or sacrilegious and whether absolution was given or not.[34] No exception is allowed for breaking this seal without the permission of the penitent, not even to save someone's life or to promote the common welfare. This teaching was first promulgated as follows by the Fourth Lateran Council:

> Let him (the priest) constantly take care, lest by word or sign or any other way whatsoever he may at any time betray a sinner. But if he should need more prudent counsel, he should seek it cautiously without any mention of the person, since he who shall presume to reveal a sin entrusted to him in confession, we decree not only must be deposed from priestly office but must also be thrust into a strict monastery to do perpetual penance.[35]

24. Whence come confessional boxes or "confessionals"?

Confessionals were instituted by the Church in 1611 as a means of insuring the anonymity of penitents. Such anonymity was deemed particularly necessary for women guilty of sexual offenses.[36]

25. What changes did Vatican II effect in penitential practices?

In 1963, Vatican II called for the renewal of the liturgy that would be more in conformity with the tradition of penance in the Church and at the same time more properly responsive to the needs of the people. Ten years later, to accentuate the public reconciliation of the sinner with the Church also, the Sacred Congregation for the Sacraments and Divine Worship authorized three rites of penance—one private, one semiprivate and one public. The private rite was an adaptation of the former Tridentine rite that was to be administered in a confessional, or, under the proper circumstances, in a face-to-face setting. The semi-private rite began with a prayer service consisting of hymns and readings from the Scriptures, after which the members of the congregation made individual confessions to the priest. The public rite was to be reserved for emergencies or cases in which the number of penitents, who would have no other opportunity to receive the sacrament for a long time, was too great for the number of confessors *(Misericordiam Suam,* 31). It consisted of an opening ceremony of prayers, Scripture readings, silent confessions of sin to God, an invocation for forgiveness, and a pronouncement of absolution.

26. *How do Catholics make an act of auricular confession?*

The penitent enters the confessional and kneels before the priest himself or a screen that separates the priest from the penitent, who makes the sign of the cross and says, "Bless me, father, for I have sinned." He (or she) then relates the time of his last confession. The priest invites the penitent to have confidence in God's forgiveness. The penitent next delineates his sins in an integral manner, listing the offense and the number of times it was committed. The priest then imposes a penance, which usually consists of the recitation of a number of prayers, and asks the penitent to make an act of contrition. This act consists of the recitation of the following prayer:

> O my God, I am heartily sorry for having offended you, and I detest all my sins, because I dread the loss of heaven and the pains of hell, but most of all because I have offended you, my God, who are all-good and deserving of all my love. I firmly resolve, with the help of your grace, to confess my sins, to do penance, and to amend my life. Amen.

The priest blesses the penitent and says: "I absolve you from your sins in the name of the Father and of the Son and of the Holy Ghost."

27. *Is it permissible for Catholics to receive Communion before going to confession?*

Not if the communicant is in a state of serious sin. Vatican II, in its document "On the Eucharist Mystery" *(Eucharist Mysterium),* as promulgated in 1967, stated the following: "The precept 'let a man examine himself' (1 Cor. 11:28) should be called to mind for those who wish to receive communion. The custom of the Church declares this to be necessary, so that no one who is conscious of having committed mortal sin, even if he believes himself to be contrite, should approach the holy Eucharist without first making a sacramental confession."

28. What is the difference between mortal and venial sin?

A "mortal" sin is a willful transgression of the law of God. Such a transgression is called "deadly" because it kills the grace in the soul of the believers. In the early Church, as previously stated, apostasy, murder, and adultery were looked upon as deserving everlasting punishment. This list was considerably expanded with the emergence of canonical penance in the fourth century. By the twelfth century, such sins were distinguished from "venial" or "pardonable" sins, which do not separate believers from the grace or fellowship of God. This often fine distinction between mortal and venial sin gave rise with the advent of the exact sciences in the seventeenth century to painstakingly scrupulous analyses of the quantitative and objective aspects of sin. In certain penitential works of this period, priests were instructed that the theft of one to five ears of corn from a rich man's harvest constituted no sin; the theft of six to ten ears venial sin; and any amount beyond that mortal sin.[37] The Church maintains such fine lines, and in every age, sometimes drawing on Scripture, sometimes on the nature or circumstance of the dead, sometimes on the intention of the evil-doer, teaches what kinds of gravely evil acts merit eternal separation from God.

29. What kinds of sins would be considered mortal today?

The Church continues to view the following sins as mortal: deadly violence against another human being, grand theft, denial of the faith, marriage outside of the Church, blasphemy, false oath taking, adultery, abortion, fornication, contraception, regularly missing Mass, and other flagrant violation of the commandments of God and the Church. However, in several "progressive" Catholic communities,

confessors are apt not to speak of mortal or venial sins but of fundamental options.

30. What is the "fundamental option"?

Fundamental option, according to Bernard Haring in Free and Faithful
in Christ (Volume One) is a phrase to describe a persistent attitude or
will that shapes a person's life.[38] For example, a person can choose a
fundamentally selfish lifestyle, which leads him or her to a series of
evil acts against God and others, or a lifestyle that is basically loving
and disposes him or her to good for God and others. This system of
classifying lifestyles does not easily permit the categorizing of sins into
mortal or venial transgressions. A person, for example, may be engaged in a array of sinful activities, but as long as he or she is true to a
basic stance for good, he or she is not in a condition of mortal sin. In
1975, the Sacred Congregation for the Doctrine of the Faith in its
"Declaration on Certain Problems of Sexual Ethics" (Personae
Humanae) condemned this view by saying: "It is scarcely correct to say
that individual actions are not sufficient to constitute mortal sin."

31. Are Catholics still faithful in receiving this sacrament?

Nowhere is the malaise within modern Catholicism more apparent
than in the decline of the sacrament of penance. In a recent Gallup
poll, less than 18 percent of the practicing Catholics surveyed admitted
to going to confession within the last month. Indeed, the practice of
confession, according to the 1986 National Conference of Catholic
Bishops, has come perilously close to total disappearance.[39] Many
older Catholics say they will never return to it. Many of the young
have never heard of it. "The keys to the kingdom," quipped one
commentator, "are growing rusty."

NOTES

1. Joseph Martos, Doors to the Sacred (Garden City, New York: Image Books,
1982), p. 312.
   2. Ibid.

3. Origen, quoted in Thomas Bokenkotter, *Essential Catholicism: Dynamics of Faith and Belief* (Garden City, New York: Image Books, 1985), p. 222.

4. St. Cyprian, "On the Lapsed," 28, translated by Ernest Wallis, in *Fathers of the Third Century*, Vol. V, *The Ante Nicene Fathers*, edited by Alexander Roberts and James Donaldson (Grand Rapids: William B. Eerdmans Publishing Company, 1981), p. 445.

5. Tertullian, *De Pudicitia*, 21, in *Early Latin Theology*, translated by S. L. Greenslade, Vol. V, *The Library of Christian Classics*, edited by John Baillie, John T. McNeill, Henry P. Van Deusen (Philadelphia: Westminster Press, 1956), p. 75; St. Cyprian, "On the Advantage of Patience," 14, in *Fathers of the Third Century, op. cit.*, p. 488.

6. St. Cyprian, "Letter LXXIV," 16, in *Fathers of the Third Century, op. cit.*, p. 394.

7. St. Cyprian, "Letter 69," in *Early Latin Theology, op. cit.*, p. 157.

8. "The Shepherd of Hermas," Mandate III, in *The Apostolic Fathers*, translated by Joseph M. F. Marique, Vol. I, *The Fathers of the Church*, edited by Ludwig Schopp et al. (New York: Cima Publishing Company, 1947), p. 264.

9. Tertullian, "On Repentance," X, translated by S. Thelerall, in *Latin Christianity, Its Founder, Tertullian*, Vol. III, *The Ante Nicene Fathers*, (edited by Alexander Roberts and James Donaldson (Grand Rapids: William B. Eerdmans Publishing Company, 1980), p. 664.

10. *Ibid.*

11. Martos, *op. cit.*, p. 317.

12. Hermias Sozomen, *Ecclesiastica Historia*, VII, 16, quoted in *Ibid.*, pp. 324–25.

13. Henry R. Percival, trans. and ed., *The Seven Ecumenical Councils of the Undivided Church*, (New York: Edwin S. Gorham, 1901), p. 25.

14. Martos, *op. cit.*, p. 321.

15. St. Augustine, *Enchiridion*, 65, in *St. Augustin: On the Holy Trinity, Doctrinal Treatises and Moral Treatises*, translated by J. F. Shaw, Vol. III, *Nicene and Post Nicene Fathers*, First Series, edited by Philip Schaff (Grand Rapids: William B. Eerdmans Publishing Company, 1956), p. 258; *Ibid.*, p. 322.

16. St. Basil, "Letter CCXVII," in *The Nine Homilies of the Hexaemeron and the Letters of St. Basil The Great*, translated by Blomfield Jackson, Vol. VIII, *Nicene and Post-Nicene Fathers*, Second Series, edited by Philip Schaff (Grand Rapids: William B. Eerdmans Publishing Company, 1955), pp. 256–59.

17. William A. Bausch, *A New Look at the Sacraments* (Mystic, Connecticut: Twenty-Third Publications, 1984), p. 172.

18. Martos, *op. cit.*, p. 330.

19. Bausch, *op. cit.*, pp. 174–75.

20. Martos, *loc. cit.*

21. *Ibid.*

22. Bokenkotter, *op. cit.*, p. 225.

23. Ladislas Orys, *The Evolving Church and the Sacrament of Penance* (Denville, New Jersey: Dimension Books, 1978), p. 44; Also cited in *Ibid.*

24. "The Fourth Lateran Council," Canon 21, in *Disciplinary Decrees of the General Councils,* edited and translated by H. J. Schroeder, O.P. (St. Louis: B. Herder Book Company, 1937), p. 259.

25. Will Durant, *The Age of Faith* (New York: Simon and Schuster, 1950), p. 753.

26. Martos, *op. cit.,* p. 331.

27. *Ibid.,* pp. 332–33.

28. Bausch, *op. cit.,* p. 175.

29. John F. Clarkson, S. J. et al., trans., *The Church Teaches: Documents of the Church* (St. Louis: B. Herder Book Company, 1957), p. 305.

30. Bokenkotter, *op. cit.,* p. 227.

31. Luther's "Letter to Osiander," quoted in Martos, *op. cit.,* p. 346.

32. *Canons and Decrees of the Council of Trent,* translated by H. P. Schroeder, O.P. (London: B. Herder Book Company, 1955), p. 92; see also *Ibid.,* p. 351.

33. Martos, *Ibid.,* p. 352.

34. Hardon, *op. cit.,* p. 406.

35. "Fourth Lateran Council, Canon 21," in *Disciplinary Decrees of the General Councils, loc. cit.*

36. Martos, *op. cit.,* p. 353.

37. Bokenkotter, *op. cit.,* p. 304.

38. Bernard Haring, *Free and Faithful in Christ,* Vol. I, (New York: Seabury Press, 1958), p. 177–88.

39. Bokenkotter, *op. cit.,* p. 234; John J. Gallen and James J. Lapreski, "Penance in Crisis," in *America,* October 10, 1987, p. 217.

NINETEEN

The Doctrine

# of Purgatory

We believe in eternal life. We believe that the souls of all those who die in the grace of Christ—whether they must still make expiation in the fire of Purgatory, or whether from the moment they leave their bodies they are received by Jesus into Paradise like the good thief—go to form that People of God which succeeds death, death which will be totally destroyed on the day of the Resurrection when these souls are reunited with their bodies.

Pope Paul VI, "The *Credo* of the People of God," 1968

1. *Discuss the development of the doctrine of Purgatory.*

The doctrine of Purgatory has a long and complicated history. One source comes from the ancient Judeo-Christian practice of praying for the dead. This practice is mentioned in the Second Book of the Maccabees, a work which is included in the Catholic, albeit not the Protestant, canon of Scripture. The key text for Purgatory in Maccabees concerns the aftermath of a battle in which a number of Hebrew soldiers, all of whom committed the sin of wearing amulets of the idol Jamnia, were slain by the enemy. Before burying these soldiers, Judas Maccabee prayed that their sinful deed might be blotted out. Moreover, he ordered a collection to be taken among his troops to provide for an expiatory sacrifice. The account continues by saying: "In doing this he acted in an excellent and noble way, inasmuch as he had the resurrection of the dead in view; for if he were not expecting the dead to rise again, it would have been useless and foolish to pray for them in death" (12:39–44).

This practice persisted in primitive Christianity. Tertullian, circa 190, praised the salutary custom of making oblations for the deceased on the anniversary of their deaths. However, he added: "If you look in Scripture for a formal law governing these and similar practices, you will find none. It is tradition that justifies them, custom that confirms them, and faith that observes them."[1]

A second source for Purgatory is found in a passage from the Gospel of Matthew in which Jesus speaks as follows about the possibility of redemption in the world to come:

> Therefore I tell you, every sin and blasphemy will be forgiven men, but the blasphemy against the Spirit will not be forgiven. And whoever says a word against the Son of man will be forgiven; but whoever speaks against

the Holy Spirit will not be forgiven, either in this age or in the age to come (12:31–32).

These strands of Scripture and tradition were woven together by St. Augustine in the following passage from his "Confessions" in which he prays for the soul of his mother:

> Therefore, O my praise and my life, O God of my heart, I put aside for a while all her good deeds, for which I give thanks to you with joy, and I now beseech you in behalf of my mother's sins. Hear me for the sake of him who hung upon the tree, of him who now sits at your right hand and makes intercession for us. I know that she was merciful to others and that from her heart she forgave her debtors their debts. Do you also forgive her her debts, if she contracted any in so many years after receiving the water of salvation. Forgive her, Lord, forgive her, I beseech you. Enter not into judgment with her. Let your mercy be exalted above your justice, for your words are true, and you have promised mercy to the merciful. Such you made them to be, for you will have mercy on whom you will have mercy, and you will show mercy to whom you will show mercy.[2]

In his "Commentary on Genesis Against the Manicheans," he spoke of this possibility of forgiveness in the afterlife in connection with a correctional fire *(ignis emandatorius),* which he carefully distinguished from the ever-lasting fire of hell.[3] St. Augustine emphasized the difficulties inherent in this idea of a purgatorial fire and noted that the whole question of redemption in the world to come was an obscure one *(obscura quaestio).* Nevertheless, he argued, ". . . it is not impossible to believe that some believers will pass through a purgatorial fire, and in proportion as they have loved with more or less devotion the goods that perish be less or more quickly delivered from it. . . ."[4]

Throughout the Dark Ages (i.e., the time from the death of St. Augustine in 430 to the death of St. Anselm of Canterbury in 1109), theologians were not sure where this place of purgation was located. Some said the entrance to heaven, others a second level of hell. A third group (including St. Gregory the Great) thought that souls in need of purgation are obliged to return as ghosts to the earthly places of their transgressions. This overall uncertainty was expressed in a letter by

Cardinal Robert Pullus, who served as the chancellor of the Church in 1145:

> But where does this correction take place? Is it in heaven? Is it in hell? Heaven does not seem appropriate to tribulation, but torture does not seem appropriate to correction, particularly not in our time. For if heaven is appropriate for the good alone, is not hell appropriate only for the wicked? And if evil is entirely banished from heaven, how is it that hell can accept some good? Just as God made heaven for the perfect only, so it seems that Gehenna is reserved for the godless alone; the latter is the prison of the guilty and the former the kingdom of souls. Where are those who are supposed to do penance after death? In purgatorial places? Where are those places? I do not know.[5]

In response to this dilemma, Peter Comster (d. 1178) and Odo of Ourscamp (d. 1171) located Purgatory as a separate place between heaven and hell where souls were sent for the completion of unpaid penances and the purgation of all venial sins.[6] This teaching was refined by Peter the Chanter (d. 1197), who taught that after death the virtuous go directly to heaven and the wicked to hell. He added, however, that those who must make just reparation for their offenses and who have been less than perfect in their day-to-day life are sent by God to *Purgatorium* for a period of greater or lesser duration.[7] Therefore, the word was finally coined and its place in the afterlife pinpointed to the satisfaction of the Church.

Throughout the thirteenth century, the doctrine continued to be refined. Theologians began to espouse the belief that the time of a departed soul's suffering in Purgatory could be shortened by the good works of the living. The most effective forms of such suffrage, according to St. Thomas Aquinas, were gifts to the poor, the recitation of certain prayers, and, above all, the celebration of the Mass, since the Eucharist was the fount of all charity.[8]

In 1274, the year of St. Thomas's death, the doctrine of Purgatory was formally promulgated as follows by the Second Council of Lyons:

> Because of various errors which have been brought up, sometimes in ignorance, sometimes in malice, the Church asserts and preaches that those

who fall into sin after baptism are not to be rebaptized, but to receive forgiveness of sins through true penance. If those who are truly penitent die in charity before they have done sufficient penance for their sins of omission and commission, their souls are cleansed after death in purgatorial or cleansing punishments, as Frater John has pointed out to us. The suffrages of the faithful on earth can be of great help in relieving these punishments, as for instance, the Sacrifice of the Mass, prayers, almsgiving, and other religious deeds which, in the manner of the Church, the faithful are accustomed to offer for others of the faithful. The souls of those who have not committed any sin at all after they received holy baptism, and the souls of those who have committed sin, but have been cleansed, either while they were in the body or afterwards, as mentioned above, are promptly taken up into heaven.[9]

2. Do Catholics still offer suffrages for the suffering souls in Purgatory?

Yes. Vatican II in its "Constitution on the Church" *(Lumen Gentium,* 50) encouraged Catholics to continue this practice by stating: ". . . the Church in its pilgrim members, from the earliest days of the Christian religion, has honored with very great respect the memory of the dead; and 'because it is a holy and wholesome thought to pray for the dead that they may be loosed from their sins' (2 Mac. 12:46), she offers suffrages for them. . . ."

Prior to Vatican II, the efficacy of various forms of suffrage was described in temporal measurements of days, months, and years. For example, the recitation of five decades of the Rosary remitted the punishment of a dearly departed soul in the agonizing flames of Purgatory by five years; the reading of an approved litany by seven years; and the visitation to a church during the Forty Hour Devotion of the Blessed Sacrament (along with the recitation of the prescribed prayers) by fifteen years.

3. Does the Church sell Masses for the dead?

The Church officially does not "sell" devoted or "votive" Masses that may be applied to shorten the stay of a loved one in Purgatory. However, it expects the faithful to provide a suitable financial "stipend" for the celebration of such private rites. These stipends are to be understood as a willingness by the faithful to participate more intimately in the eucharistic sacrifice by making, in the words of Pope Paul VI's "Apostolic Letter on Mass Stipends" (July 13, 1974), "a form of sacrifice of their own by which they contribute in a particular way to the needs of the Church and especially to the sustenance of its ministers."[10]

NOTES

1. Tertullian, *De Corona Militis*, 3, in Jacque Le Goff's *The Birth of Purgatory*, translated by Arthur Goldhammer (Chicago: University of Chicago Press, 1981), p. 47.

2. St. Augustine, *Confessions*, translated by John K. Ryan (Garden City, New York: Image Books, 1960), p. 227.

3. St. Augustine, *Enchiridion*, 69, in *St. Augustin: On the Holy Trinity, Doctrinal Treatises, and Moral Treatises*, translated by J. F. Shaw, Vol. III, *Nicene and Post Nicene Fathers*, First Series, edited by Philip Schaff (Grand Rapids: William B. Eerdmans Publishing Company, 1956), p. 260.

4. St. Augustine, quoted in Le Goff, *op. cit.*, p. 68.

5. Robert Pullus, quoted in *ibid.*, p. 150.

6. *Ibid.*, pp. 156–59.

7. *Ibid.*, p. 165.

8. St. Thomas Aquinas, *Summa Theologiae*, Part III (Supplement), Question 71, Article 9, translated by the Fathers of the English Dominican Province, Vol. 20 (London: Burns, Oates and Washbourne, Ltd., 1921), p. 61.

9. "Decree of the Second Council of Lyons (appendix to the constitution *Cum sacrosancta)"* in *The Church Teaches*, translated and edited by John F. Clarkson, S. J. et al. (St. Louis: B. Herder Book Company, 155), pp. 348–49.

10. Pope Paul VI, "Apostolic Letter on Mass Stipends," quoted in *The Teachings of Christ: A Catholic Catechism for Adults*, edited by Ronald Lawler, O.F.M. Cap.; Donald W. Wuerl; and Thomas Comerford Lawler (Huntington, Indiana: Our Sunday Visitor, 1983), p. 418.

Index